THE PRESENCE PROCESS

MICHAEL BROWN

THE
PRESENCE
PROCESS

A Journey Into

Present Moment Awareness

Revised Edition

MICHAEL BROWN

namaste

PUBLISHING

Vancouver, Canada

LIBRARY AND ARCHIVES CANADA CATALOGUING IN PUBLICATION

Brown, Michael, 1962-
The presence process / Michael Brown. -- Rev. ed.

ISBN 978-1-897238-46-2

1. Awareness. 2. Self-actualization (Psychology).
3. Spiritual life. I. Title.

BF637.S4B775 2010   158.1   C2010-901922-9

Published in Canada by
NAMASTE PUBLISHING
P.O. Box 62084
Vancouver, British Columbia, V6J 4A3
www.namastepublishing.com

Distributed in the United States and Canada by
Publishers Group West

Cover Design by Ivan Rados
Typesetting by Steve Amarillo / Urban Design

Printed and bound in Canada by FRIESENS

This book is written for you.

CONTENTS

ACKNOWLEDGEMENT / xi

FOREWORD   William Hayashi / xiii

PREFACE   Dr. Judith Kravitz / xxi

REAWAKENING / xxiii

PART I   **ATTUNING TO THE PROCESS** / 1

What Is Present Moment Awareness? / 5
The Heartbeat of Reinforcement / 9
Aligning Intent / 12
Mechanics of the Process / 18
Consciousness of Questions / 25
Movement Beyond Motion / 29
The Pathway of Awareness and Seven-Year Cycle / 34
Emotional Imprinting / 43
Emotional Charge / 46
Beyond Addiction and Affliction / 51
Trading Results for Consequences / 59

PART II   **PREPARING FOR THE JOURNEY** / 71

The Process Trinity / 74
An Integrative Approach / 81
Level of Entry / 91
Navigational Guidance / 94

PART III   **THE PRESENCE PROCESS** / 111

Insight and Felt-Perception / 113

WEEK ONE / 116
Activation and Maintenance / 116
The Consciously Connected Breathing Practice / 119
Into the Breath / 122
Presence and Individual Expression / 127
Experiencing Presence / 131
Onward, Inward, and Upward / 132

WEEK TWO / 135
Identifying Messengers / 135

WEEK THREE / 148
Receiving Insight / 148

WEEK FOUR / 157
Feeling Unconditionally Integrates / 157

WEEK FIVE / 164
Integrating Our Childhood / 164
Integration of the Child Self / 171

WEEK SIX / 175
Integrating Charged Emotion / 175
The Mechanics of Reactivity / 180
The Emotional Integration Procedure / 183
Into The Water / 185

WEEK SEVEN / 188
Embracing Physical Presence / 188
Feeling Our Way Through / 192

WEEK EIGHT / 199
Peace Is a Vibration We Feel / 199
Realizing Peace Through Forgiveness / 201
Praying for Forgiveness / 209

WEEK NINE / 211
Integrating Our Unconscious Definition of Love / 211
Manipulation / 216
Giving Unconditionally Is Receiving / 218

WEEK TEN / 224
Consciously Entering the Unified Field / 224
Living on Purpose / 233
Appreciating Appreciation / 236

PART IV   **POSSIBILITY** / 241

Where There's a Gardener, There's a Garden / 243
Fruits and Flowers / 244
Radiating Present Moment Awareness Responsibly / 272
The Story of Clive and Nadine / 279
The Organic Unfolding of Present
　　Moment Awareness / 283

PART V   **CONTINUANCE** / 287

Freedom Is Responsibility / 290
Roses Have Thorns / 294
The Capacity of Presence / 296
A Parting Gift / 299

ACKNOWLEDGEMENT

My deepest appreciation to Constance Kellough,
Kathy Cholod, David Robert Ord, Lucinda Beacham,
and Nora Morin for taking such loving care of this book.
Thank you for making sure this revised edition shines.

FOREWORD

This being human is a guest
house. Every morning
a new arrival.

A joy, a depression, a meanness,
some momentary awareness comes
as an unexpected visitor.

Welcome and attend them all:
Even if they're a crowd of sorrows,
who violently sweep your house
empty of its furniture, still,
treat each guest honorably.
He may be clearing you out
for some new delight.

— Rumi

I HAVE ALWAYS LOVED RUMI'S POEM. Later on, a wise friend counseled
me, "Acceptance is the doorway to transformation."

Again, the same message: welcome the guests inside you without judgment, without resistance, and they will change you, "sweep you clean," from inside. The question was, "How?" Especially when they appeared dark, unfriendly, even mean-spirited.

Reading Michael Brown's *The Presence Process* some years ago provided a clear and safe way. Michael often tells us, "Don't kill the messenger. Receive the message." The "messengers" are the people and situations that "upset" us, seem to thwart and diminish us. The "messages" are the unintegrated, not-yet-resolved emotional memories and wounds from early childhood that are being played out through these current "adult" experiences. Like neglected children, they won't leave us alone but continue to "out-picture" in our daily life as the individuals, events, and circumstances that cause us pain and discomfort. Often they express through one of three core emotions: anger, fear, or sadness/grief. Our usual, habitual response is either mental or physical. We try to figure it out with the mind or distract ourselves through physical activity and avoidance. We may eat, run, overachieve, or simply get into our head to avoid engaging. Yet, the scared, wounded kid place in us continues to suffer, desperately wanting and needing attention and acceptance. To approach these wounds, often our oldest and most tender, requires a method that's both safe and effective. Fortunately, The Presence Process™ provides us with both.

Michael wisely begins by offering us two approaches to the book: to read/study, or else experience directly. I personally found it helpful to first get familiar with the method by reading Parts I and II, which provide a kind of overview and acclimatization to what is to come. All the developmental psychological history, the various techniques and methods to be used, the possible reactions and what to do are clearly spelled out and addressed in this instructional section, which helps get us ready for the actual journey. When we enter the experiential portion, the approach is again gentle, slow, and step by step. We have ten weeks to complete the process and each week is a gradual deepening and amplification. We have ample time to feel, question, and integrate. As with the "bath immersion exercise" of chapter 7, we are invited to slowly and gradually lower ourselves ever more deeply into the "warm healing waters" of this powerful process.

I was delighted to hear that Michael had written a revised version of his original manuscript and was pleased when invited to write a preface to it. The question, of course, was how this version is different and what has been strengthened. I would say first off that the original has the look and feel of an instructional manual, with italicized Presence Activating Statements to practice and Next Week Assignments at the end of each chapter. The current version feels less formal, less "teachy." The Presence Activating Statements have been changed to Conscious Responses without italics, and there are no formal "assignments" for the following week. I don't feel I am being "instructed by a watchful prof," but rather "kept company by a wise friend." The voice has more warmth and heart to it. I feel more seen and personally addressed by Michael.

Also, this text seems to flow more readily and communicate more clearly and effectively. Michael has added a section title to each of the weekly experientials not present in the original. These titles zero in on the core focus for each chapter. Also, at the start of each chapter, we are given the "conscious response for the next seven days," the phrase we are to repeat like a mantra throughout the week to help us internalize the week's focus. This focus is then broken down into several key ideas and expanded in the text to enhance our understanding, and we are given specific exercises or practices to bring these ideas alive in our body. Each chapter ends by identifying challenges that may emerge and how to work with them. In this way, each chapter elegantly and organically unfolds, skillfully integrating what has come before and gracefully leading to the next stage in the process, always clearly, always gently.

The key to "working" The Presence Process is to stop running from, or projecting onto others, the unresolved emotional charges from childhood that keep resurfacing in our current life situations. Instead, we learn to gently be with them, giving them our unconditional attention and support. As with angry, hurt, or frightened children, we don't scold or abandon our wounded child parts, and neither do we try to control or manipulate them. To do so would be to upset them further. Rather, we quietly keep them company with our benign presence and unconditional, loving support, until they in due course calm down. We don't need to say or do anything, but simply let them feel our resonating empathy.

Learning to identify and rest in Presence is the essence of this process. In this new version of *The Presence Process*, Michael puts particular emphasis on this. In the first six weeks of the experiential section, he shows us how to recognize our "shadows," our unresolved emotional charges, and how to identify them with wounded child parts – as well as how to welcome, hold, and reintegrate them through loving Presence. In the last four chapters, seven through ten, he shares more meta-level Presence skills. He starts by showing us more generally how to move out of our head and away from our mental stories, away from physical diversions and sublimations, and instead develop our "felt-perception" – our "inner body feeling," as Eckhart Tolle would say. It isn't through our mind or our emotional drama that we can sense into and be with our unresolved emotional resonances. We need to learn to develop felt-perception, "vibratory heart knowing," so that we can sense into and resonate with the energetic charges that keep our scared inner kids so off balance. We must also learn to identify the stories and beliefs that hold these uncomfortable vibratory frequencies in place. We begin to recognize the generic nature of these stories. We learn to forgive ourselves and others by recognizing that we all suffer from the double bind of desperately seeking unconditional love from hopelessly conditional and unstable sources outside ourselves. Rather than judging ourselves for having these unmet needs, we learn to accept them as inevitable and offer them the one abiding source of unconditional love, the ever-available embrace of our own conditionless and abiding Inner Presence. Once we can begin to give this to ourselves, we can also start offering it to the scared, wounded child parts of others as well.

Perhaps the most difficult stories to recognize and release are the unconscious definitions of love we create to explain our early frustrations with love. Michael tells us that we all have "one primary dramatic theme," one particular Achilles heel in love, that we keep recreating and reliving. This begins as a particular felt-resonance, an energetic imprint received during childhood, an energetic holding pattern of continual resistance. Because of this imprinting, or "charge," we continuously recreate the same circumstances as our initial childhood love wounds, hoping that this time we will be able to work them through. Unfortunately, because we amass the same types of characters and life situations, we simply repeat the same dramas and losses. It's Freud's "repetition compulsion" all over again. In my case, my story or "unconscious definition of love" was "here today, gone tomorrow." Because of early childhood losses in love, I unconsciously chose people who would love me for a time, but who would inevitably leave me behind. I had to first recognize the pattern, the story, and then let myself feel, accept, and release the charged energy of this debilitating life script. I had to learn to unconditionally give myself the love that I was so desperately trying to "get" from parental prototypes who were utterly incapable, due to no fault of their own, of giving me what I needed. Once I was able to release this story, this compulsively repeating energy pattern, and reintegrate the formerly bound or charged energy into my being, I was able to find abiding love.

Week Ten, the experiential culmination of this unfolding method, is entitled in this version, "Consciously Entering the Unified Field." Michael boldly identifies the final goal of his transformative process, entering into non-dual lived experience, abiding in felt-oneness with total and abiding Presence. He offers a number of extraordinary insights into this reality. First, he affirms the law of cause and effect, "ask and you will receive, seek and you will find." Backed by the laws of quantum intentionality, "as you believe, so it is," he says that the felt-quality of our beliefs about love inevitably determines our actual experience of love. Indeed, there is a perfect matchup between our inner resonance concerning love and the external circumstances of our love life. He places complete creative responsibility on our shoulders: "For this reason, whenever we don't feel in harmony with the quality of our life experience [in my case, my love circumstances] it's our responsibility to integrate the imprinted condition that's the cause of this situation."

Later, Michael explains how and why, though we live in a continuously "unified field of human experience," we know separation and non-love, isolation and aloneness. He says that as long as we feel we have "separate" physical bodies, brains, emotional and vibratory bodies, we feel a "gap" between ourselves and all others. The "world" comes into existence inside this gap, this space between these apparently diverse forms. We also begin to give importance and significance to the items, or "stuff," we place inside this gap. In this way, our mental, emotional, and physical focus becomes the individual objects and persons that seem to make up our world and the gap between us that holds it all. As long as we perceive in this way, we will continue to feel separate, individual, isolated. And, as within, so without. However, once we have learned to be with, accept, and quiet the mental and emotional charges keeping us separate and unintegrated within ourselves, and become the unified field of Presence that we essentially are, then we can begin to sense it as also present outside ourselves, underlying the apparently diverse and separate shapes and forms that seem distant and apart from us. We begin to feel the "shared Presence" we have in common, the "unified field" and "oneness in diversity" that connects and sustains us through our awareness and appreciation of essential and abiding being-aliveness. Eventually, we invite this awareness of Presence to be continuously with us, by consciously recognizing and celebrating it in the here and now. We activate this through cause and effect by consciously looking for experiential evidence that we are one unified body, one unified mental matrix, one unified heart, and one unified vibrational field. By looking for evidence of it, we perceive it, because cause and effect states that we perceive what we are looking for. As we continuously seek to "see and appreciate Presence," we are given continuous opportunities to feel and celebrate it both in its ongoing totality and its unique and individual expression in this moment, right here, right now. Although these ideas and transmissions appear in the original *Presence Process*, they resonate so much more clearly and coherently in the revised version, with its additions, edits, and restructuring.

At the end of this version, Michael has added a "parting gift," a concluding meditation that he recommends we do daily to help us stay connected with felt-Presence. By having us consciously feel and hear the breath, sense into and live the extended gap between inhalation and exhalation, tune into and resonate with the various sensations arising in the field around us, one-pointedly focus our awareness on the third eye and the sounds vibrating first outside and then within us, he invites us to intimately know and abide "with," "in," and "as" lived Presence. By simultaneously having us repeat the mantric intention, "I am here now in this," he has us simultaneously create/live the experience we are asking for, "say it, do it, say it, be it." He shows us we can instantaneously enter the realm of Presence by remembering and honoring it whenever we wish. Though we may need to return occasionally to work with our shadow, he wants us to keep our focus on our true and abiding identity, the vibrating light and joy of the one great Self, the Divine's ongoing Presence within and all around us as the unified quantum field.

(Bill) Gorakh Hayashi
Professor of Humanities & Psychology
Columbia University, Chicago

PREFACE

AFTER DOING INTEGRATIVE BREATH WORK for over 35 years and leading the largest breathing school on the planet, I was introduced to and began The Presence Process about a year ago. After going through the first two cycles, I realized that The Presence Process is the missing link in integrative breath work.

It was a pleasant gift and honor to preview Michael Brown's new edition of *The Presence Process*, and thus do my third round using this new text.

I have been absolutely amazed by what The Presence Process has done for my life and the full scope of the work I do, which includes training several hundred breath work facilitators a year, as well as working with thousands of newly conscious breathers. It has also been remarkable to observe the shifts in those individuals, facilitators, and their work as a result of their participation in The Presence Process.

Interestingly, I noticed a big change in my experience of doing the first two cycles of The Presence Process with the first edition, and my third cycle with the new, definitely improved model.

There seems to be a greater ease in reading and digesting the concepts in this new version, yet it took me deeper and was more to-the-point. To me, this truly reflects the improved clarity and shifts in the author's consciousness, which get passed on to us in this new edition.

I have also noticed that the levels of my emotional integration increased in intensity. This new version seemed to "cut to the chase" of my causal emotional body and take me to new places of healing and freedom. It took me beyond the nitty-gritty of my past suppression and offered me final resolution of many old emotional and behavioral patterns.

The new edition of *The Presence Process* is a gift and indeed a necessity for any who truly want to experience Presence more fully. Providing us with a powerful path that is precise, it leads us to an authentically joyful life.

Thank you, Michael.

Breathing in Love,
Dr Judith Kravitz
Founder and Director, Transformational Breath Foundation

REAWAKENING

IT IS DEEPLY SATISFYING TO KNOW that The Presence Process™ is available to you. This process is designed to accommodate anyone who chooses to reconnect with our shared Presence. The process is safe, gentle, and simple to follow. The benefits are real and the effects lasting.

The Presence Process is a guided journey that provides the practical techniques and perceptual tools required to extract our attention from the trappings of a time-based mentality, allowing us to gradually re-enter the present moment in which our experience is unfolding.

The Presence Process is the result of a quest that consciously began in the Arizona desert in 1996. It was here, possibly for the first time since early childhood, that I reunited with my authentic *beingness* and experienced the profound radiance of such communion. Throughout this text, I refer to this authentic *beingness* as "Presence" and call the radiant experience that becomes possible when this divine essence takes the reins of our life "present moment awareness."

Before these encounters with my beingness, for almost ten years I had been preoccupied with the task of coping with and healing myself of an acutely painful neurological condition called Horton's Syndrome. This condition, which started in 1987, manifested as multiple daily occurrences of excruciating agony. It isn't necessary for me to go into detail concerning the symptoms, other than to share that I was informed by one of South Africa's leading neurosurgeons that this ailment has no known cause or cure. He also warned me that, because of the severity of my condition, I was a candidate for drug addiction and even suicide.

In an attempt to find relief, I first used a variety of prescription medications. As my desperation increased, I explored a wide variety of alternative modalities, exposing myself to anything that promised a chance of healing. This included having cortisone injected into my face, the removal of my wisdom teeth, visiting a South African Xhosa Sangoma, and many fascinating encounters with "healers." Nothing brought relief, release, or resolution.

In 1994, after years of pursuing endless modalities that led nowhere, I was confronted with the possibility that nothing and nobody "out there" could alleviate my suffering. My options at this point were either to *check out* – or *check in.*

Since I wasn't yet ready to die, I embarked on a quest to heal *myself.* This began with a study of Swedish massage and qualifying as a Reiki Master. As I experimented on myself with various physical, mental, and emotional techniques, I discovered that when I maintained what I then called "a high personal energy frequency," I lessened the intensity of my pain and the rate of its reoccurrence substantially. This was the first whisper of what I now call present moment awareness.

My first significant encounter with Presence and the radiance of present moment awareness came in 1996 in a Native American sweat lodge in Tucson, Arizona, through the guidance of a Yaqui Indian Medicine Man. I shall never forget crawling out of the sweat lodge doorway on my hands and knees after a two–hour journey through heat, steam, drumming, singing, and praying. As I stood there in the cool night air, everything in and around me vibrated with life – as if I had just been born. This particular moment was my first taste of what it felt like to "show up" in my life.

After exiting the sweat lodge, I stood by the crackling fire in reverent silence, remaining long into the night, feeling warm blood flowing through my veins, crisp breath massaging my lungs, and the comforting rhythm of my heartbeat. For hours afterward, I experienced direct connection with Presence and the radiance of this *beingness* vibrating in every cell of my physical body, which I now began to understand as simply a vehicle for the manifestation of Presence. In fact, I often refer to the body as our "body-vehicle," so when I use the word "body" in this text, it's in the sense of the body as a vehicle.

My second encounter with Presence and present moment awareness came a few months later, facilitated by ingesting a tea brewed from peyote cactus. Peyote is one of the most alkaline substances on the planet. It's also undisputedly one of the foulest tasting liquids my mouth has ever encountered! Native Americans who ingest this plant as a sacrament in their Native American Church ceremonies refer to it as "the medicine." My initial experience of ingesting "the medicine" was profound. After an hour of increasing discomfort and nausea, I awoke, as if from a deep and dark dream, into an experience of present moment awareness. Although it was only fleeting, I experienced the undeniable sense of wholeness that comes from connecting intimately with Presence. I felt physically present, mentally clear, emotionally balanced, and vibrationally "in tune."

As with my initial sweat lodge experience, being able to feel and consciously commune with Presence throughout this peyote experience reunited me with the precious part of my authentic nature that had been obscured by the noise, busyness, and distractions of daily life. The peyote enabled me to step through a perceptual veil, on the other side of which life revealed itself as connected by a single intimate, intelligent, shared Presence. I saw how the breathtaking, luminous beauty of the natural world is hidden from us because of our preoccupation with unintegrated past trauma and fearful future projections.

In that moment, I became aware that my painful condition was no mere chance, but was purposeful. My painful neurological condition revealed itself not as my enemy, but as my friend and facilitator. It was Presence calling me back from a state in which I had

unconsciously attached my attention to the mental web of time, causing my attention to become scattered.

During this encounter with "the medicine," it became obvious
that the most important quest I could undertake would be to discover
a practical way to increase my experience of present moment awareness. Unless I discovered a means of accomplishing this for myself,
my usefulness to others would remain limited because I was *inau-*
thentic.

It was also apparent that experiences such as sweat lodges and peyote aren't for everyone. The mechanisms of a journey into present
moment awareness have to be as natural as possible – a pathway anyone can follow, no matter what their circumstances. Hence one of the
questions I asked Presence was: *How can present moment awareness be*
achieved primarily through inner work, instead of having to rely on exter-
nal conditions, substances, tools, ceremonies, rites, and rituals?

The first clue to achieving this was revealed the same year. I was
introduced to the obvious but somehow overlooked technique of consciously connected breathing. Consciously connected breathing is the
practice of breathing deliberately without a significant pause between
our in-breath and our out-breath. In other words, there are no breathless gaps between breaths.

After my first few consciously connected breathing sessions, I realized that using this modality produced an increasing sense of wellbeing, gained through enhanced personal presence. Also, for reasons I
didn't then comprehend, this breathing led to a gradual but consistent
decrease in the intensity of my physical pain. For the first time in
many years, I experienced a glimmer of hope for a genuine resolution
of the Horton's Syndrome from which I was suffering.

These breathing sessions also produced explosive insights. For
example, by enabling me to experience moments of detachment from
the goings-on of my daily routine, this natural breathing practice
helped me discern a distinct difference between what Presence is and
my unfolding human experience. I hadn't possessed the perceptual
capacity to identify this difference before commencing consciously

connected breathing. I was so enmeshed in my day-to-day experience that what I was going through had become the be-all and end-all of what I identified with.

As a consequence of using this breathing technique, I began noticing that whenever I encountered Presence, I knew a wholeness and completeness of being. This was an experience of effortless peace in which I was in perfect harmony with whatever transpired in my life. I realized that it was my unfolding physical, mental, and emotional *experience* that had become acutely unbalanced and in need of adjustment, not what I actually *am*. The notion that "our Presence requires healing" revealed itself as humorous.

By using consciously connected breathing to become increasingly present, I found myself making choices that restored my sense of wellbeing. For instance, I began responding to situations instead of reacting. This one simple shift in my behavior affected every facet of my experience. My encounters with the world around me, including other people, increasingly manifested both harmony and a feeling of comfort.

At the same time, the intensity of my painful condition continued to subside. After years of suffering from this neurological agony – and the frustration, anxiety, anger, grief, and depression it seeded – a light was now shining in the darkness.

It dawned on me that there was no greater healing tool at my disposal than consciously connected breathing, coupled with the awareness of Presence this technique evokes. To discover more about this tool, I began facilitating others in this breathing practice, closely observing the effects.

Another key insight that came to me was that my intent to heal myself – to "get rid of my discomfort" – was misguided. Perhaps this was why I hadn't succeeded despite my best efforts. In due course, I dropped my use of the word "heal" because of its connotation that something was wrong and had to be fixed. Instead, I began using the word "integrate," which to me meant there was a part of my experience that was unconscious – a part of my experience that I resisted, controlled, and sedated – which was asking to be incorporated into the whole. Whereas healing felt like I was excluding something from my experience, integration felt like I was embracing everything I experienced.

These significant moments in which I was introduced to present moment awareness became a yardstick by which I measured subsequent explorations into what became for me the art of integration. When anything I explored led to an increase in present moment awareness, I embraced it as authentic. When it didn't, I wasted no more time on it. To this day, the experience of present moment awareness remains my trusted barometer, assisting me in brushing aside inefficient activities and glamorized but impotent modalities that are nothing more than window-dressing.

In addition to exploring consciously connected breathing, I also began investigating the shamanic paradigm. Over a period of four years, I apprenticed as a Fire Keeper in the Native American Peyote Church. I also crossed the Arizona border into Mexico and participated in ceremonies with the living ancestors of The Peyote Way, the Huichol Indians. Whenever the opportunity presented itself, I used myself as a laboratory for experimenting with activation of present moment awareness, and my subsequent experience became an arena for observing the effects of becoming present.

This personal odyssey may appear romantic to some, and I certainly had plenty of fun along the way. However, it was seldom easy and the path was often unclear. Initially there was no point of reference for communicating to others what Presence and present moment awareness are. I didn't have a vocabulary to explain what I was discovering and seeking to achieve. I placed one foot in front of the other, following a trail that often made sense only to me.

There were numerous occasions when I became confused and disheartened. There were moments when I doubted my insights. Fortunately I always had a way to reconnect with my quest: by connecting my breathing and re-entering the radiance of Presence. Each time I did so, I remembered that my quest was a simple one. I was unable to verbalize it back then, but I can now: *How may I become increasingly present in such a way as to leave a trail for others who also intend to show up in their life experience?*

I didn't realize that by embarking on such a quest, I was ultimately searching for *a specific procedure*. However, hindsight reveals that as a consequence of my intent, I was steered experientially toward uncovering the practical techniques, perceptual tools, and profound insights that have today evolved into The Presence Process.

In essence, I dragged my intent to reunite with Presence and to achieve present moment awareness out of the mental realm, rooting it on this Earth as a practical, methodical, integrated process that balances the physical, mental, and emotional aspects of our experience.

In 2002, after nine years away from South Africa, I returned knowing I had accomplished the first step of my quest: acquiring the raw materials for a procedure that enables activation, maintenance, and continuation of the process of accumulating present moment awareness. Later that year, fifteen years after I had crumpled onto the side of a gravel road in the Transkei during my first attack of Horton's Syndrome, I began consciously living my purpose by sharing The Presence Process with others.

No matter how many individuals I personally facilitated through The Presence Process, and no matter how often I share it through instruction and subsequent writings, I remain in awe of what this process accomplishes for everyone who is willing to enter it. The Presence Process is a rare jewel. It offers us a methodical approach for resolving unintegrated past trauma and a fearfully projected future, which distract us from experiencing that which we all share – Presence, and the profound experience of living in present moment awareness.

The Presence Process is an invitation to step onto a pathway that liberates us from the prison of unconscious mental distraction. I have witnessed how many who commit to completing this journey are perceptually reborn, become available as ambassadors of life itself, and now live among family and community as authentic peacemakers.

As a result of facilitating others through this process intensively for about four years, it became clear that the option of training people to be Presence Process facilitators wasn't an approach I was willing to take. It seems to me that such an approach opens the door to the possibility of diluting the impact of this procedure, misinterpreting its intricacies, and turning it into a means of income for facilitators who specialize in "the business of spirituality." I have realized through experience that only life itself can prepare us to have the integrity to facilitate another, and that life accomplishes this by inviting us to first develop this integrity through facilitating *ourselves*. In line with this insight, The Presence Process focuses on the art of self-facilitation.

My intent is that The Presence Process be an accessible tool of emotional integration for everyone. Therefore, instead of transforming The Presence Process into a modality to be shared through the medium of trained facilitators, I choose to make it directly available to you through this book. This way you have it in its purest form. *The Presence Process* is written and presented in a manner that will enable *you* to become the facilitator of *your* journey into present moment awareness. Now everyone who seeks to awaken from the distracted dream-spell of a time-based mentality has access to this process for the price of a book. Having said this, I still encourage you to be companions to each other as you embark upon this magnificent journey. May the essence of this companionship be experienced through example, free of any assumed authority.

I am grateful to the teachers who laid their experience before me so I might uncover this profound procedure. The Presence Process makes it possible for anyone to experience Presence and present moment awareness without having to take the long, challenging path I had to take. In hindsight, I realize much of my journey was about learning what *not* to do. By following the simple instructions in this text, you are invited to navigate your way to an experience of Presence without spending unnecessary time and energy exploring the consequences of misguided intent.

It's also now apparent that even though respectful application of plant medicines and ceremonies activates an awareness of Presence, for most of us these tools are best viewed as signposts, not the road itself. Few are called to be "medicine people" as a way of life. I embrace these tools, ceremonies, medicines, and their dedicated caretakers as allies. I shall always feel this way about them. I know they have been placed on the human path to assist us in remembering what has been forgotten, and to provide us with a glimpse of what's possible. However, I don't adhere to their approach as *the way for everyone.* The mechanisms of *the way for everyone* are already embedded within each of us, discovered as an inner design, a deliberate blueprint, and an intended birthright.

Although rituals and ingested substances initiate an awareness of Presence and enable us to experience present moment awareness, thereby providing much insight for humanity's evolution, their impact decays substantially after a while. Because they don't necessarily foster the accompanying day-to-day experience required for maintaining awareness, they are potentially as misleading as they are useful. Consequently, those who use this approach repeatedly to achieve and maintain awareness, without simultaneously using willpower and discipline to develop this capacity naturally, risk succumbing to the contradiction of *developing outer reliance in the name of inner development.*

It's my experience that, for most of us, developing an authentic open-door relationship with Presence and present moment awareness is best accomplished naturally, through the conscious and sober accessing, accumulating, and applying of personal willpower and sustained discipline. Achieving present moment awareness is a way of life, a daily approach to living on this planet, not a one-time quick fix. It's a journey, not a destination. This natural approach is what The Presence Process now makes possible for all.

The beauty of The Presence Process is that it paves the way for us to return to our authentic state in a manner that requires no artificial instruments or external activities – no elaborate ceremonies, rituals, dogmas, or beliefs. It only requires a conscious and disciplined use of attention and intention. Entering this process experientially – and for many of us, repeating it about three times – gradually activates the capacity we all have in common, enabling us to accumulate an awareness of Presence and the subsequent radiance of present moment awareness. This can now be accomplished safely within the structure of our mundane experience, no matter where or how we are placed in this fast-paced, complex world. It doesn't on any level require a departure from where destiny has us right now.

The Presence Process also introduces us to a concept that's foreign to the world of changing conditions, which is that *Presence knows no order of difficulty*. By this I mean that Presence has the miraculous capacity to manifest in our daily experience the exact circumstances required to integrate the dysfunction that currently prevents us from experiencing present moment awareness.

Like many of you who are now drawn to this text, I too initially entered this adventure because of symptomatic discomfort. My suffering caused me to turn inward in search of what was causing my distress. I have personally witnessed this process impact symptomatic conditions within myself and others – conditions such as depression, phobias, drug and alcohol addiction, grief, anger, fear, allergies, lack, and many other external indicators of internal discomfort. It also supports the repair of physical injuries, enhances sporting and creative abilities, and enlivens practices from yoga to meditation.

This process demonstrates that it's our deeply suppressed emotional imprints that unconsciously distract us from an awareness of the present. It's the confused mental states that arise from these unintegrated emotions that lead to the physical manifestations of discomfort that become symptoms of disease.

In essence, The Presence Process is a practical pathway that guides us into taking responsibility for the integration of our emotional blockages. In other words, it's a way to consciously "grow up."

When we deliberately initiate emotional integration, we invariably realize that the great gift of this process isn't the symptomatic relief it often brings, but the capacity it endows us with to take full responsibility for determining the quality of our overall experience.

Engaging intimately with Presence and accumulating present moment awareness is an intensely rewarding journey that appears to know no limits. It continues today for me with the same intimate resonance as when it began through my sweat lodge and peyote experiences. It activates a *way of being* that empowers us to respond to life instead of reacting to it. It leads us into an awareness of what we share, rather than focusing on the things that cause us to experience separation. But until we consciously initiate our personal journey into present moment awareness, the experience of Presence remains hidden by the mundane demands and distractions of the world.

Activating an experiential awareness of Presence is one of the greatest gifts we can give ourselves. It's also a responsible way of contributing to humanity because, by entering present moment awareness, we bring the profound capacities of Presence into all our interactions and activities.

The Presence Process is an invitation to activate our shared Presence, allowing it to guide us into a deepening awareness of *what is*. It's a gift that empowers us to transform our perception of life's possibilities. For this reason, it's recommended we not hurry through either the book or the process. We aren't well served when we are driven by desperation to "finish as quickly as possible."

It isn't useful to treat this process as something we are required to get through in order to arrive somewhere else. Everything we seek has already found us and is available within us. The Presence Process is an opportunity to experience personal confirmation of this.

And yes, I have successfully resolved the emotional state that manifested as my painful neurological ailment. I accomplished this by entering an intimate relationship with Presence, and by allowing this "inner knower" to take over as my guide into present moment awareness.

This same omnipotent quality is also within you, for it's what we share – an aspect of what we *are*. This state of *beingness* is readily accessible to you. May this magical, mystical, and mysterious journey bless the quality of your entire experience as it has mine – and as it has for the many who have already accepted the invitation to show up fully in their experience.

In the fast-paced world of today, present moment awareness is an unknown frontier as much as it's an ever-open doorway into personal liberation. Presence is our trusted guide for entry and continuance. Like you, I'm a curious explorer. Onward, inward, and upward.

Thank you for giving yourself this gift.

Kindest regards,
Michael

PART I

ATTUNING TO THE PROCESS

THE TEXT OF THIS BOOK is designed to support the experiential procedure called The Presence Process™. By reading it, we are gently led into this process, invited to experience it, and guided into a transformed everyday life.

Through experiencing Presence, we become *present*.

By completing this process, we are trained as self-facilitators of our ongoing journey into present moment awareness. We are reconnected with an aspect of our *beingness* that's continually available to guide us, which frees us from seeking this guidance from outer sources.

The Presence Process is a journey we take *into* ourselves. It takes us through forgotten memories and into unfamiliar emotional territory. As it does so, it equips us to integrate the suppressed fear, anger, and grief that seep into our daily experience. This emotional terrain may at first appear alien to us, but it's this forgotten energetic landscape that reunites us with our inherent innocence, joy, and creativity.

Even though it may appear we are taking this journey alone, we are not. Part 1 of the text assists us in realizing this, since it's written to awaken a direct relationship with Presence. Although we may not know where we are heading right now or how we are going to move in this direction, there's an aspect of our *beingness* that does know because it knows everything. It's what's inviting us to embark on this inner pathway. This Presence knows what we seek and what's required to attain it.

Presence is our best friend and closest companion, our champion and guard of honor. It carries our flag and supplies. It sends us off enthusiastically and it's present to greet us as we access present moment awareness.

Part I of The Presence Process prepares us to be receptive to communication from Presence. Through reading this text, we learn the language of authenticity, which is the language in which Presence communicates.

It isn't necessary to memorize any part of this written material. However, it's to our benefit to read it as often as possible, especially in quiet moments when we are feeling relaxed and receptive.

If at any point we feel overwhelmed, this is an indicator we should close the book and allow ourselves the space to *integrate* what we are reading. In this context, "integration" means giving ourselves the quietness and space to physically, mentally, and emotionally take in the content we are reading, along with digesting the experience this text sets in motion so we absorb the nutrition it offers. Accordingly, let me emphasize again that we aren't to hurry. It's essential we read these words carefully and allow ourselves the time required to process them.

So as to be accessible to everyone, The Presence Process has two levels of entry: introductory, and experiential. The first level is entered simply by reading the text. The second level involves an experiential procedure that gradually unfolds over a period of ten weeks. Part 1 of this book assists us in making an informed choice as to which level is suitable for us. Part 2 aligns us with the overall intent of The Presence Process, opening the door and pointing the way. By formulating our intent, focusing our attention, and activating our inner guidance, it readies and encourages us.

WHAT IS PRESENT MOMENT AWARENESS?

Present moment awareness is a state of *being* as opposed to something we *do*. The simplest definition of present moment awareness is *to be fully aware of the moment we are in* – or, *to be present in the moment.*

The emphasis isn't on *the moment,* but on *the beingness* we bring to bear on our life experience when we pay full attention to the moment.

A reliable indicator we have entered present moment awareness is if our experience, no matter how comfortable or uncomfortable it may feel at any given moment, is infused with *gratefulness.*

When I speak of gratefulness, I'm not referring to the kind of gratitude that's founded on comparison, such as feeling grateful we are in better health or have more wealth than someone else. Neither is it the sort of gratitude that arises because life is unfolding how we want it to and everything is easy. Rather, it's gratitude that requires no reason – gratitude for the invitation, journey, and gift of life itself.

Gratefulness is the one single marker we can depend on as an indicator of how present we are in our experience. When we lack gratitude for simply being alive, it's because we have strayed from the present into an illusory mental state called "time."

Because we are born into a culture that exists almost entirely within a world of time, few of us are able to be continually present. This is the curse of modern civilization. We thirst for progress, but in many cases progress leads to the structuring of life in such a way that we are no longer required to be present when it's happening. The more automated our experience becomes, the less involved we are in the art of living.

In the world of time, it's challenging to be grateful because nothing appears to unfold the way we *think* it should. The past holds regrets and the future the promise of improvement, while the present requires constant adjustment. We therefore spend our waking moments reflecting on what didn't work in the past and planning those adjustments we believe are necessary to attain the peace and fulfillment we seek. Because these adjustments are oriented to a "better tomorrow," we've forgotten how to have a meaningful *today*. Consequently, the experience we are having *right now* is viewed as just *a means to an end*. Because we don't have access to a different experience to which we might compare our current predicament, living like this appears normal to us.

By living this way, we consistently leapfrog over the present. Even though the past has gone and can't be altered, and the future isn't yet manifest, we choose to mentally occupy these illusory places instead of fully entering and experiencing the one moment we actually occupy – this moment now.

By habitually dwelling in a mental state, which allows us to project our attention into an illusory past or future, we miss out on the authentic physical and emotional experience that's happening *right now*. We are all but oblivious to the only moment that contains all the vibrancy of life. We *think* we're living, but we're merely existing. We *think* we're moving forward, but we're spinning in circles. We have become mental about everything and have thereby sacrificed the experience of being physically present and emotionally balanced. Consequently, as advanced as we may believe our mental state to be, we are ridden with confusion.

We are so accustomed to this state of "not-being" – this condition of merely existing – that not only does it appear natural to us, but we even aspire to it. Of course, it isn't natural, since it knows no harmony. At some level we realize this because, in the midst of our mental leapfrogging, we sense something is amiss. Our lack of inner peace is reflected outwardly as ongoing chaos – as well as in the way we shy away from any experience of stillness and silence. The theme of this mental age is *let there be noise and movement.*

Because we can't remember what we've lost, we don't know what we are missing. We can't find it because we seek it either in pictures of the past or by scanning the future. Our insatiably needy behavior, which is forever seeking something, is testimony to the emptiness our current approach to living can't fill. The word "enough" has no relevance for us.

In our angst, we are turning over every piece of this planet in a desperate search for an awareness of peace, yet nothing we do brings the awareness of peace into our state of frantic "doing." This is because we have long since forgotten that peace isn't "a doing" but a feeling. It's something that can't be enforced or mechanically installed, but that's only realized by entry in a felt manner into *this moment*.

Our state of internal unrest manifests as external physical, mental, and emotional symptoms of discomfort and disease. No matter what we take for it, where we run in an attempt to escape it, and how we distract ourselves from it with endless "doings," relief constantly appears just out of reach. Even as a sleep-deprived person inevitably enters physical, mental, and emotional breakdown, our neglect of the oasis of present moment awareness also quickly leads us into ever-increasing planetary and societal disintegration.

This mental condition of "living in time" – relentlessly running from yesterday and frantically chasing tomorrow, without rest and stopping to feel peaceful – is the predicament that The Presence Process addresses and soothes. By assisting us to recognize the cause of our predicament, this process provides us with a way out of our dilemma. It throws us a rope of awareness and empowers us to pull ourselves out of our distraction by past and future, allowing us to return to the only solid, safe, and peaceful ground – the present.

The behavior we generate in order to feel safe and accepted in the world is a substitute for real peace and isn't who we are. The Presence Process guides our awareness to the authentic Presence we really are. It accomplishes this by encouraging conscious dismantling of the inauthenticity and pretence we engage in to shield ourselves from the fear, anger, and grief we endure as a result of our alienation from the present moment.

The ten-week process we are about to enter demonstrates that the way to really change our experience of the world is by liberating ourselves from the virus of "living in time." Liberating ourselves from this mental disarray is the greatest act of service we can perform *right now*.

No matter what the future promises, the moment that's actual – *this-here-now* – has nothing to do with yesterday and what may happen tomorrow. As long as we react unconsciously to the events of life, focusing primarily on *that-there-then*, we aren't even seeing what's right in front of us. Instead, we are in a mentally driven dream spell, recoiling from ghosts of the past and projected future phantoms. This is no way to live. In fact, it isn't living at all because the vibrational resonance of what life *really* is cannot enter time. Our current time-based experience is a perceptual hell guarded by the bars of our unintegrated fear, anger, and grief. It doesn't take us anywhere. It never did, and it never will. In "time," nothing authentic happens – we only *think* it does.

The good news is that although this may be the only quality of experience we are currently aware of, it's definitely not the only experience available. There's another paradigm that runs parallel to the world of time. We call it "the present moment." Its holy governor is our shared Presence, and its eternal expanse is experienced through present moment awareness. We know it exists because we seek it even when we don't consciously realize this is what we thirst for. We know it exists because many ordinary human beings from different walks of life have already re-entered and are living it right now. There's a growing community of shared Presence on this planet, enjoying present moment awareness. This book and the process it contains is your personal invitation to join the party.

Present moment awareness is accessible wherever we are. We don't have to go anywhere or embark on any outer "doing" in order to activate it. But we can't consciously enter it as long as we unconsciously cling to unintegrated past trauma and fearful future projections.

A joyful, healthy, and abundant life is pouring itself upon us all right now. However, when we "live in time," the vessel we really are is upended. In this upside down state, we mistakenly spend our experience *trying to get something* instead of simply *receiving that which is already and eternally given.*

Present moment awareness isn't a concept – it's an *experience*. The fact that more and more of us are entering it now is a consequence of our accelerating evolution. For anyone willing to receive its blessings, its invitation is here, now, in *this* moment, *this* set of circumstances. It calls to us in a silent voice that says: "*Stop. There's nowhere to go and nothing to do. There's simply everything to be.*" This is the invitation, the journey, and the gift that The Presence Process makes possible.

We are now at a place to embrace a more complete understanding of present moment awareness as *a state of being in which we effortlessly integrate the authentic Presence we are with each given moment we are in, so that we are able to respond consciously to each experience.* Our response is one of gratitude, whose flow washes us of illusions.

Entering such a state may sound challenging and complicated when we are so used to living in time. However, because present moment awareness is our birthright, to live this way is natural for us and hence effortless. It's the kingdom of awareness through whose gates the prodigal children, now awakened, return.

THE HEARTBEAT OF REINFORCEMENT

The Presence Process functions from the premise that *what we authentically are isn't mind.* We are eternal Presence.

Within the context of The Presence Process, "mind" is the vehicle through which we interact with our transient human experience. It's composed of physicality (our body), mentality (our thoughts), and emotionality (our emotional states). In other literature, when people talk about their "mind," they're generally referring only to their thoughts.

The Presence Process is an experience of present moment awareness delivered in the form of a book. For this reason, it's written and structured in a manner we may not be accustomed to. Although it employs the thinking aspect of mind as a tool (which is referred to throughout this text as "the mental body"), it isn't written for the purpose of encouraging us to think. Because the thinking aspect of mind operates primarily within a time-based paradigm, it struggles to comprehend present moment awareness. Thinking and present moment awareness seldom cohabit.

As we enter present moment awareness, one of the indicators this is occurring is a steady decrease of mental analysis. However, because we've become servants to the thinking aspect of mind instead of it serving us, achieving this quieting of mental activity requires deliberate intent – a process of perceptual "undoing." This is also what The Presence Process is – a process of *undoing*. For this reason, the rhythm of this text may in places appear unorthodox.

Our mental body may struggle with the tempo of this text. It may declare, "This is too repetitive. This particular explanation has already been given, so why are we going through it again? Does the author assume we lack intelligence?"

The reason our mental body is likely to react to this text is that, as long as we are perceptually entrenched in a time-based paradigm, the thinking aspect of mind is all about "understanding." Seeking understanding through thinking is currently the most common application of the mental body. Indeed, understanding is practically godlike to the mental body!

If the thinking aspect of mind believes it already understands something, it becomes offended and is bored when the subject matter is repeated, especially if it's repeated in exactly the same way. The thinking aspect of mind sees no purpose for information beyond its role as a tool of understanding and analysis. Yet the information contained in this book has a deeper purpose than merely assisting us to understand. The information on these pages enables us to gently move "in formation" (information) with the flow of this intricate procedure.

When the thinking aspect of mind encounters a book, it assumes the book is written for *it*, and it therefore wants every sentence to be new and exciting, and each chapter to end with a cliffhanger. Hungry for and addicted to constant change and excitement, it wants to be continually entertained. It can't comprehend the silence and stillness inherent in cyclic experiences, especially the depth of the silence and stillness out of which Presence arises and into which it invites us.

To the thinking aspect of mind, cycles are meaningless repetition. This is why the thinking aspect of mind often has difficulty sitting on a beach and quietly watching waves, savoring the silence of a sunset, or enjoying the stillness in the company of a tree. Repetition tends to annoy it and cause it to complain, "What's the point of repeating this?" It reacts this way despite the fact that most of the thoughts it entertains *are* meaningless cycles of repetition!

Life at its vibrational core isn't new. Life is already complete in what it is and doesn't change from its essential nature. In this light, life in this world is an endless stillness and silence flowing in and out as forms upon a tide of ongoing cycles. However, these cycles aren't mere repetition. They are reinforcement, emerging from an eternal dance of expression. In this world of phenomena, these cycles of reinforcement are the heartbeat of our shared *beingness*.

The Presence Process isn't written to entertain the mental body, but rather to realign and inspire it. What appears to the thinking aspect of mind as repetition is reinforcement that results in the gradual awakening of present moment awareness. The task of our mental body in this journey is to assist us in reading, and to enable us to contain this information so we can assimilate it into the fabric of our physical and emotional experience. *Thinking* about it is neither required nor desirable. We can't *think* our way into present moment awareness. We can't think outside the box when thinking *is* the box!

Why the text flows as it does, and why certain information cyclically re-enters the pages we are reading, will make greater sense in hindsight. However, before we fully enter the text, it's useful to be aware of some of the structural intent that steers it. This calms the thinking aspect of mind and shields us from its tendency toward boredom, annoyance, and resistance.

The Presence Process is designed to cause unconsciousness to surface into our awareness. This enables us to undo misguided perceptions that mask our awareness of Presence. As this unconsciousness surfaces, it's helpful to have certain information repeatedly reinforced so we remain aware that what's transpiring is valid.

The text also gently activates an awareness of what may be called our "child self" – a vital aspect of our *beingness* that was abandoned when we departed childhood. As this aspect surfaces for integration, reinforcement of certain information helps our child self know it's safe to leave *that-there-then* and join us in *this-here-now*. In other words, in addition to speaking to the part of us that's consciously turning these pages right now, the text simultaneously communicates with this child-like self, along with other aspects of our *beingness* that are still unconscious to us. Children require this reinforcement, as do adults who are embroiled in unconscious behavior.

Once we embark on The Presence Process, we are actually beginning not only a ten-week procedure but also a lifelong adventure. Presence is something with which we grow more intimate from day to day as our present moment awareness increases. The Presence Process is a river of experience-activating information that carries us into the eternal ocean of present moment awareness.

It's essential to realize that we aren't served by jumping around from section to section of the book or by skipping sentences and paragraphs. The information presented is deliberately delivered in layers in a specific order of importance. By attending to the simple instructions, going page by page, day by day, we gently cleanse our perception and permanently anchor present moment awareness in every aspect of our experience. When approached consciously and consistently, *routine* becomes what the structure of the word reveals – our *route in*.

ALIGNING INTENT

Activating present moment awareness and the unlimited possibilities of Presence is the overall intent of The Presence Process. Because Presence knows no order of difficulty, activating this capacity enables us to process any unintegrated experience.

The paradigm of Presence and present moment awareness can't

be found in or validated by concepts. We cannot enter this paradigm through another person's explanation. On the contrary, we are required to experience Presence and present moment awareness first-hand before we can even grasp what the word "Presence" implies. Everything in this book is therefore offered as *an invitation into an experience*. It's an invitation to open a doorway and enter this state of Presence ourselves, so that we know through personal involvement what the gift of present moment awareness is.

It actually doesn't matter whether we think the information contained in this book is valid. What matters is whether the experience activated by reading and applying what we are reading redirects our attention from a time-based mentality into present moment awareness.

To see how this works, consider how the words a mother uses to sing a lullaby to a newborn child are irrelevant, since the child's mind can't comprehend them. The effectiveness of a lullaby is determined by whether its *emotional* content soothes the child. In the same manner, the effectiveness of this text is determined by whether it activates an awareness of Presence and initiates the experience of present moment awareness.

By entering The Presence Process experientially, we simultaneously make a commitment to ourselves to complete this process. This commitment is of necessity unconditional because we really don't know what the experience of The Presence Process is until we reach completion. Part 1 of this text is designed to provide the information and encouragement we require to make this unconditional commitment to ourselves.

The Presence Process guides us through places within ourselves with which we may not as yet be familiar. Consequently, *we will inevitably have experiences in which we feel as if we don't know where we are going or what's happening*. This is normal and is supposed to occur. Accelerated personal growth unfolds during these moments of "not knowing."

Even when this process reaches completion, it may still be challenging to explain to another what has occurred. Because much of the process is about felt-perception, not our mental understanding of what's unfolding, this is also normal. In fact, The Presence Process is primarily a process for awakening felt-perception. Upon completion, we will have no doubt this experience has been a precious and loving gift to ourselves.

Also, *there is no specific experience we are supposed to have* as a result of entering this process.

Having said this, upon concluding The Presence Process, we are left with no doubt that this process activates *an experience*. Whatever experience it activates *for us* is valid. The information delivered to us through this text is designed to assist us not only in navigating this experience consciously, but also with integrating the experience.

Once we are able to digest the insight that emanates from our experience, we are liberated. We no longer need to analyze the experiences and insights of others as a means of navigating our way through life. *Our experience is now our teacher.*

It's important to recognize that our experience is *always* valid. Indeed, every aspect of our experience is presented to us precisely because it's *what we currently need to learn*. This is what our experiential journey through The Presence Process reveals.

In life, we grow physically by putting the appropriate nutrition into what I prefer to speak of as our body-vehicle, but for the sake of simplicity, as mentioned earlier, refer to here simply as our "body." Our mental growth is also catered to when we enter the basic experience of schooling. However, our emotional development, which usually slows drastically at about seven years of age, receives little or no deliberate attention as we move into and through adulthood.

We humans have proven ourselves remarkably physically adaptable to our environment. In the last century, we have also become mental giants. Sadly, we remain emotionally impotent, and the turbulent state of the world is testimony to the fact that it's the playground of the emotionally undeveloped. The journey we embark on throughout The Presence Process is therefore essentially a journey of acquiring emotional development through activating awareness of our physical presence, coupled with mental clarity.

The experience of physical presence occurs when we discover how to anchor our awareness in our physical body. Many of us believe we occupy our physical body, though we seldom do. Thinking about the past and the future involves the mental realm, which isn't confined to the location of our physical brain but extends as far as we are able to think. When we are thinking about a friend in another country, perhaps revisiting a memory of our last encounter, we assume we are still present in our physical body, even though we clearly aren't. *We are where our attention is.* Something may be unfolding right in front of our eyes, but we are oblivious to it because we are wandering around in our thoughts. We are definitely not present in our physical body!

Although the physical body symptomatically reflects past experiences and future projections, the body itself is *always* fully present. It's fully present in the intricacies of its functioning, as witnessed by the fact that each beat of our heart takes place only in the present. However, the *experience* of physical presence is only activated when we enter present moment awareness. For example, when we experience physical presence, we are able to *feel* our heart beating.

Sadly, often the closest we come to experiencing physical presence is by default, such as when we almost have an accident and feel fright. In the moments following the onset of fright, our awareness fully enters our body, so that we feel blood pumping through our veins and our heart beating in our chest. When we spend our days in the mental realm thinking, we aren't even aware we have a heart, let alone able to hear and feel it.

The Presence Process instructs us in a breathing practice that consciously anchors our awareness in our physical body. From this point of increased awareness, we then set about achieving mental clarity and emotional integration. Achieving emotional integration through first gaining physical presence, then mental clarity, is an effective way to initiate emotional development, as will become evident further on in this text when we examine in detail why our intent to initiate emotional development is the natural way to integrate symptoms of physical and mental discomfort.

Emotional development is challenging. The necessity for it is seldom understood, let alone supported, by those around us. Although the instructions given throughout this text are intended to make this experience gentler, the process itself isn't intended to be easy. Neither does it initially make us feel "better" or feel "good."

Feeling "better," "good," "nice," "fine," "okay," and "all right" are terms we use when we are emotionally numb. For the duration of this experience, we are encouraged not to judge our progress by how good we feel. *However* we feel throughout The Presence Process is *valid.*

The Presence Process is about remembering how to feel *authentically.* This initially tends to include experiencing suppressed emotional states such as fear, anger, and grief. The Presence Process specializes in assisting us in gently accessing suppressed emotions – emotions we ordinarily prefer not to acknowledge. During the process, we deliberately allow this to occur because *these suppressed emotions are the unconscious energetic causal points of those behaviors and experiences that no longer serve us.* By accessing and releasing the charge of these suppressed emotions, we reinstate the resonance of authenticity in the quality of our experience.

This process conveys *experientially* – above and beyond our capacity to *comprehend* why such an endeavor is necessary – the reason we commit to the task of emotional development. As we also discover along the way, mental understanding is seldom part of emotional integration. Like any journey into the unknown, we perceive where we are and why certain circumstances unfold as they do only when we reach a point of completion, which gifts us with the capacity for reflection.

Throughout The Presence Process, the word "emotion" is an abbreviation for "energy in motion." Emotional development requires that we first free suppressed and blocked emotions, then learn to channel this energy responsibly so it enhances the quality of our experience. To accomplish this, we use some simple perceptual tools. These serve us through all our experiences, enabling us to navigate our way through life consciously no matter what.

The Presence Process isn't about changing what we already are, which is impossible. Rather, it's about *releasing our attachment* to a *manufactured* identity, so that we gently return to an awareness of authentic Presence. By releasing us from our manufactured identity, it consciously connects us with an aspect of *beingness* that remains constant and continually present from the moment we enter the world.

In other words, The Presence Process *moves us from pretence into Presence.*

The Presence Process isn't about becoming *something or somebody else.* It's about remembering and experiencing *what we already are.* Neither is The Presence Process about changing the nature of what the "stars" may have marked on our forehead, hands, and feet. Rather, it's about waking up to the fullest potential of each moment as it unfolds *right now,* responding to life with Presence instead of reacting to it as if something else were supposed to be happening.

The Presence Process reveals that our desire to manipulate every experience we have so that we feel more comfortable is born of an inability to show up and fully enjoy the wonder of our experience *exactly as it is.* The Presence Process awakens within us an awareness that it's in how we interact with what's happening *in this moment* that we sow the seeds for what's to come beyond the borders of our present experience. It helps us see that the quality of the seeds we sow in any given moment depends on whether we choose to *react* or *respond.*

Reacting to our experiences means we make decisions based on what we believe happened yesterday and what we think may happen tomorrow. In contrast, we *respond* to our experiences when we make choices based on what's happening right here, right now. This response draws on the *wisdom* we derive from past experience, whereas reactivity is driven by the *unresolved trauma that's embedded in us.* Once we integrate the energetic patterns that underlie our behavior and beliefs, it's possible to respond to all our experiences rather than reacting.

Since The Presence Process can't be experienced *for* someone else or *to please* someone else, and since activating present moment awareness is our individual responsibility, this is an experience that by its nature is immune to comparison and judgment. In other words, because this is a journey driven by commitment, curiosity, and intention, there are no failures in The Presence Process. Whatever experience we have as we move through it is valid. Other than following the simple instructions to the best of our ability, there is no "correct" or "proper" way of moving through it – there is only *our* way of moving through it.

As we move through The Presence Process, we discover that *our* way of moving through this process *is always a fractal that reflects how we engage our overall life experience*. In other words, our journey through The Presence Process serves as a mirror of how we approach our everyday experience.

The Presence Process isn't an "end" to anything, as if something about us should never have been. Rather, it's simply the *continuation* of a lifelong journey we are already making into the heart of Presence and present moment awareness. As we enter this leg of life's journey, let it be our intent to commit to our emotional development for the rest of our human experience.

It's worth taking a quiet moment to carefully consider the following question before reading further: What is *my* intent in entering The Presence Process?

MECHANICS OF THE PROCESS

Instead of being about outer "doing," The Presence Process introduces us to a technique of perceptual response called "not-doing" or "undoing."

"Not-doing" isn't to be confused with inactivity. Life invites action and expresses itself through us as momentum. However, there is *reactive* momentum and *responsive* momentum. Reactivity is momentum driven unconsciously by an unintegrated felt-charge and emanates from suppressed inner discomfort. Responsive action is momentum rooted in taking charge of our inner discomfort, which involves simply "being with it," allowing it to be fully in our awareness without placing conditions on it.

Within the context of The Presence Process, *doing* is momentum – whether physical, mental, or emotional – whose intent is sedation and control of our inner discomfort. In contrast, "undoing" and "not-doing" are momentum – whether physical, mental, or emotional – whose intent is a response to inner discomfort.

All the mechanics that make up the structure of this process are intended to be *not-doings*. For example:

- We are already breathing. This process now empowers us to breathe consciously. Nothing is added to what's already unfolding other than responsive awareness.

- We are already mentally active. This process empowers us to consciously embrace thought processes that serve us. Nothing is added to what's already unfolding other than responsive awareness.

- We are already feeling. This process empowers us to consciously engage with what's currently suppressed and sedated. Nothing is added to what's already unfolding in our experience other than responsive awareness.

- We are already spending some time in our daily experience reading. This process provides us with a text that directs our awareness into the present. Nothing is added to what's already unfolding other than responsive awareness.

- We are already utilizing various means of perception. This process empowers us with tools that enable us to perceive the world as it is, instead of perceiving it through interpretations and beliefs drawn from unintegrated past experiences. Nothing is added to what's already unfolding other than responsive awareness.

Instead of requiring us to engage in practices that aren't part of our experience in most cases, such as standing on our head, The Presence Process simply adds *the resonance of awareness* to *what already is*. Awareness is the only tool required for authentic transformation of any aspect of our experience.

The Presence Process is structured as a series of ten graduated sessions, each seven days in length. These ten seven-day periods provide the necessary time and space for gathering the required experience from our ordinary day-to-day life interactions. These ordinary day-to-day interactions assist with integration of the insights we receive through this procedure. These insights, when confirmed through daily experience, become personally acquired knowledge. When this personally acquired knowledge is the frequency on which we base our felt-perceptions, thoughts, words, and deeds, we enter the resonance of wisdom. In this light, The Presence Process invites us to accumulate experiences that awaken wisdom.

In week one of this process, we are instructed in the practice of consciously connected breathing, which we engage in for fifteen minutes twice a day for the duration of this journey. This breathing practice is the backbone of this process. It fosters daily accumulation of present moment awareness through integration of the energetic patterns that keep us trapped in a time-based mentality.

Throughout the process, we consciously wield the perceptual tools called *attention* and *intent*. Attention is the tool of the mental body and is the *what* of our focus. Intent is the tool of the emotional body and is the *why* of our focus. We utilize attention and intent to navigate toward, through, and out of all our experiences. Normally we wield these perceptual tools unconsciously, which is why The Presence Process is designed to bring awareness to our application of attention and intent. The quality of our experience is determined by how consciously we wield these tools.

With each week, in addition to our daily breathing, we are given a statement to activate mental clarity. We call these statements "conscious responses." We apply each week's conscious response to the daily life experiences stimulated by this process. In addition to the conscious responses, we also read weekly allotments of text that contain perceptual tools and insights whose purpose is to awaken us to our unconscious behavior.

The Presence Process isn't about being "fixed" by anybody or anything "out there." Instead, it focuses our attention on developing our internal capacity. Through this process, we take full responsibility for accessing present moment awareness.

By instructing us how to detach from our experience and observe it, this process enables us to realize there is nothing wrong with us — that what we authentically *are* isn't broken. This enables us to see that it isn't *us,* but rather the quality of the *experience* we are having, that needs to be brought into balance. In this way, The Presence Process assists us in recognizing that there's a difference between *what we already are* and *the experience we are currently having.*

There's no magic or mystery about how and why The Presence Process succeeds. It's simply a perceptual technology that's aligned with the natural flow and tendency of the mechanics of our human awareness. It honors and applies the moment-by-moment flow of cause and effect. Through personal experience of the process, we come to realize that the mechanics and insights contained in this process are obvious and natural.

What distinguishes this experience from many other introspective procedures is the absence of external rituals, ceremonies, and dogma. There are no toys or "power objects" to cling to. It requires no belief system, no religious concepts, no awareness of any established human philosophy. The less preconceived notions we bring to the process, the more efficient it is.

Everything we accomplish in this process is through disciplining our willpower to consciously wield our attention and intent. We trade time spent in the corridors of endless thinking for an integrated physical, mental, and emotional experience. We are provided with a continual opportunity to *experience* each insight because these insights are presented to us during the course of this process as events, circumstances, and encounters within our day-to-day circumstances. By applying ourselves as instructed, then witnessing the consequences, we realize through personal experience that *nothing has more lasting impact on how we feel than developing a conscious relationship with our shared Presence.*

The Presence Process invites us to *enjoy a personal encounter with what we already are.* This is why it isn't an experience we can enter into for someone else, and why we don't enter into it to prove something to someone else. Having said this, it's possible that the desire to enter and complete this journey might *initially* arise as a reaction to symptomatic discomfort and external circumstances. However, throughout this experience, we are instructed how to source our intent and willpower directly from within. By discovering how to take full responsibility for the quality of our experience, we release our victim-victor mentality.

The Presence Process enables us to embrace the insight that *authentic growth comes from what we don't know.* This cannot be overstated. It also can't be understood mentally. The thinking aspect of mind either assumes it already knows everything it needs to know, or it believes that anything not yet known can be acquired through the application of thinking and analysis.

Since authentic growth requires a voluntary stance of "not knowing," thinking we know exactly what's going on in each aspect of our experience makes it challenging to surrender to The Presence Process. As we enter this journey, we therefore open ourselves to the possibility that we don't know what we are, what we seek, or how to bring about this awareness. Indeed, we may be mistaken about everything we thought we understood.

We've seen that the intent of this journey isn't to "feel good," but rather to feel what's actually unfolding within us right now. In other words, *our intent isn't to feel better, but to get better at feeling.*

Our authentic state of Presence is joyful, harmonious, and peace-loving. However, to awaken to an ongoing awareness of this Presence initially requires journeying through the current condition of the emotional body. This journey takes us into suppressed fear, anger, and grief. These uncomfortable emotional states are suppressed because we believe that whenever they surface, something is wrong. This belief doesn't serve us.

Our attempts to *try to feel good all the time* stem from a desire to suppress the fact that what we are actually feeling is afraid, angry, and full of grief. As we enter The Presence Process, we intend these suppressed emotional states to surface.

As we experience the surfacing of these suppressed emotions, people around us predictably become concerned and instinctively try to make us "feel better." By doing so, they encourage us to *re-cover* (to cover up our surfacing suppressed emotions again). Our task isn't to *recover,* but to *discover.*

When we experience the surfacing of suppressed emotional states, to express ourselves to individuals who have no point of reference for what we are engaged in only invites unnecessary interference. As we make this journey, it's recommended we use discernment in discussing our experience with others. This is called "containment." Be alert not to use surfacing emotional discomfort as a means of gaining attention. Projecting our drama may initially help us to feel better – to *recover.* But it can't help us to become better at feeling – to *discover.*

Bringing awareness into our breathing is an integral part of The Presence Process because our breath is both an efficient and readily accessible tool for anchoring our attention in the present. Initially, we might imagine that the breathing practice used throughout this process is like breath work and rebirthing. While the breathing practice used in The Presence Process isn't aligned with the intent and practices of breath work and rebirthing, it is consistent with much about these fields of exploration and may be viewed as an accompaniment to them. However, the intent of consciously connected breathing is unique to The Presence Process.

Also, this process isn't intended to be Pranayama Yoga or any other technique that seeks to magnify our awareness of breathing with the intent to activate and access vibrational experience. *This process doesn't concern itself with breath control, but rather with releasing unconscious control over our breath so as to establish a normal and healthy breathing pattern.*

The primary intent of consciously connected breathing is the activation and accumulation of Presence and present moment awareness through the integration of unconscious emotional blockages that inhibit our current experience.

How does consciously connected breathing activate present moment awareness? Many of us spend our waking hours thinking either about circumstances from the past or events yet to occur. Indeed, the thinking aspect of the mind is almost exclusively engaged in such activity. Thinking about the past and future is a mental addiction that imprisons humanity in a distracted internal dream state, reflected outwardly as ongoing planetary conflict, chaos, and confusion.

Throughout this text, we call this addictive dream state "living in time," a condition devoid of present moment awareness and thus of the consciousness of consequence. We can't be responsible for the quality of our experience, be available to support others, and experience our connectedness with all life unless we enter present moment awareness.

Without present moment awareness, it's challenging to perceive the energetic connection between cause and effect. We remain oblivious of the unified field in which we are all dancers. However, when we are authentically present, we can't knowingly cause harm to another because the intimately connected nature of present moment awareness equips us with the capacity to *feel* the consequences of our behavior. Insensitive behavior indicates absence of both present moment awareness and the felt-perception that arises out of it.

Fortunately we aren't completely lost within the dream state of the time-based paradigm. A lifeline into present moment awareness resides within us all: our breath. There's no way to breathe in the past or in the future. We can only breathe in the present. By becoming aware of our breathing, we activate a tool that facilitates withdrawal of our attention from both the past and the future. By focusing our attention and intent on connecting our breathing, we encourage an aspect of our awareness to remain anchored in the moment.

The Presence Process brings unintegrated and suppressed memories to the surface as gently as possible, while it simultaneously facilitates safe integration, the gaining of required insight, and the neutralizing of the destructive impact of our suppressed emotional charge on the quality of our current experience. By accomplishing this, it answers two questions we all ask in one way or another beginning in childhood: *What happened?* and, *How can I stop this from happening again?* As long as these two questions remain unanswered, they deflect our attention from the present into past trauma and a fearfully projected future. Left unanswered, these questions are a springboard into continual anxiety. The Presence Process calms and resolves this anxiety at its causal point.

This procedure isn't intended to be a "spiritual" process or a "spiritual experience," although it undoubtedly impacts our vibrational awareness. It's more accurately viewed as an integrated physical, mental, and emotional technology that facilitates emotional awakening, emotional growth, and ongoing emotional development.

In other words, The Presence Process is about *showing up* by *growing up*, and *growing up* by *showing up*.

CONSCIOUSNESS OF QUESTIONS

To assist us in activating the attitude of surrender required to enter into The Presence Process, we first change our relationship with the way we respond to questions. We place our focus on *the asking of the question*, not on attempting to think up answers. We allow the answer to manifest unexpectedly, organically, trusting it to arise in the moment we require the realization. This opens up our capacity for receiving.

One of our greatest errors is the assumption that the thinking aspect of the mind is the only avenue available to us when we are confronted with challenging questions. Whenever we are asked a question about a past experience, notice how the mental body examines our memory for the answer. There are answers we access immediately without the need to think, and there are answers that appear to require a measure of thinking before they can be accessed. However, there are other questions whose answer is inaccessible no matter how much thinking we do.

The mental body keeps searching until a particular self-limiting thought arises, such as, "I don't know" or "I can't remember." The moment the mental body entertains such a self-limiting thought, the thinking aspect of mind brings closure to its investigation.

Once we accept that the answer to a question about our past appears inaccessible by thinking about it, there arises within us a self-judgment such as, "I can't remember because my long-term memory isn't good," "I can't remember because it isn't significant to me," "I can't remember because it's too painful," or "I can't remember because it happened long ago." The mental body punctuates its inability to answer a question by thinking about it with a self-judgment because this conceals the fact it doesn't know everything. Instead of embracing the unknown, the mental body blames external circumstances for its apparent lack of ability to access information through thinking. Whenever this happens, we inadvertently shut our experience off from the "knowing" that comes from Presence. This shutting-off occurs because Presence is non-interfering. Its communication is continuous, but this communication is hidden from us when we insist on gaining information only through the process of thinking.

Accessing information without the application of thought may seem foreign to us because of the mentally dominated approach of our current educational system. However, contrary to popular assumption, the thinking aspect of the mind isn't the be-all and end-all of our capacity for insight. On the contrary, we have an ability to receive insight when we least expect it.

We have all had the answer to a question come to us when it feels like we "can't quite get it." Because the answer feels accessible, as if it's just out of reach, we don't terminate our mental search for it but instead tell ourselves something like, "I know that I know this," "It will come to me," or "It's on the tip of my tongue." The result is that it *does* come to us. While our attention is diverted to something else, the answer mysteriously pops into our awareness as though it had always been available.

Similarly, many inventors testify that the crucial piece of information that made their invention possible surfaced when they took their attention off the task at hand and occupied themselves with something else, such as a relaxing nap.

These types of experiences reveal that all the relevant information we seek about our past experience is available when we apply the correct method of access, which doesn't necessarily require thought. Instead, it requires *being open to receive the answer from an aspect of ourselves that knows everything.*

As we currently conceive of ourselves, we don't know everything. But there is an aspect of our *beingness*, which we may so far be unaware of, that does. It knows everything without having to think about anything. Presence is a silent witness to each experience we go through and it remembers everything in each moment of these experiences as if they are still happening. To Presence, all the experiences we ever go through are as if they were happening in the now, because *beingness* resides in present moment awareness, which knows no time. Presence is a constant witness to all experience as if all experience were unfolding simultaneously.

Throughout The Presence Process, we are encouraged to ask many questions about our experience. So as not to lessen the potential of our questioning, we are encouraged to approach the asking of questions *without resorting to thinking about the answers*. Either we know the answer to a question or we don't. Thinking about it doesn't alter this. Thinking may entice conjecture, but it's impotent when it comes to activating *knowing* if knowing isn't already self-evident. When we rely solely on thinking, we invariably make up stories that are inauthentic.

In contrast to mentally understanding something, knowing requires that we enter an integrated physical, mental, and emotional *experience* of what it is we seek to know. If we have no memory of such an integrated experience, thinking about it won't make any difference. By asking a question without trying to think of the answer – by asking a question sincerely, then letting it go and allowing the answer to be given – we invite a manifestation of the required answer through physical, mental, and emotional experience. Presence oversees the manifestation of the answer as and when required.

A question and its answer have the same relationship as any cause and its effect. At the moment of asking a question, we are operating from causality. Consequently, we are already connected into the answering experience. When we don't terminate this moment of causality with self-limiting reactivity, the answer is delivered to our awareness in some form or another exactly when required (though, I emphasize, *not necessarily when we wish)*. The question is the cause, while the answer is the effect. They are already intimately connected because they are part of each other. The one guarantees the other. This is the approach we are invited to take toward any question before us during this process.

Don't be even slightly concerned when you have no immediate recall in answer to a question in this text. Our task is complete once we sincerely ask the question. When the answer isn't immediately apparent, we simply keep an open mind on the matter and allow the answer to arise without effort through our day-to-day experience. It arrives when required, not when we wish it would.

The mental body is a useful mechanism for conveying insight, but it isn't *the means with which to access insight.* Presence accesses insight and delivers it to us through the mechanics of the mental body, precisely when and how we require it. Our task is to open ourselves to its unlimited capabilities by not trying to figure everything out mentally.

Asking significant life questions from the point of awareness allows the energy of inspiration and insight to awaken in our daily experience. It allows us to enter the resonance of *knowing without having to know why.* This is especially useful during The Presence

Process because we will be accessing experiences that occurred prior to the development of our mental capacity – before we had the ability to attach mental concepts to everything. Many of these experiences are now only accessible to us through felt-perception as emotional states, energetic vibrations, and physical sensations. They are felt "energies in motion," vibrational experiences that occurred in the womb and shortly after we were birthed, that we engage directly through our capacity for felt-perception. When we insist on mentally understanding the "why" of everything, we inhibit our ability to access these early felt-memories so that their impact on our current experience can be integrated.

The questions we choose to ask throughout this emotional processing experience are significant. Their answers liberate. As with cause and effect, when we ask a question and simultaneously keep ourselves open, the answers always manifest in some form. Throughout The Presence Process, we are invited to explore the experience of allowing ourselves to *receive* answers, as opposed to *getting them*.

MOVEMENT BEYOND MOTION

Often we embark on the type of experience we are about to begin in The Presence Process because we seek to "change ourselves."

If we mistakenly believe we *are* our experience, instead of realizing we are Presence *having* an experience, we are likely to attempt to "heal ourselves" by changing our behavior, appearance, or circumstances. These are merely an *expression* of what we are and represent an experience we are currently moving through.

Not realizing this truth – not being able to differentiate between what we already are and the experience we are currently moving through – leads us into endless external doing.

Though we can't change *ourselves*, we can change *the quality of our experience*.

As we enter The Presence Process, we are asked to adjust our perception of what we think of as "movement." Generally, when we speak of movement, we are referring to a physical event, as in movement from one physical location to another. As far as the physical world is concerned, there's no possibility of a journey without physical movement.

The Presence Process involves a different kind of movement that doesn't result from physical activity – movement that isn't simply motion, but that results in a shift in the quality of our life experience, a shift that's always in the direction of increased *authenticity*.

To illustrate the difference, consider what we usually do if we are dissatisfied with the quality of our experience. We may change our circumstances by changing the person with whom we are partnered, changing our job, or moving to another town, city, or even country. These kinds of changes require a lot of physical motion.

Running around and getting nowhere is the movement endorsed by the world as a means to rectify the dissatisfaction we feel with the quality of our day-to-day experience. The trouble is, once we are settled in our new location, we invariably discover that despite our altered physical circumstances, our dissatisfaction resurfaces. This is because, despite rearranging our situation, we haven't initiated authentic movement *within* ourselves. As has been said, "Wherever we go, there we are."

We've all gone through this frustrating experience in one form or another. This type of rearranging of our day-to-day experience is nothing but pointless commotion – a better word for which is perhaps "drama," the word used throughout this text to describe this type of pointless movement. Drama is physical, mental, and emotional activity that focuses on and fiddles with effects without impacting causality.

The Presence Process leads us out of drama by activating authentic movement in our experience. Much of our unconscious approach to life arises from a Catch 22, which is that until we activate authentic movement in our experience, we reactively resort to drama. But as long as we reactively resort to drama, we don't attempt to activate authentic movement. The Presence Process shows us how to release ourselves from this Catch 22 by instructing us how to integrate blocked *emotions*. Once these blocked emotions are liberated, the effect is reflected automatically in our physical, mental, and emotional experience.

By raising our capacity for causal adjustment – also referred to as "alchemy" – we activate authentic movement throughout our experience without resorting to drama. Only when we realize the effectiveness of this alchemical approach are we prepared to drop drama. Through authentic alchemy, the pointlessness of all drama becomes self-evident. Once we realize this, the dharma of all drama is accessed.

When we enter The Presence Process, we begin moving from "doing" to being, looking to seeing, hearing to listening, discomfort to balance, separation to being unified, reacting to responding, inauthenticity to authenticity, fragmentation to integration, seeking happiness to allowing joy, revenge and blame to forgiveness, incorrect perception to correct perception, complaint and competition to compassion, behaving unconsciously to behaving consciously, and "living in time" to experiencing present moment awareness.

All the above movements are variations of the same shift—from pretence to Presence. This shift is achieved solely by using our attention and intent to adjust our felt-perception.

Because of the example set for us by the world, it's challenging to comprehend achieving authentic change in our current circumstances without drama. For instance, as we enter this experience, we may already be adding unnecessary drama. We may intend to give up smoking and other addictions, place ourselves on a special diet, and add a workout program to our daily routine – all while experiencing The Presence Process!

When we attempt to change any aspect of our experience as a means of feeling better, we automatically engage in drama. Drama places the focus of our attention on fiddling with effects, not on causality. By entertaining the possibility that what we require now isn't more drama, but rather the activation of authentic movement, we save ourselves the wasted energy of attempting to complement our experience of this process by embarking on any unnecessary outer activity.

As we enter The Presence Process, we are asked not to judge our experience by *how good we feel* as we move through it. We are encouraged not to expect this journey to be *easy*. Instead, we are invited to intend an *authentic* experience for ourselves, even when this may be uncomfortable.

We are invited to entertain the possibility that the key to restoring harmony to the quality of our life experience lies in personal emotional development. We are also invited to consider that personal emotional development comes from surrendering ourselves to an experience of "not knowing."

Our appearance, behavior, and circumstances as they are *right now* are the accumulated consequences of the current condition of our emotional body. If we don't like an aspect of this, we have the ability to change it. However, authentic movement that brings about lasting change in our experience is only realized through adjusting the point of causality. Fiddling with our behavior, appearance, or circumstances may bring us temporary relief, but not permanent resolution – not integration.

Resorting to making drastic external changes is a manifestation of our unconscious desire to control and sedate what's unfolding. Such reactive behavior breeds commotion. It leads us into taking on too much too soon, which is an unconscious way of sabotaging ourselves. The Presence Process reveals experientially that it's by adjusting causality – by activating authentic movement within the current condition of our emotional body – that enduring change in our experience is realized.

As we enter this journey, we are wise to be discerning about any intent to simultaneously make major outer adjustments to our behavior, appearance, or circumstances. If such sudden adjustments can wait until after our completion of the process, it's recommended we give ourselves permission to take a break from outer drama. Be cautious of entertaining impulsive behavior that's intended to bring about drastic changes. Throughout the duration of this process, see the words "impulsive" and "drastic" as indicators of drama.

No one can tell us what's required of us. However, our *heart* knows the difference between forcing something and allowing it to unfold organically. Don't push the river! While moving through this process, *thinking and engaging in outer physical "doings" move us away from direct felt-perception.* If we feel we are receiving insights that direct us to make any major adjustment to our appearance, behavior, or life circumstances, let's agree to simply "be with" such insights for a while before acting. Allow this urge to "do something" to breathe, so we may discover whether it's a valid response or a reactive reflex. Such impulses for drastic action often erupt during the course of emotional processing as a reaction to unconscious emotional imprinting that's surfacing for integration.

Journeys in which we mistakenly attempt to change ourselves by fiddling with our behavior, appearance, or circumstances are like moving a radio around a room as a means of tuning into a desired station. In contrast, the journey initiated by The Presence Process, in which we discover how to adjust the quality of our experience at its causal point, requires us to leave the radio exactly where it is. Instead, we focus our attention and intent on turning the tuning dial. This is a much simpler approach than resorting to drama, and it enables us to tune into the music, which brings us exactly what we require.

The experience of present moment awareness is nowhere "out there" in the world. Present moment awareness is an inner accomplishment – an inside job. Having said this, once present moment awareness is activated by emotional integration, the results are automatically reflected in our experience of the world.

Activating awareness of Presence is free and available to all, regardless of external segregation caused by color, caste, or creed. It requires no rites, rituals, or dogma. Our capacity to be causally responsible is our birthright.

Our journey through The Presence Process is simple, so let's not complicate it by *trying hard* to do this heart work properly or correctly, to the point of bringing in increased activity. Such drama is wasted energy. It's like throwing dust at an oncoming gust. All that's required of us is our consistent attendance to the breathing practice, the conscious responses, and reading the allotted text containing the perceptual tools.

THE PATHWAY OF AWARENESS AND SEVEN-YEAR CYCLE

THE PATHWAY OF AWARENESS

Acknowledging and operating in line with a pathway of awareness that's native to all humans is why The Presence Process is perceptually impactful, oftentimes obvious, and – considering all that is accomplished – borders on effortless. Within this text, we call this "the pathway of awareness."

Our experience manifests mostly through an unconscious application of attention and intent along this pathway. It is, therefore, second nature to all – though it remains hidden until brought into awareness.

To be acquainted with the simple dynamics of this pathway assists us in integrating the fact that it's necessary to access and adjust the emotional core of our experience in order to initiate authentic transformation in the mental and physical. Once we recognize our footprints on the pathway of awareness and identify the seven-year cycle in our life experience, we are better equipped to integrate the causal points of uncomfortable experiences.

The pathway of awareness is easy to identify: just observe the natural development of a newborn. Even though the emotional, mental, and physical capacities are already evident and developing simultaneously alongside each other from the moment of birth, there's a specific pathway our individual awareness uses to move consciously through them. First a child cries, smiles, and coos, which is emotional. Next it learns to communicate in a variety of ways that eventually include speech, which is mental. Only then does it learn to walk, which is of course physical. The pathway of awareness is therefore *from the emotional, through the mental, to the physical.*

When we leave the womb, we are primarily emotional beings. All we are able to do is emote. We don't have a verbal language to conceptualize our experience or communicate with it. Nor do we have the motor skills to physically participate in anything independently. Our experience of the world is one of *energy in motion,* with which we engage primarily through felt-perception. We remain in this mostly emotional state – bathed in felt-perception – until we recognize something and deliberately begin interacting with it.

Our next step along the pathway of awareness, the mental realm, unfolds as we discover how to deliberately use emotions to achieve a particular outcome. When this occurs, emotions are no longer just a reactive reflex to our circumstances. They now become a means to consciously interact with our experience. The moment we use crying and smiling as tools of deliberate communication, we are no longer primarily emoting but are also participating mentally. This entry into mentality is concretized when we verbalize our first word. This first word is an act of naming something – an act of recognition. Being able to call upon aspects of our experience and recognize them indicates the door is now open for us to take the next step along the pathway of awareness, which is into the physical realm.

When we can recognize and call upon aspects of our experience, it's because these aspects no longer appear only as *energy in motion.* The moment we name anything, we are able to do so because its appearance as energy in motion subsides and it begins to appear as solid matter. We name something because it "matters" to us.

Our recognition, and the subsequent capacity to name, is the consequence of acknowledging that what was once flowing energy is now transformed into what appears as solid, dense, and stationary matter. Part of entering into human experience is to be equipped with the perceptual capacity to "make everything matter." We then become addicted to this capacity to the point that we are no longer aware of what our experience was like before everything "mattered" to us. This addiction is what enables us to perceptually enter into and have solid physical encounters with circumstances that are in reality pure vibration. We "stop the world" so we can move about in it.

As children, once our perception stops the world and we start naming the individualized pieces, we crawl curiously toward what we've named and engage in a personal encounter with it. This outward movement of attention and intent, triggered by curiosity, leads us out of a primarily emotional and mental experience into the third step along the pathway of awareness, the physical realm. Curiosity is necessary for us to make the effort to take baby steps into "a world that matters to us."

This pathway of awareness from the emotional, through the mental, and into the physical, which we all move along to enter our experience of the world, is clearly acknowledged in the way the world behaves toward us, although this behavior is primarily unconscious. Recognizing how the world acknowledges the pathway of awareness unveils the seven-year cycle.

SEVEN-YEAR CYCLE

The primarily emotional development that begins the moment we leave the womb tapers off and, for most of us, ceases altogether as we approach the age of seven. By seven, childhood is officially over. We are now young girls and boys. This is why formal education really gets underway around the age of seven, as we are informed that it's time for us to "grow up."

This seventh-year transition point marks our exit from the accentuated emotional body development of childhood into a greater focus on our developing mental capacity. From seven to fourteen years of age, we are trained to mentally grasp and develop the basics of communication skills: speaking, reading, and writing. We are also instructed in appropriate behavior for the society into which we are born.

Around fourteen years of age, we encounter another transition point. Our mental development becomes focused on what others anticipate is required for us to take up a meaningful physical role in society. This adjustment of our focus is simultaneously marked by an increase in physical awareness of our environment and the relationships we have within it and with it. This refocusing from primarily mental to physical expression is punctuated in our physical body by the experience of puberty.

Puberty marks our departure from our seven-year mental socialization and acclimatization cycle, signaling our entry into our third seven-year cycle. This third seven-year cycle intensifies the development of our relationship with the physical world. We are now teenagers. During this third seven-year cycle, we become increasingly aware of our own physical body and our physical interactions within the world. We become attracted to and repelled by other human beings. We choose our group. Emphasis is placed on mentally mapping out how we are going to fulfill our roles as physically responsible and capable humans. The closing of this third seven-year cycle is often acknowledged by celebrating our 21st birthday. We are now young adults.

The Presence Process demonstrates through personal experience that in view of the natural flow of the pathway of awareness and the three initial seven-year cycles, the cause of our current physical experience doesn't lie in our present physical circumstances. Neither does it lie in our current thought forms. By first instructing us how to activate physical presence, then mental clarity, The Presence Process reveals experientially that the first emotionally-driven seven-year cycle of childhood is the cause of our current uncomfortable experiences.

Emotional seeds, planted primarily energetically through felt-perception during the first seven-year cycle, sprout into ongoing discomfort unless they are consciously integrated. Out of this ongoing discomfort, we then manufacture reactive mental states – thought forms – which in turn manifest as the unbalanced conditions and circumstances we experience physically. Throughout this text, we call the mechanics of this causal seeding "emotional imprinting."

A profound insight The Presence Process offers is that, emotionally, *since we exited our first seven-year cycle, nothing new has occurred.* Even though we may daily appear to be moving through new physical circumstances and mental experiences, *on an emotional level nothing changes unless we consciously integrate it.*

Emotionally, each seven years we repeat the same cycle that was imprinted in our emotional body during our first seven-year experience. As we teach ourselves to identify the emotional undercurrent that runs through all our mental and physical experiences, we realize it only *appears* we are growing up and having a variety of different experiences.

By age fourteen, our attention and intent are habitually *transfixed* on the physical circumstances of life. We are in a mental *trance, fixed* on a world that matters. As adults, we only perceive the solid surface of things. Because the physical world, with its inherently cyclic nature, appears to be constantly changing and seems to make itself anew in each moment, an illusion of continuous change is established. But this appearance of continuous change is a trick of the physical world. This is the great illusion. In the East, this slight of hand by the physical world is called *maya.*

By instructing us how to look beneath the surface of things, The Presence Process reveals the physical world's sleight of hand. This is achieved by using our felt-perception to peer beneath the physical circumstances and the mental story we tell ourselves about them, and there "see" the emotional content of life. This "seeing" is accomplished by *allowing ourselves to feel aspects of our experience that we've long suppressed.* When we accomplish this seeing – this felt-perception – we realize we are all diligently, albeit unconsciously, repeating a pattern imprinted in our emotional body during childhood.

Repeating this emotional pattern unconsciously gives rise to the experience of "living in time." We then realize it isn't possible to enter present moment awareness by, as it were, "removing our wristwatch" – that is, by making purely mental and physical adjustments to our current circumstances. We enter it by integrating the energetic impact our uncomfortable childhood experiences had on our emotional body.

Moving through The Presence Process enables us to identify the repetitive and stagnant condition our personal energy makeup reveals, which shows us that we are indeed living in the past and constantly writing a future that obediently replicates the emotional content of our past.

Moving through The Presence Process also reveals that we died an emotional death when we were approaching seven years of age. This is the causal energetic death point from which we are invited to reawaken. Our repetitive emotional patterns are the dream that, on the surface of things, appears to be reality. As we learn to see beneath the surface of this dream state, we discover something startling: adults living in a mentally driven, physically transfixed, time-based paradigm are "dead children."

Dying to our child self to become an acceptable adult is a coping mechanism, not a necessity. We are only pretending to be dead. It's up to us to break through the self-manufactured perceptual prison bars of adulthood and free our child self from the dungeon of pretence. By gaining the experience necessary to rescue our innocence (inner sense), we equip ourselves to enter a whole new paradigm – one in which inner sense and outer experience abide in harmony on balanced scales of wisdom.

"I don't know why this keeps happening to me," we say as a situation appears to repeat itself yet again. Or we may ask, "Why does this keep happening over and over again?" By taking a conscious journey into the dynamics of our emotional undercurrents, we realize why we have heard ourselves and others make such statements or ask such questions. It isn't our physical circumstances or the repetitive stories we tell ourselves about these circumstances that we are inquiring about, but our *felt-state* when things keep happening in our life experience. This felt-state is a reaction to the emotional cycles of childhood, which are reoccurring in our current experience. The unintegrated emotional content of our experience constantly repeats and causes manifestations of mental and physical discomfort.

Once we realize we are consistently but unconsciously recreating the emotional resonance of childhood, we take the first step into awakening ourselves from this dream state. We realize that if we are to initiate authentic change in the quality of our life experience, it's pointless to meddle with our physical circumstances. For a while we may habitually fiddle physically with these experiences, or we may try to change the story we tell ourselves, but we will ultimately realize that such activity, motion, and commotion is drama and accomplishes nothing.

One of the reasons the emotional experience of our first seven years remains undigested is that our human experience isn't solely an emotional one. It also has mental and physical components. To fully integrate any experience requires embracing it emotionally, mentally, and physically. During the first seven-year cycle, we have the ability to interact emotionally, but our mental and physical capacities aren't yet sufficiently developed to participate in an integrative process. This is why the world steps in when we are around seven years old, emphasizing formal education and thereby all but freezing our emotional development. Unless it did this, we wouldn't focus on developing mental and then physical capacities, all of which are necessary so that in due course we may become fully integrated.

The Presence Process isn't concerned with manufacturing "another experience" for us outside the one already in play. We aren't aspiring to "bliss" or "enlightenment." Our intent is the full embrace of *this-here-now,* not moving beyond it or seeking something else. We are instructed how to show up in *this* experience, *here* and *now.* We accomplish this by listening to the felt-communications of our emotional imprinting. We discover how to use attention and intent to return our awareness to the place where our emotional development ended abruptly – to where Presence became obscured by pretence.

By accomplishing this, we realize firsthand why an intentional journey beneath the physical illusion and mental confusion is required to reactivate and revitalize the energies responsible for authentic movement. On this journey, we consciously travel seemingly backwards along the pathway of awareness, deactivating the charged emotional impact the seven-year cycle has on our present experiences. The veil of past trauma is torn, together with a projected future, allowing the joy and beauty inherent in the present to be revealed. This is no small task, but when we undertake it, we realize why it's one of the most significant quests set before us.

Journeying "backwards" isn't an apt description of this process. It only makes sense because we are living in the mentality of linear time and therefore perceive ourselves as constantly moving forward. Until we integrate our past, we spin in energetic circles like a puppy attempting to catch its tail. A more appropriate way to describe the journey activated by The Presence Process is that we are commencing a movement "inward" toward vibrational awareness.

The outer shell of our experience is physical and remains physical as long as everything "matters" to us. As we discover how to take steps inward, we move through the mental, then through the emotional, which is one step away from the vibrational. Unless we consciously integrate our charged emotional condition, we don't develop the capacity to contain vibrational awareness. We may use physical and mental processes to pop in and out of vibrational awareness, but without emotional integration we remain impotent in terms of an ongoing experience of vibrational awareness.

Our inward journey along the pathway of awareness isn't unfamiliar to us. Whenever we wish to make contact with our source, we automatically take this journey. To see this in action, watch a child pray. First it kneels down and puts its hands together (the physical). Then it speaks to source (the mental). Then its words of innocence touch our heart and activate felt-states (the emotional). The return journey into source-awareness along the pathway of awareness is from the physical, through the mental, through the emotional, and into the vibrational.

The Presence Process not only makes us aware of the pathway we took when we left our childlike emotional innocence for the adult world, it instructs us how to revisit our first seven-year cycle with the intent of integrating experiences that were imprinted in our emotional body. Unless we return along the pathway of awareness and bring peace to our child self, we remain unintegrated as adults. Authentic movement in our current experience isn't activated, and neither is harmony restored to our mental and physical states.

The seven-year cycle is continually adjusting itself in line with the present acceleration of our evolution. For instance, today some children experience cycles that may be shortened to six and even five-year periods, as we witness their transition from emotional into mental body development at earlier ages. However, for the purpose of The Presence Process, we refer to this repetition of energetic cycles as the seven-year cycle.

By putting ourselves through The Presence Process, we gradually integrate the emotionally charged impact our first seven-year cycle has on the quality of our present experience. Repeating this process more than once dismantles this energetic cycle altogether because it removes the internal perceptual barrier that resulted from the emotional death we experienced when entering adulthood.

Once this cycle is sufficiently dismantled, we stand at the edge of possibility. Our programmed awareness of having a past and a projected future fades into the eternal moment of Presence. Our energetic experience of polarities then dissolves, and our awareness consciously merges into the unified vibrational field.

NOTE: Don't be concerned that you may not yet be able to discern the evidence of the seven-year cycle in your experience. It isn't necessary to understand this cycle mentally in order to integrate it. Through The Presence Process, we integrate these patterns whether we grasp them mentally or not. Identifying our seven-year cycle is best accomplished through insight, not understanding. Relevant insight is acquired once we develop the capacity to contain it.

To contain an insight such as this requires detaching our attention from the surface events of our experience and becoming aware, through the development of felt-perception, of the emotional undercurrent that runs throughout our experience. This requires accumulation of present moment awareness. The Presence Process empowers us to accomplish this at the pace that's most beneficial for us. When we are patient, all is revealed as required.

EMOTIONAL IMPRINTING

Emotional imprinting is the term we use in The Presence Process to describe the unconscious passing on to us of our parents' or caregivers' unintegrated emotional condition. By the time we reach seven years of age, we are emotionally picking up where they left off.

The unavoidable consequence of childhood is that we all receive this emotional baton from our parents so that we may take our part in the human race. Imprinting is an unfolding of a sacred agreement we have with each other. Imprinting is therefore not something *done to us* by our parents, or something we *do to another* when playing the role of parent. It's an experience we *enter together*.

This initial seven-year period of passing the emotional baton from parent to child may also be regarded as the deliberate process of "destiny downloading." This is because the content of our first seven-year emotional cycle establishes an energetic pattern that contains the potential of our emotional, mental, and physical circumstances.

Our potential for our life experience is downloaded *vibrationally* during the last seven months of womb life, *emotionally* during the first seven years after birth, *mentally* between seven and fourteen years of age, and *physically* by the time we turn twenty-one. Each dimension of this transference occurs through imprinting, like osmosis. This imprinting, which is primarily delivered to our energetic systems via felt-perception, occurs through a whole range of interactive physical, mental, and emotional experiences.

In the first seven months, we are mainly imprinted by the felt-vibrations we experience in our mother's womb. This occurs as we sense her heart beating, lungs breathing, blood pumping, body movement, the resonance of her voice, and so on. In the first seven years, we are imprinted primarily through interactions with our parents and immediate family, though also through our felt-encounters with every aspect of our environment. During the years from seven to fourteen, educators, encounters at school, and peer groups imprint us mentally. From fourteen to twenty-one, our first lovers and interactions with our broader physical environment imprint us. By the time we are twenty-one, the energetic potential of our destiny is imprinted vibrationally, emotionally, mentally, and physically in the fabric of our multi-dimensional experience.

While we "live in time," these imprinted experiences and energetic potentials surface continually as physical, mental, and emotional manifestations that seemingly occur randomly and haphazardly. However, there is nothing random or haphazard about them.

A barometer of the extent of our entry into present moment awareness is the degree to which we perceive how deliberately each and every experience we have is unfolding.

If imprinting occurs vibrationally in the womb, we may wonder why we only focus on integrating the emotional imprinting received between our birth and seven years of age. The answer is that integration of both our vibrational and emotional imprinting requires felt-perception. Unless we are able to feel vibrations, we are unable to integrate them. By focusing our attention on integrating our emotional charge – by facilitating ourselves so we *feel this energetic condition without condition* – we reawaken and develop felt-perception.

Once felt-perception is developed, we are endowed with the perceptual capacity to consciously participate in our vibrational unfolding. Indeed, attaining present moment awareness through the integration of our emotional imprinting automatically delivers us onto the perceptual platform on which we effortlessly merge with the train journeying into the vibrational.

Until we awaken to the point that we adjust this seven-year cycle at an emotional level through unconditional felt-perception, we are enslaved by it. It's our willingness to awaken to an awareness of the mechanisms of our imprinted destiny that empowers us to direct our pathway consciously and responsibly.

Only at this point do we reestablish and explore what we now conceptually *think* of as "free will." Participating consciously in our destiny becomes possible as we integrate the discomfort in our emotional body by decreasing charged emotion. Once we are no longer driven into compensatory experiences by charged emotion, our interaction with the emotional body is restored to its highest potential.

In other words, we *take charge* of our experience by *taking the charge out of it,* which then enables us to live on purpose. Taking responsibility for the quality of our experience by integrating charged emotion is the doorway into authentic personal freedom.

This level of emotional integration is only possible when we decrease our pain and discomfort to a point where we view all emotion as "energy in motion," instead of deeming some emotions as threatening and to be avoided, while we find others so seductive that we are driven uncontrollably into activity because of them. To experience authentic emotional integration means we move beyond favoring one emotion over another. Full emotional integration precipitates a state of felt-acceptance within ourselves, in which we no longer have an agenda concerning which emotions we seek to experience.

Remember that before we started naming energy – before the energy "mattered" to us – it was primarily experienced as "energy in motion." This was before we attempted to make sense of it, while we were in a state of *pre-sense.* Returning to present moment awareness is an adjustment to our perception that restores our neutral relationship with energy. Through this shift, all "energy in motion" becomes fuel for authentic movement in the quality of our experience.

EMOTIONAL CHARGE

The main characteristic of charged emotion is that we perceive it as *uncomfortable*. This is because it's trapped, blocked, sedated, and controlled energy.

Because this charged emotion has been with us from childhood, we are for the most part numb to it. However, our resistance to emotion's inherent compulsion to move causes friction, and this friction causes heat to seep into various aspect of our experience. We then manifest a reflection of this charged inner heat, which causes our life experience to become hellish.

Our human experience is currently acutely combustive. We mold our circumstances by heating them up, boiling them, and burning them. We heat practically all our food. Many of the liquids we drink, from coffee to alcohol, generate heat in our internal experience. Many of the substances we are addicted to, like sugar, cause heat within the body. We even manufacture cigarettes as a means to burn and heat up the air we inhale. Our current modes of transportation cannot move without combustion.

This continual heating up of our human experience is a manifestation of our collective, unconscious, internal combustion. Our intense resistance to being authentic fans these flames. Because we feel more comfortable entertaining pretence instead of Presence, we feel more comfortable living in "a world on fire." Because we can't perceive the energetic mechanics of our internal heat, we can't perceive what "living in the fires of hell" is about.

We describe the felt-aspect of this charged emotional condition by a variety of names, but the trinity that includes them all is fear, anger, and grief. Fear, anger, and grief are mental definitions of the heat arising from emotionally charged resistance. Comprehending the relationship between heat and charged emotion, as well as that the emotional body is symbolically associated with the element of water, gives us a new appreciation for many of the expressions in our language that describe emotional overload:

"In the heat of the moment"
Self–esteem (self is steem)
"Hot under the collar"
"Going to blow my top"
"Blowing off steam"
"Loosing my cool"
"I'm in hot water now"
"Blowing my top."

Aside from the hellfire imagery generated through this emotionally charged experience, this predicament manifests in two ways:

1. **DRAMA:** The first consequence of charged emotion is drama. *Drama is reactive projection* – whether physical, mental, or emotional – which we use to gain the attention from others that *we don't yet have the capacity to give ourselves.*

   We all have a range of tried and tested acts we conceived when our authentic behavior was discouraged – when we were entrained into resisting being spontaneous. These acts are our re-act-ions.

   A spontaneously joyful and creative child is pure energy in motion. To incorporate us into the adult world – into "living in time" as we call it in The Presence Process – our parents and environment start to weed out much of our spontaneous behavior. As part of our emotional imprinting, we are subjected to experiences in childhood in which our authentic behavior is discouraged and reshaped into calculated appropriateness. This occurs so we become socially acceptable in the adult world. In this way, the child's Presence is replaced by adult pretence.

   Although spontaneous behavior such as running around naked in public is deemed cute for a two-year-old, it becomes inappropriate for an eight-year-old, and in many societies even illegal for an eighteen-year-old. Whether spontaneous behavior requires tempering (note the pun) isn't the point under discussion, since we are focusing on the consequences of this behavior.

The reshaping of spontaneous behavior is usually accomplished by parental use of words such as "stop" and "no." What isn't apparent is that *the energetic activity underlying spontaneous behavior never stops when interrupted by enforced discipline. It merely transforms into something else*, becoming energetic resistance that manifests as calculated drama.

Calculated drama is successful in that it makes us acceptable to the adult world, while in the same breath it renders our own authenticity unacceptable to us. This rejection of our inner being triggers energetic conflict, and this conflict is projected and reflected outwardly in the many acts we conjure up to gain attention and acceptance.

This rejection of ourselves is followed *by seeking others to accept us on our behalf. We then desperately try to "borrow" a sense of ourselves as acceptable from these individuals.* This is the inspiration for many of our dramas. Our underlying desire for attention and acceptance is a longing to have the discomfort and heat generated by charged emotion numbed. Projected drama arises from the mistaken belief that someone "out there" can relieve and remove this discomfort on our behalf.

As we realize that certain aspects of our authentic behavior are no longer acceptable, and we manufacture little acts to gain acceptance, our gauge on whether these acts work is based on how much attention they draw from our parents and immediate family. Often any attention, even when it's uncomfortable and has unwelcome consequences, is better than no attention. Hence our repertoire of behaviors leads to both negative *and* positive attention.

This desire for attention and acceptance can be positively and creatively channeled, as in many aspects of the performing and creative arts. However, being authentic within a craft entails first learning how to give ourselves the unconditional attention we seek from others.

2. **SELF-MEDICATION – sedation and control:** The second consequence of charged emotion is also a type of dramatic behavior that arises out of a reaction to inner discomfort. However, instead of being aimed outward at others to gain attention, this behavior is aimed inward at ourselves in an attempt to decrease our experience of our internal discomfort. Throughout The Presence Process, this behavior is called "self-medication." It manifests as *sedation* and *control.*

   Whenever circumstances arise that cause charged emotion to seep into our awareness, so that we start feeling uncomfortable within ourselves, we attempt to either sedate or control the experience. Let's examine these two types of reactivity:

   > **Sedation** is a dysfunction of the feminine side and an attempt to numb our awareness of our emotional charge. For example, the habitual need and use of alcohol is intended to sedate discomfort. We are drowning out our authentic emotional state. The expression popularly used is "drowning our sorrows."

   > **Control** is a dysfunction of the masculine side and an attempt to gain power over discomfort – to overpower it. The habitual need and use of cigarettes is intended to control our emotional charge. Whenever we don't know what's happening and feel out of control, we reach for a cigarette because, by smoking, we at least know what's going on: We are having a cigarette. Being able to reach for, light, and smoke a cigarette allows us to live in the illusion we are in control of our emotional charge.

   Smoking marijuana habitually is a popular tool for self-medication because it simultaneously achieves both sedation and control.

Behaviors associated with sedation and control range from blatant to subtle. Until we substantially decrease our charged emotion, we are self-medicating on one level or another. Our quest for "happiness," to "have it good," and to "have it be easy" are all behaviors associated with control and sedation.

By not entertaining habitual or addictive behavior, we instantly discover the felt-identity of the charged emotion that lies beneath our habits and addictions. The felt-state that erupts from abstinence reveals the nature and intensity of the charged emotion that's driving our self-medication.

Addictions, which are a form of self-medication, are energetically implanted in our field through vibrational, emotional, mental, and physical imprinting. Integrating charged emotion is the only authentic, causative treatment for addiction because any self-medicating habit is an effect of an internal emotional predicament.

Quitting self-medicating behaviors without integrating the associated emotional charge is ineffectual and accomplishes nothing. When we focus on the manifestation of the emotional charge instead of on its felt point of causality, we inevitably replace one self-medicating behavior with another. This is called "transference."

The extent to which we integrate charged emotion is what separates those who are authentically "in charge" of the quality of their experience from those who are "carrying a charge" that manifests in their experience.

When anyone enters our field of awareness, it may not be immediately apparent whether they are *in charge* of the quality of their experience or *carrying a charge*. However, observing their behavior over a period of time reveals all: Anyone carrying a substantially charged emotion sooner or later exhibits physical, mental, and emotional drama. They also entertain habits and addictions – self-medicating behaviors established as a means of sedation and control. Society's acceptance of alcohol and cigarettes enables us to self-medicate openly without feeling awkward about our inability to integrate an uncomfortable emotional charge.

BEYOND ADDICTION AND AFFLICTION

In the context of The Presence Process, addictions and afflictions (chronic illness and disease) are the same. Both are outer manifestations of an unintegrated charge within the emotional body.

Although we don't discuss allergies specifically, they are considered in the same light as addictions and afflictions. An allergy is the polar opposite of an addiction. When we are addicted, we pull a specific experience toward us. When we are allergic, we repel a specific experience. The causes of both are an unintegrated charge.

In The Presence Process, addiction is defined not only as something we do uncontrollably and habitually, but also as *seemingly random activity we are magnetically drawn toward when faced with specific emotional triggers.*

The Presence Process is efficient in instructing us how to integrate the causality of addictions and afflictions, no matter how long we have entertained them and how acutely we have allowed them to color our experience. The Presence Process doesn't instruct us in how to achieve integration by promising "a cure," because a cure is *a destination.* It instructs us how to enter an ongoing inner journey toward complete emotional integration, which gradually leads us beyond the manifestation of these outer experiences.

None of us are immune to "living in balance," no matter how acute our ailment! It's a matter of personal will, commitment, and *consistency.* When we intend activating Presence, and when this intent remains in the forefront of our awareness, integration of charged emotion is inevitable.

The Presence Process demonstrates that addiction, whether to illegal drugs, alcohol, food, sex, gambling, or legal prescription medications, is self-medicating behavior that we manifest to sedate and control the charge within our emotional body. Without self-medicating, an addict inevitably manifests an affliction. When an affliction is successfully suppressed by ongoing prescription medication, the same condition manifests as addiction. Both conditions are manifestations of an unintegrated emotional charge. Whether an unintegrated emotional charge manifests as an addiction, affliction, or allergy – or a combination of the three – depends on our individual circumstances.

When charged emotion is sufficiently integrated, there's no longer a foundation for addiction and affliction. Based on this simple realization, this process takes what may be considered an unusual and controversial stance in restoring harmony to those of us who have resorted to addictive behavior and prescription medications as a means to sedate and control the charge within our emotional body.

We aren't expected to cease our self-medicating behavior to commence The Presence Process. Even as it's recommended that we not invest in additional external activity, which is simply drama, during The Presence Process, so also forcing ourselves to quit addictive behavior and suspend prescription medication before commencing this journey for the first time is also not required.

Addictive behavior is *an effect*, and up to this moment in our experience may also constitute a necessary act of self-medication. When we attempt to quit self-medication ahead of the reduction of charged emotional content, we risk spiraling into states of unconscious behavior in which it becomes impossible to continue attending to our procedural commitments. Becoming deeply unconscious, we forget our "tools." We then become overwhelmed and discouraged, with the consequence that we invariably return to our addictive behavior more intensely than before we entered this process.

It is of course recommended, when possible, not to self-medicate while attending to our daily breathing practice and the required reading for each week.

MEDICAL ADVISORY: Those of us who suffer from afflictions are asked not to change prescription medication or any other prescribed therapeutic practice when commencing this procedure. We are to continue as per our doctor's recommendations. However, it's recommended that we closely monitor the impact of the prescription medication on our experience as we move through the process. If our response to our medication changes, it's recommended we immediately consult our medical practitioner, requesting an examination and review of our status. The reason for this is that as charged emotion related to our ailment commences integration, so does our relationship with medication. One of the ways this becomes apparent is when our medication starts feeling as if it's too strong. We may then request re-evaluation and a subsequent decrease of our prescribed dosage.

The reason we aren't asked to quit medications before starting our initial journey through The Presence Process is that we can't change anything by fiddling with an effect. Addictions and afflictions are effects, and therefore our addictive behavior and relationship with prescription medication is also an effect. Rather than putting energy into forcing ourselves to quit anything, it's more beneficial to focus on integrating the cause of the condition.

This being said, it's also not practical to attempt to benefit from The Presence Process if we are sedated to the extent we are unable to attend to our reading material, conscious responses, and breathing practice. Under such circumstances, it's recommended we first enter rehabilitation therapy to detoxify and regain the level of clarity necessary to attend to the requirements of this process. When severely addicted, rehabilitation therapy delivers us into a state of "recovery" in which our level of perceptual comprehension is stabilized.

However, let's be honest with ourselves: The precarious state referred to as "being in recovery" is one of ongoing quiet desperation. It's called "re-*covery*" because it's a state of continual *doings* designed to keep the causality of our predicament *covered* from our awareness. Nevertheless, being in recovery – being in a "covering up" mode – does enable us to behave in a more lucid and therefore disciplined manner. Hence once we have completed rehabilitation therapy, it's recommended we enter The Presence Process directly so we can take the necessary steps to integrate the cause of our experience.

By completing The Presence Process experientially to the best of our ability, we commence integration of our emotional charge. We also equip ourselves with the perceptual tools to enable us to live in a manner that constantly integrates our charged emotion. This journey, once initiated, gradually restores harmony to the quality of our experience. How long it takes to restore harmony depends on many factors, such as our capacity for emotional development, our current level of felt-perception, how long we have been addicted or afflicted, what the nature of the lesson is that we are to learn from an experience, how long we choose to remain in a victor or victim mentality, and what our capacity for integration work is.

The more we integrate our charged emotional condition, the less severe our afflictions, and the less we require medication. At some point, if we abuse alcohol, our alcohol turns to castor oil, our smoke (if this is our addiction) to ammonia, and our opium (if this is our addiction) to acid. Self-medication has a pleasurable and calming effect only when required. When no longer required, its pleasure sours and the comfort it provides turns into discomfort.

In other words, the more present we become in our physical, mental, and emotional experience, the more we feel what the medication and drugs really do. There's nothing pleasurable about ingesting toxic substances whose side effects require the ingestion of more toxic substances. Only because of ongoing discomfort within our emotional body does such behavior appear beneficial.

It's important to be clear that by using the word "required," we aren't legitimizing such behavior. We are acknowledging we engage in it because we are suffering and haven't yet reached resolution. By integrating the charged emotions that drive our imbalance, we dismantle the foundations that support it.

If we have been self-medicating or using prescription drugs for a long time, it's recommended we enter this process with intent to integrate the causality of our uncomfortable experience without becoming preoccupied with its *effects*. As addicts, we may feel shame and guilt. This is natural but unnecessary. We self-medicate because society's healthcare systems aren't physically present enough, mentally clear enough, or emotionally mature enough to show us how to integrate our imprinting. However, this isn't a reason to blame society for our condition. *We* are responsible for our predicament. Addiction is an experience of self-medication *we* are having. Our experiences are susceptible to change. By taking responsibility for our experiences, we embrace our ability to change them.

It's also recommended that, during The Presence Process, long-time addiction be given a compassionate amount of time for integration to occur. Addiction programs generally convince us we are *forever addicted*. They assert that unless we attend group meetings regularly, forever and ever, we will relapse into using again. Because addiction support groups are impotent when it comes to integrating causality, the belief that we are fated to an existence of desperation becomes a self-fulfilling prophecy. But it isn't the truth, and when we embrace such a perception as truth, we unconsciously transfer our addiction from substance abuse to reliance on group meetings. We become addicted to our addiction group. Our reliance on our addiction group becomes our affliction.

The Presence Process invites us to challenge this self-defeating belief system and our inevitable self-imprisonment in the victim mentality supported and maintained by endless group meetings. It also invites those of us who attend these meetings to observe how addicts who are supposedly abstaining and recovering transfer their addictive behavior to other aspects of their experience. For instance, *recovering* alcoholics smoke more, *recovering* cigarette smokers eat more, and *recovering* heroin users turn to painkillers. All these transferences are *covering up* causality instead of functioning as a means of *discovering* causality.

Recovery – a way of living designed to constantly cover up charged emotion – leads to living in quiet desperation. Discovery – consciously embracing our charged emotional content through felt-perception, using it as raw material for emotional growth – leads to present moment awareness and Presence. As happens with medication, the need to attend endless support group meetings diminishes in proportion to the integration of charged emotion, until it ultimately ceases. Addiction isn't a life-sentence. It's an experience, and experiences change.

The Presence Process invites us to consider the possibility that we are on the brink of a healthcare evolution. Instead of running to another for insight into our own condition, looking to this person to initiate the changes required for integration, we are invited to consider that all these capacities are present within each of us.

Until now, the paradigm of Twelve Step consciousness has been required, otherwise it wouldn't be with us. It enables many to tread water instead of drowning. However, in Presence and present moment awareness, we have something solid to stand on. Establishing an experiential relationship with Presence is the solid ground that empowers us to step onto dry land again. The possibility we are invited to consider is "a 13th step" – a step *not accomplished by moving outward into the world,* but by *returning into ourselves.*

This doesn't in any way negate the experiences that have brought us to this point. We acknowledge them as a required part of our evolution. But as with any journey, unless we lift our foot off the step we are currently on, we can't place it on the next step – the one that invites us to evolve from recovery into discovery, and from subdued acceptance of our predicament into the possibility of integration of the causality of our addicted or afflicted plight.

The Presence Process also invites those of us with chronic, incurable, and supposedly terminal afflictions to challenge the current belief system of the allopathic and psychiatric community. Imagining that what we suffer from is incurable just because doctors tell us so is nothing more than a belief system. In the language of authenticity, the word "incurable" means, "I don't know what to do for you." Yet doctors use it to mean, "You are going to die and there is nothing I, you, or anyone can do about it." Challenge all belief systems, because they only scratch the surface of life.

The allopathic profession is magnificent for containing, controlling, and sedating physical, symptomatic trauma. For example, if we are in a car accident and physically injured, or if the symptoms of a diseased condition or addiction escalate to a point where living becomes unbearable, going to a medical specialist is necessary. They know how to mend bones and suture wounds. They know how to sedate and control physical, mental, and emotional symptoms to stabilize our situation.

However, if we intend to integrate the causal charged emotion that unconsciously drives us to manifest experiences that physically, mentally, and emotionally debilitate us, a medical practitioner isn't the person we approach. This is because their training instructs them to seek physical explanations for all states of disease. Their expertise is in treating effects, not in causality. A large portion of the conventional medical community doesn't comprehend the causality of addictions and afflictions. Their emphasis is on attempting to contain addictions and afflictions with medication and therapy.

The Presence Process takes a confident step in a new direction. It demonstrates to all who are willing to dive into their emotional abyss that, by sincerely applying ourselves to the journey of emotional integration, we discover the causality of addiction and affliction. Unlike drugs, pharmaceuticals, and unnecessary operations, which *are* the easy approach, this is neither an easy nor quick approach. Emotional integration is challenging for our emotionally undeveloped, mentally confused, and physically distracted world. However, as challenging as it is, it's preferable to dependence on support group meetings. It's also preferable to living with the discomfort of a physical disease, whose discomfort is compounded by the side effects of medication. The Presence Process equips us to move beyond these uncomfortable predicaments.

In the final analysis, no matter what form it may take, an addiction is an affliction, and an affliction is an addiction. Society still postulates that addiction is caused by poverty, laziness, a lack of education, weakness of character, and drug pushers. These so-called "causes" of addiction are effects, and therefore cannot be the cause. The cause of addiction is our unintegrated emotional condition. Realizing this is liberating.

Depending on the severity of our condition, it may take moving through The Presence Process several times to integrate the causal charge within our emotional body. It may even take a lifetime of integrative work. How long it takes isn't something to obsess about.

We only have two choices: We can journey inward along the pathway of awareness, taking responsibility for our experience; or we can journey outward along the pathway of awareness into ongoing ineffectual (in-*effect*-you-all) behavior that attempts to compensate for our emotional state, along with reliance on others and added substance abuse.

Journeying through The Presence Process for the first time instructs us in the art of responding to our charged emotion. We become our own self-sufficient support group. The first time through also assists us in commencing integration of our overall charged emotional condition. It's therefore recommended that on entering this process for the second time, we wield our willpower and common sense by commencing extraction of ourselves from the routines and rituals of our addictive behavior. We are to gradually but deliberately put our fix aside.

The consequence of decreasing or halting our self-medicating behavior is that the charged emotion related to this behavior automatically arises into our awareness. We then consciously engage these felt-predicaments through breathing, use of the perceptual tools, and insights offered throughout this text. When we become aware of these emotional signatures, we develop the capacity to *be with these uncomfortable felt-resonances without condition.*

As we move through The Presence Process for the second time, we also have the experience accumulated from already having moved through it once. We may falter and fall along the way, and this is to be expected. Our capacity to respond consciously to our discomfort isn't acquired instantly through a mental decision, but developed gradually through consistent application. It isn't our faltering or falling that matters, but our consistency in picking ourselves up and continuing. After moving through the process a second time, it's recommended we take a break for a period of three weeks, then re-enter the process.

With each encounter with this process, we empower ourselves to journey more deeply inward. The first time through is often primarily an experience of increasing physical awareness. The second time through, we experience greater mental clarity. The third time through, we expand our capacity for emotional integration.

By experientially engaging in this journey, we realize that the events of the past – each detail of these events – served to bring us into the wholeness of present moment awareness. We realize that our guilt, shame, and regret for the years spent self-medicating is founded upon a misinterpretation. Addictive behavior and severe affliction are no reflection on *who we are,* but are *experiences we are having.* Once we receive the insight offered us through these experiences, we also acquire the capacity to overcome them and move onward into new ones.

As we approach present moment awareness, we feel increasing gratitude for each aspect of the journey, especially the rough parts. All of our past reveals itself as steppingstones that led us into present moment awareness.

TRADING RESULTS FOR CONSEQUENCES

We often don't say what we mean or mean what we say. For example, when many of us speak of abundance, we mean money. When we speak of health, we mean appearance. When we speak of joy, we mean happiness.

The difference between experiencing abundance, health, and joy – in contrast to money, a good appearance, and happiness – is huge. The former are inclusive, while the latter are exclusive.

Abundance is being grateful for all the physical, mental, and emotional experiences flowing toward and away from us. Abundance arises through the realization that *we always receive exactly what we require for the integration and evolution of our experience.*

Health arises when we attend to each aspect of our physical, mental, and emotional experience by responding consciously to its cause. Health arises through responsibility.

Joy is the state that arises when we allow ourselves to experience *everything* as it is unfolds, without judgment. It arises when we are *being – without condition.*

In contrast, money only represents one tiny aspect of our overall energy flow. Appearance, when it's all that matters, is only skin deep. Happiness requires that "this or that happens," or doesn't happen.

The Presence Process isn't concerned with whether we accumulate money, perfect our appearance, or attain happiness. Rather, it's a means of preparing the garden of our experience to plant, nurture, and bear the fruits of *present moment awareness* – an awareness of what abundance, health, and joy actually are.

Because of our ongoing desires, we likely enter this journey with specific and therefore exclusive intentions. This is natural. However, this process isn't about satisfying our specific desires, but about opening our awareness so we consciously receive *what we require in order to initiate emotional integration.* It's about experientially accessing the realization that *if something is happening to us, it's required.* It's about embracing the fact that *our unfolding experience, exactly as it is, is always valid.*

We may not appear to desire what's currently unfolding in our experience, but the fact that something is unfolding reveals that it is indeed a requirement. Within the context of this text, we identify requirements by the fact that *they happen regardless of what we think we desire.* Once we realize this, our choice is either to respond or to react.

As we move through The Presence Process, it's natural we would expect "results." We grow up in a world where each aspect of our experience is flaunted unashamedly as a means to an end, and where the consequences of almost all of our activities are held up to some form of measurement. It's therefore unlikely we know how to behave unconditionally. Because of this, we naturally monitor our progress and measure our success throughout this process by watching for the fulfillment of our desires in our circumstances, even though we are asked not to do so.

We are asked not to be preoccupied with *results* because initially we simply don't know where to look, or what to look at, to see the real consequences of entering The Presence Process. Because of this, we inevitably examine the wrong aspects of our experience for signs of progress.

In this process, there is no standardized measurement by which to gauge success, other than the unexpected and seemingly unintended shifts in our experience. What we require almost always comes to us as something unexpected and unintended. False expectations about satisfaction of our desires dampen our effort and instill doubt.

Looking for results – and the yardstick we use to determine our success – is motivated by the niggling of our unintegrated emotional charge. No matter how much we may perceive ourselves as different from others, as long as we suffer from unintegrated emotional discomfort, we are all really seeking the same thing. We want to fill the big black hole within our heart. It's natural therefore that we initially gauge our progress by whether we feel better. But remember, this heart work isn't about feeling better. It's about getting better at feeling, which entails feeling emotions we have long suppressed.

The Presence Process isn't about satisfying desires that arise from within our unintegrated emotional charge. These can never be satisfied. An unintegrated emotional charge that we attempt to pacify is never resolved. When fed, it lives on as long as the feeding continues.

The Presence Process isn't about satisfying desire by feeding the desire, but about *resolution of this seemingly unending inner hunger through integration of its cause.*

Having said this, an awareness that "something is happening" as a consequence of entering this process is essential. By following the instructions given throughout this journey, we receive ongoing experiential confirmation that something is indeed happening.

This confirmation occurs because this process is causal and therefore impacts our experience. However, the initial consequence of entering this journey isn't that we feel better and things are easier. No matter how physically prepared we believe we are, no matter how mentally agile we think we are, and no matter how emotionally mature and vibrationally aware we may perceive ourselves to be, when an awareness of our emotional causality arises, *we feel it.*

This feeling is what we run from through all addictive, controlling, and sedating behavior. There is seldom anything pleasant about facing what we have been running from. Feeling these emotional states isn't what we may desire, though it is what we require.

Ever since we departed childhood, the extent to which we have been able to subdue our emotionally generated yearnings has served as our barometer for achievement. When we don't subdue this restless inner hunger, we assume we aren't accomplishing anything.

In the past, we may have attempted to quiet this inner hunger by adjusting our physical circumstances through fasting and exercise routines, or with prescription medication or addictive self-medication. We may have tried to quiet our longing through food, sex, work, and charitable activity. We may have attempted to impact our confusing mental condition through mind-control techniques, hypnosis, and positive thinking. We may have read numerous self-help books, attended health retreats, gone to workshops, and participated in hours and even years of verbal or other forms of therapy. However, none of the "results" brought about by these external approaches are ever permanent. Their impact on our experience is akin to camouflage, in that they appear to assist us by temporarily covering up our awareness of the cause. Like treading water, they tire us but take us nowhere. *They are incapable of achieving anything lasting.*

Through diligent effort, we may remain for long periods in states of recovery. However, when we falter, we realize the precariousness of this emotional status quo. A "recovering addict," even after sixty years, is still at risk of betraying their sobriety. This is because the act of recovery is one of engaging in *the artificial peace of quiet desperation.*

Recovery is not *discovery*, and without authentic discovery, there is no causal transformation.

Recovery places its attention on the effect, while discovery courts causality. We don't impact causality by fiddling with effects. The prize for engaging in recovery is always and inevitably self-deceptive quiet desperation. The Presence Process seeks out causality, knowing that *when causality is impacted, the effect is automatic and the transformation permanent.*

This is why The Presence Process isn't concerned with results, but with *consequences.*

Because results aren't something that can be guaranteed, they are concerned with a *hoped-for* outcome, not certainty. Results are graded, and therefore involve seeking acknowledgement and approval. They are measured by the temporary quieting of inner hunger, not its resolution.

In contrast, a consequence is an *effect*, and therefore inevitable. Consequences unfold in direct response to the causal impact of The Presence Process. Indeed, everything about this process is causal. The Presence Process therefore invites us to trade in our result-oriented mentality for a consequence-oriented mentality.

The consequences of entering our emotional body and integrating charged emotion through connected breathing, initiating mental clarity, and awakening felt-perception aren't initially what we may expect. On the contrary, they are unexpected! Actively becoming aware of charged emotion isn't an experience we normally invite, since at first it doesn't feel good. This is because it impacts our experience in a very real way. Just consider what the word "impact" *feels* like.

The main reason we aren't experiencing the vibrational qualities of *effortless joy, abundance, and health* right now is *our unintegrated emotional charge.*

Charged emotion is blockage in the emotional body, causing resistance. Because we don't know how to integrate this, we further resist by suppressing our awareness of it. This resistance upon resistance accumulates and manifests as heat, and this heat arises within the felt-aspect of our experience as physical, mental, and emotional discomfort. To compensate for this discomfort, we "try to be happy," to appear to others as if "everything is fine," and to make enough money to "feel good about ourselves" – that is, as good as possible given our predicament.

As long as charged emotion dominates our capacity for feeling, thinking, speaking, and doing, we experience life as a constant laboring to satisfy the seemingly insatiable appetite of our inner hunger. Under such circumstance, authentic joy, abundance, and health remain unrealized.

Unlike the endless quest for happiness, money, and a perfect appearance, authentic joy, abundance, and health aren't a means to an end. They are only experienced when we are at peace with *this moment* – when we perceive this moment as valid. Joy, abundance, and health are automatic byproducts of present moment awareness. Like Presence, they are already within us. When we are unaware of them, it's because our attention is anchored elsewhere.

One reason we might enter an experience such as The Presence Process is that we secretly hope for a magical quick fix that makes everything "all right" by dissolving our current difficulties. This is expected because we live in a society that demands instant gratification. We have also been suffering with emotional discomfort for a long time and are on some level living in quiet desperation.

Desperation seeds destination consciousness.

Fortunately, as our past reveals, there is no quick and easy way around our present circumstances that has any authentic and therefore lasting impact on the quality of our experience. There are plenty of escape routes, but there is no realizing peace through any of them. They are all cul-de-sacs.

This is the challenging truth about our unintegrated emotional body: There is no way *around* it. The way out is *through,* and the way through is *in.*

Grasping the authentic nature of this quest saves us from unnecessary drama, false expectations, and bowing out because of unexpected physical, mental, and emotional discomfort.

Growing up and becoming "normal" citizens of our communities results in a storm raging within us. This is because what's accepted as normality is a state of quiet desperation in which we exist as a consequence of the denial of our authentic being. As much as we might wish to deny the existence of this controlled and sedated inner storm, it can't be hidden. It's the storm of duality, the war between authenticity and inauthenticity, the perceptual divide between Presence and pretence. It's the vast canyon of fear, anger, and grief that lies between the adult and child self. By gazing across the planet, we perceive the causes of this charged condition everywhere.

When we seek to realize authentic peace, we are asked to enter this storm consciously. For this, we require inward momentum. We don't need to take up the issues of the world because the way to have an impact on the cause of all our perceived chaos lies *within us.*

The Presence Process invites us to willingly plunge into our inner storm like a bungee jumper leaping off a bridge. Presence is the harness that guides our bravery and foolishness. It steers us into the eye of this inner storm and facilitates its integration. Entering this storm consciously enables us to grow in ways we have never imagined. Its winds blast the fog of "living in time" from our experience, while its torrential downpour washes us clean of illusion.

This inner emotional storm isn't accidental, but is both an invitation and a deterrent. It functions like a doorway, restricting those not yet ready from entering, convincing those who still require rest to remain in the sleepy dream of time. Entering our inner emotional storm consciously is a rite of passage – the right passageway for impacting causality and, through this, entering the vibrational.

The Presence Process isn't primarily an outer journey, but an inner exploration. We may not yet fully comprehend what this means. But through experience, the full implication of what we mean by an "inner journey" dawns. An inner journey implies nothing is going to be tampered with out there in the world. We leave the world alone. We don't clean the mirror to remove the blemishes from the face reflected in it. We use the mirror – our experience within the world – as a tool to perceive our blemishes. All adjustments are then initiated *within,* through *felt-perception.*

By deliberately impacting the cause of charged emotion, we simultaneously manifest physical, mental, and emotional experiences that mirror what we are focusing on internally. For this reason, as we move through The Presence Process, it's beneficial to keep reminding ourselves that our worldly experience is *an effect* – all of it. It's important to remember this so we don't become sidetracked with mirror-cleaning drama.

For many of us, the effect of consciously impacting the cause of charged emotions is that we start feeling uncomfortable. As we initially journey into The Presence Process, it may appear that our overall experience is worsening. It may appear our desires are not only being ignored, but are also being exaggerated.

None of this is real, but it's all valid. None of this apparent "worsening" is true, but it's all required. It's a reflection of unintegrated childhood experience, which is now being projected onto the screen of the world and perceived through our adult eyes. The reason it's projected onto the world is that we don't yet have the capacity to perceive it inwardly.

Because of our addiction to believing and behaving as if the effect is the cause – as if the world is the reason we don't feel at peace within – we are prone to react to this shift in our circumstances. For this reason, *when our experience appears to deteriorate into increasing discomfort and strangeness, we are to remind ourselves that this is occurring because, by entering The Presence Process, we are deliberately placing attention on our emotional blockages.* We are to remind ourselves that the turbulence we are experiencing is beneficial!

In contrast to feeling good and having everything become easier, these unexpected shifts are authentic signs of initial progress. They aren't the results we may want, but they are the consequences we require. We are also to keep in mind that there's an unintegrated childlike aspect within us that desires happiness, seeks to appear good, and wants to make lots of money to buy stuff so we can feel better. To this childlike aspect, sudden unexpected shifts within our outer circumstances feel threatening. It feels like "the end of world."

On one level, it is – it's the end of a world of pretence. Pretence dissolves as Presence reawakens. As we go *through* these shifts, we are therefore encouraged to be patient and demonstrate compassion for ourselves. This is why we are invited to *trust the process*. This is why we are told, *"The way out is through."* This is why it's recommended we complete the process *no matter what*. It's better not to start this journey than to run away just as our focus begins zeroing in on our emotional blockage. When we choose to disengage from this experience during weeks 5, 6, 7, or 8, we are running away from an awareness of our unintegrated emotional content.

Know that the sudden outer shifts in our physical, mental, and emotional experience *pass*. Remember that as we integrate causality, this becomes reflected as beneficial shifts in our circumstances. Just because we are becoming increasingly uncomfortable doesn't imply we are doing the process incorrectly. On the contrary, the opposite is the case. *When we are struggling physically, mentally, and emotionally through this process, it's because we are being impacted by it in a beneficial manner.* This is the opposite of what the world teaches us to perceive as accomplishment, the opposite of what it holds up for us as a barometer of success.

Only by witnessing firsthand how we move into, through, and out of these uncomfortable experiences do we come to the place of *knowing* we are responsible for the quality of our experience. By accomplishing this, we realize that taking care of our emotional development is one of our fundamental responsibilities. Through this journey, we understand that when we experience an emotional charge in our world, it's a reflection of our inner condition. By moving through this experience, we *witness* firsthand the capacity of Presence to manifest exactly what we require to facilitate integration. In this manner, The Presence Process uses our personal experience as a means of validation. Our experience becomes our teacher.

The invitation placed before us by The Presence Process is to learn through firsthand experience not to fear and resist the inevitable discomfort that arises from emotional processing, and not to react to emotional processing by behaving like "the world is ending." Instead, we are invited to embrace the discomfort of emotional processing as a sign that we are having an authentic impact on the cause of our discomfort. The invitation is to willingly ride our inner dragon, and to discover from personal experience that our inner dragon is only tamed when we choose to ride it.

Anyone who attempts to convince us that we can accomplish authentic, lasting adjustment to the quality of our experience without encountering what the mental body perceives as discomfort is to be viewed dubiously. Our willingness to consciously engage our imprinted discomfort is the alchemy that fuels transformation. This doesn't mean we need to suffer unnecessarily. It means that when we seek to activate authentic movement in the quality of our experience, we are required to face whatever is unfolding within us. When our inner condition is uncomfortable, facing the discomfort is what authenticity is, not pretending it away.

The Presence Process is the battleground of emotional warriors. It's an opportunity to willingly step forward and unsheathe the sword that cuts us free from our emotionally programmed time-based mentality. It quickly separates wheat from chaff. This work isn't about "easy" and "good." It isn't about happiness, appearances, and money. It's about becoming authentic, growing up emotionally, and reclaiming integrity. It's about grasping life intimately, with both hands, and raising ourselves up from being "the emotionally dead." The mental body finds a million excuses to quit this process – especially during weeks 5, 6, 7, and 8.

Remember also that there's an aspect of our experience that doesn't intend to be changed – the mental body, especially when it believes itself to be in control. The mental body is the voice that whispers "better the devil you know," ushering us away from authentic change. Though it initially encourages us when we ask for change, it's bluffing. It pretends to be on our side so we don't perceive its ploy. It pretends because the mental body not only prefers familiarity, but is addicted to familiarity. This is why habits are so challenging to defuse.

The mental body doesn't approve of change in any form, even though it appears to encourage it and comes to our aid by suggesting approaches we can take to change the quality of our present circum-

stances. But the moment we attempt to apply any of these sugges-
tions consistently, the mental body changes its tune. The moment our
experience becomes unfamiliar, the mental body tells stories, using
words like "bad," "wrong," "dangerous," "harmful," "evil," and
"uncomfortable." These words persuade us to feel afraid, and the fear
then incites us to doubt and question the new direction in which we
are moving. The mental body then encourages us to scramble back to
the familiar, thereby restoring our sense of comfort even when this
means reinstating a habit that's killing us. "Better the devil we know,"
it claims. Whenever the mental body is in control of our experience,
it is devilish.

When we use the mental body as a means of gauging the consequences of our attempts to make an authentic change in the quality
of our experience, we enter another Catch 22:

We ask for change.

We are given the opportunity to change.

We embrace the opportunity.

We start feeling different.

Then the mental body tells us that this strange feeling is "wrong."

*We subsequently mentally interpret this strange feeling, which
is actually the surfacing of our emotional signature, as a "gut feeling" or a "red flag" telling us we are headed in the wrong direction.*

*By listening to these stories, we turn against that which is
changing our experience, returning to what's familiar and safe.*

Nothing is accomplished.

We feel more frustrated and disillusioned than before.

The mental body grows stronger, and we become disheartened.

This is why it's recommended we commit to completing The Presence Process *no matter what*. Take stock only upon completion of your journey through the process, not in the midst of it. Finish this process no matter what experience arises.

NOTE: Every experience that arises as we move through The Presence Process, whether it's understood by the mental body or not, is valid. We complete the journey no matter what the mental body tells us because we realize this aspect of mind is the last to embrace the changes required as we face up to our emotional discomfort. Not completing the process gives the mental body added strength and dominance. It isn't called the "mental" body without good reason. As we move through this experience, we intend to listen to the heart, not to the thinking aspect of mind.

PART II

PREPARING FOR THE JOURNEY

BEFORE EMBARKING ON ANY JOURNEY, it's beneficial to prepare carefully. Preparation impacts the overall quality of our experience and ensures successful application of the procedural requirements. Part II informs us what this journey entails through a more detailed examination of the Process Trinity, which encompasses the breathing practice, the conscious responses, and the text containing perceptual tools.

THE PROCESS TRINITY

I. THE BREATHING PRACTICE

Consciously connected breathing is the heart of The Presence Process because it's our primary tool for accessing experiential awareness of Presence and accumulating present moment awareness.

We attend to the breathing practice, which is taught during the first week of the process, twice a day for a minimum of 15 minutes because its integrative power is accessed through consistency. The importance of consistency cannot be overemphasized. Erratic attendance to our breathing practice leads to unnecessary difficulties. By surrendering to consistency, we receive undeniable grace in that we feel as if we are "carried." Avoiding consistency leads to feeling as if we have to make unnecessary extra effort to carry ourselves. It also leads to resorting to drama and commotion so we feel as though something is "happening."

Two key processes unfold simultaneously when we consciously connect our breathing:

(i) The first is the gathering of present moment awareness. This is an automatic byproduct of breathing without pausing, which means there are no unnecessary gaps between our breaths. For each moment we spend focusing both our attention and intent on breathing without pausing, we accumulate present moment awareness. Our intent during a breathing session is not to pause between breaths for the entire session, and by so doing accumulate as much present moment awareness as possible.

The mental body gives us a hundred and one physical, mental, and emotional reasons to stop and pause during breathing sessions. Our task is to breathe without pausing no matter what. This in turn strengthens our will. Nothing is more significant during this process than attending to our breathing practice twice every day.

It's interesting to note that we humans are the only breathing creatures that consistently and unconsciously embed pauses – unnecessary breathless gaps – in our breathing cycle. Watch a dog or cat and notice how they breathe continuously without pausing. When alarmed and frightened, their connected breathing intensifies and speeds up to bring more oxygen and present moment awareness into their body. In comparison, we humans continually pause between breaths. When we become alarmed and frightened, we even stop breathing altogether and enter an unbalanced breathing cycle that leads to hyperventilation and asthma.

This habit of pausing between breaths occurs whenever we enter the mental realm and become adrift in thinking. If we are absorbed by the circumstances of the past or a projected future, or if we exit the present by placing our attention beyond our present circumstances, we pause between breaths. When we observe others who are deep in thought or distracted, we see how they too consistently pause between breaths.

In other words, whenever we aren't present, our breathing isn't consciously connected because consciously connected breathing occurs only in the present. Breathing creatures not "living in time" – not adrift in the thinking of the mental plane – don't pause unconsciously. One of the benefits of The Presence Process is that it brings attention to the disconnected condition of our breathing mechanism. Consequently, we restore harmony to our breathing pattern.

The way we breathe, especially during our breathing practice, is a reflection of the way we live life. Are we connected and present, or are we disconnected and absent?

(ii) The second process at work during a consciously connected breathing session is oxygenation. Increased oxygenation occurs during a breathing session because our breathing pattern becomes normalized. Other than whales, dolphins, seals, crocodiles, hippopotami, and other creatures that hold their breath deliberately when they submerge, breathing creatures breathe fully and without pausing in order to maintain present moment awareness and a high level of oxygenation. As well as pausing, we humans generally use less than 20% of our lung capacity, which renders us oxygen-deprived. On a primarily physical level, oxygen is life. When contemplating this, we realize it's in our best interest to oxygenate our physical form efficiently.

NOTE: Breathing deeply and fully with each breath throughout a session is encouraged but not essential. It isn't essential because The Presence Process pivots on the gathering of present moment awareness, not increased oxygenation. Present moment awareness accumulates when we consciously connect our breathing. Increased oxygenation is an added bonus. The more present we become, the more our thirst for oxygen increases.

Consciously connected breathing isn't to be confused with hyperventilation. Hyperventilation is a consequence of an imbalance between oxygen and carbon dioxide and results from forced, unnatural, exaggerated, and traumatic breathing. Because consciously connected breathing isn't unnatural, it instills harmony. It releases trauma instead of stimulating it.

Any discomfort experienced from consciously connected breathing is the consequence of unintegrated past trauma surfacing into our awareness for integration. Discomfort experienced during a consciously connected breathing session is purposeful and valid. We welcome it as an indicator of the inner causal impact The Presence Process is having.

During the initial stages of each consciously connected breathing session, we may encounter varying levels of personal resistance. This is normal. We either overcome this, or it overcomes us. There are three levels of resistance we may experience:

(i) The first level of resistance is *physical* and is evident when we say to ourselves: "I don't feel like doing this. It's too hard."

(ii) The second level of resistance is *mental* and is evident when we say to ourselves: "I don't feel like doing this because nothing is happening."

(iii) The third level of resistance is *emotional* and is evident when we say to ourselves: "I think I can stop now because I feel 'all right,' 'fine,' or 'okay'" – or when we use any such emotionally numb words.

We know we have passed through our resistance when, in the midst of a breathing session, we honestly feel "this is fantastic. I could keep breathing like this forever."

Regardless of the experiences we have during our breathing practice, it's useful to remember that just the act of keeping our breathing connected to the best of our ability accomplishes the requirement of each breathing session. Approaching these sessions expecting some sort of profound experience is misguided. There is no prescribed experience we are "supposed to have."

The breathing sessions aren't intended to be *the* experience – *our life is*.

Our only intent is keeping our breathing connected. When approached in this manner, we discover each breathing session we enter is unique. Each session manifests as "what's required." Accordingly, every experience we have when connecting our breath is valid.

There are likely to be instances when we feel unable to stay conscious during our breathing practice and find ourselves falling asleep. Why is this?

When we consciously connect our breathing, we are anchoring an aspect of our awareness in the present instead of allowing all of it to drift into either the past or a projected future. Consequently, instead of all our attention leaving the present and journeying to some of these "places in time," some of these "places in time" are drawn toward us. They are pulled into the present. Until we have accumulated a degree of present moment awareness, some of these "places in time" still have a strong impact on our attention, which causes them to override our attempts to anchor ourselves in the present and instead drag our awareness out into a dream-like state that manifests as waves of unconsciousness. In the present, unconsciousness appears as sleep. When we are overtaken by these waves of unconsciousness, we find ourselves slipping into a sleep-like state without any apparent warning. We only realize this has occurred when we awaken and discover we have been sleeping instead of consciously connecting our breathing.

Nodding off into states of unconsciousness is normal when we attempt to extract our awareness from time. To be frustrated with this is nothing but drama. During our journey through this process, we may even become enmeshed in what manifests as sleep-loops, so that each time we sit down to breathe, we fall asleep. This is no cause for concern but a reason for perseverance. The way out of this predicament is through it. We continue to persevere until we break through the unconsciousness that's arising for integration.

Through consistent daily attention to our breathing practice, we accumulate enough present moment awareness to anchor our awareness in the present while breathing. Then these unconscious "places in time" no longer have the capacity to drag us into unconsciousness. Instead, we drag these unconscious past experiences into the present to be integrated. They are perceptual dream states and cannot survive present moment awareness.

II. CONSCIOUS RESPONSES

Conscious responses are a tool we wield in order to respond consciously to those experiences that would normally draw a reaction from us. This tool is used by the mental body to bring into our awareness the unintegrated emotional signatures at the root of our confusion.

We are given a specific conscious response for each of our ten weeks of the process, plus one to be used during every breathing session. The conscious responses activate awareness of aspects of our experience in which we are blocked. By becoming conscious of these blockages, which we do through felt-perception, we integrate them. Hence the more we apply this perceptual tool to our experience, the more efficiently we accomplish integration.

These conscious responses are also designed to replace "stinking thinking" – our unproductive thought patterns – with responsible mental processes. Whenever we aren't mentally occupied, it serves us well to repeat our conscious response for the week.

Our mental body may resist and even reject these conscious responses. This is normal. Sometimes realizing we have gone through a whole day without consciously visiting these mental statements, and thus reminding ourselves to do so, is a necessary part of this process. The process of forgetting them, then remembering to use them, is beneficial. It strengthens the mental muscle we use to draw our attention into the present and anchor it here.

Conscious responses aren't wishful thinking, and neither are they positive affirmations. They are *causal*. They don't concern themselves with the *effects* of emotional blockage, but with our capacity to *act causally*.

A person who moves through their experience mentally repeating, "I am abundant, I am abundant, I am abundant" over and over because they have no money is using mental repetition as positive thinking, which is nothing more than wishful thinking. They are deriving the fabric of their mental affirmation from a physical manifestation of their unintegrated emotional charge.

In other words, *they are using a mere effect to address an effect.*

When a person repeats, "I am abundant, I am abundant, I am abundant," their mental affirmation isn't touching the *cause* of their financial lack. Lack of money, which is their point of focus, is *an effect of emotional blockage, not its cause.* Therefore, the quality of their mental affirmation is impotent. It is in-*effect*-ual.

These conscious responses are also aligned with the realization that when we seek to anchor our awareness in a real comprehension of what peace is, we are required to become aware of the chaos we have been projecting that has obscured this realization. By resolving our projected chaos, we naturally restore an awareness of peace.

Accordingly, conscious responses bring awareness to unconscious aspects of our experience that are impacting the quality of our experience. We don't "wish" or "hope" our chaos away. Neither do we ignore it. We bring it into awareness so we may integrate it consciously and responsibly, gaining the required wisdom from it.

By taking responsibility for the quality of the experience we are having, which doesn't serve us, we liberate ourselves from waiting for the world to change so we may at last enjoy ourselves!

III. WEEKLY TEXT & PERCEPTUAL TOOLS

For each week of The Presence Process, we are allotted required reading. The wording of the text for each week's reading, as well as everything we have read up to this point, is *deliberate*. Notice how the word "deliberate" incorporates the word "liberate."

The Presence Process isn't only written in paragraphs, pages, and chapters, but also in individual sentences. The text contains insights that can't be digested with hurried scanning. It contains years of experience encapsulated in felt-insights to facilitate integration.

It's recommended we not leave our required reading until the last moment of each weekly session. These weekly readings facilitate present moment awareness. Each allotted section of text contains perceptual tools for use during that specific week. This text is designed to add gentleness to our emotional processing by enabling us to become more conscious of what's unfolding during each step of the journey. Reviewing the text at regular intervals is beneficial because the insights gained deepen as our personal level of present moment awareness increases.

The reality is that this book is *one long conscious response*. The perceptual tools shared in this text realign our behavior from reactive to responsive and simultaneously replace our unproductive beliefs with information that serves us well. Like any new venture, to gain proficiency in present moment awareness requires repeated application of these tools. Through experiencing the consequences of repeated application, we integrate the benefits.

No "doing" is involved in applying these tools. They are an internal response that empowers responsible mental processing.

AN INTEGRATIVE APPROACH

Even when we believe our childhood was good, being born into a conditional world means we have uncomfortable physical, mental, and emotional experiences. We are unconditional beings, which means that entering any conditional experience is to some degree traumatic.

When the moment arrives in our evolution that we are ready to step into full responsibility for the quality of our experience, it's into the emotional body that we journey. To do this responsibly, an integrative approach is recommended.

For the purpose of The Presence Process, we prefer to use the word "integrate" instead of "heal." This is because these two words have a different intent. *Healing* makes an assumption that something is wrong and in need of fixing. Healing often attempts *to get rid of* whatever it attempts to heal. Healing is therefore more often than not *a reaction to "what is."*

Traditionally, healing focuses primarily on symptomatic expressions of discomfort and believes nothing is accomplished until the symptomatic expression is removed. Healers therefore are individuals who, looking outward and seeing a broken world in need of fixing, believe themselves in some way chosen to fix others. More often than not, those who enter healing as a profession are individuals who project their unresolved conditions onto the world, then try to fix the reflection they perceive.

Integration begins from the standpoint that if something is happening, the fact that it's happening makes it valid and therefore required. Nothing is viewed as "wrong" and "needing to be fixed." Rather, if something appears to be out of balance, it needs to be embraced back into the whole. When responded to accordingly, it contains insight for further growth. Integration is therefore *a response to "what is."*

Integration is only interested in causality. When the world appears broken to an integrationist, they take responsibility for their perception of it and respond by restoring the health of their own perception, not that of the world's. Integration doesn't offer us any professional opportunities: no one pays us to integrate, and no one can integrate on our behalf. This is one of the reasons there are no Presence Process facilitators. Integration is the art of self-facilitation.

An integrative approach to the quality of our experience is based on the realization that *when we impact the causal aspect of our experience, we simultaneously change the condition of the whole.* Also, the effects this has on the whole unfold *organically,* in a manner best serving the wellbeing of the whole.

Throughout The Presence Process, the individual parts of our experience that we work with to activate changes in the quality of our experience as a whole are our physical body (sensations), mental body (thoughts), and emotional body (feelings). Even though this process is designed to work with all three aspects, every impact is causal in that it zeroes in on the unintegrated charge in the emotional body.

When we are dissatisfied with the quality of our experience, we attempt to make changes by rearranging our physical circumstances.

This is because the physical aspect of our experience is tangible and immediately accessible. However, even though we may be able to make relatively quick changes to our physical circumstances, these changes don't last because the physical aspect of our circumstances is an effect, not causal.

Complicating our attempts to alter the quality of our experience by rearranging our physical circumstances is the fact that change is constantly occurring in our physical experience, which means that whatever we physically force to change inevitably changes yet again in time. Also, when we use force to change something quickly, it's necessary to continuously invest large amounts of energy to maintain the changed condition, which is an impossible task. For this reason, making and maintaining physical changes in an attempt to alter the quality of our experience requires control and sedation.

We may also attempt to change the quality of our experience mentally by changing our thinking about something. "Mind power" and "positive thinking" approaches aspire to this. Changing our thinking about something may in fact lead to an adjustment in the quality of our experience – as long as we don't again change our thinking. In other words, the extent and duration of the change we are able to accomplish by making mental changes is haphazard because this approach has to continually defend its accomplishments from our unconscious thought processes. We know what our unconscious thought processes are up to by observing those circumstances we manifest in our experience that are contrary to the intent of our positive thinking!

Also, just because we consciously change our thinking about something doesn't mean we *feel* differently about it. Therefore, even when a change of thought brings about an adjustment in our physical circumstances, until we *feel* differently, no amount of mind control allows us to arrive at an authentic sense of felt-transformation. Unless our unconscious emotional states are impacted, the unconscious thought processes they breed continue to disturb our intentions.

A transformed experience isn't the result of just positive thought. Rather, underlying it is a shift in feeling. If we are to achieve our intended change, our feeling and thinking processes require harmonizing. So, like attempting to make primarily physical changes, making only mental changes in order to adjust the quality of our experience is again fiddling with an effect, not the cause.

Fortunately, we have the option of going directly to the root of our discomfort and making causal adjustments. We accomplish this by initiating change in the condition of our emotional body. This is as challenging as it is effective and rewarding. Once achieved, the impact is lasting.

Activating changes within our emotional body requires approaching it with gentleness and consistency. This takes commitment and perseverance. It's like chopping down a big tree: we chop, chop, and chop. At times the task appears endless, and it may seem as though nothing is happening. Then, without warning, we hear a cracking sound, and in seconds the tree begins falling. Once it's falling, nothing stops it. Once it's lying on the ground, we can't put it back up. Adjusting the condition of our emotional body is similar. We work at it consistently, and sometimes it may feel like we are getting nowhere. Then a shift occurs, and once it does, nothing stops it. Once this inner shift occurs, it's impossible to return the emotional body to its previous condition.

Because of the emotional body's propensity for sudden shifts, the shifting experience has the potential to be traumatic. The accelerated way to make lasting changes to the quality of our experience would be not to waste time on any physical or mental processes, but rather to zero in on our emotional body. However, diving directly into the emotional body and activating shifts just because we realize this is the point of causality isn't recommended. Instead of zeroing in on the emotional body to the exclusion of all else, which can be traumatic, our watchwords are "gentleness, patience, consistency, and responsibility."

The Presence Process is designed to physically and mentally prepare us so we are able to absorb sudden shifts in our stride. These sudden emotional shifts, when approached responsibly, are profound experiences. They lead to immediate perceptual shifts. From the moment of the shift onward, we perceive the world differently. The consequence of such an emotional adjustment then filters through our mental and physical experience along the pathway of awareness, manifesting in a change in the quality of our experience. When it does, it's lasting and requires no effort to maintain. Adjusting the condition of our emotional body allows us to step into a new experience of the world without going to another planet. Approaching the task at hand in this manner is what we refer to as an "integrative" approach.

To gain deeper insight into how changes made to our physical, mental, and emotional body affect us, let's imagine we are an adult struggling with significant excess weight. Because we are a "normal" adult, like most people we are unknowingly mentally and physically *trans*fixed by our experience in the world. Because of this, we approach the task of losing our excess weight as primarily a physical undertaking, assuming it only entails the removal of excessive fat from our body.

Pursuing a primarily physical approach, our quest for weight loss may cause us to go on a fat-free diet, while ingesting a diet formula that enables us to dissolve the fats in our system. We may also start an exercise program, or step up our current one, to burn more calories. We might even attempt radical physical processes like stapling our stomach or wiring our teeth together. Because such physical approaches involve attending to the effect and not the cause of our excess weight, they take effort. Some of them take blood, sweat, and tears, not to mention a substantial financial commitment.

However, even when the weight is lost, this doesn't guarantee the effect we are seeking. For a while we may feel better about ourselves because our appearance has improved, but this feeling wears off because the cause of our excess weight isn't physical.

All diets fail in the long-term because they fail to address the emotional causality of overweight. Stapling a stomach can't seal off the discomfort of emotional turmoil we don't know how to stomach. Wiring teeth together doesn't empower us to express ourselves authentically and thus address our suppressed emotional charge. So even though these processes may be quick, depending on how drastic they are, the sense of wellbeing achieved through them is inauthentic and therefore temporary. When the inner discomfort finally resurfaces, it may be devastating because now there appears to be nowhere to turn.

These physical procedures don't integrate the unconscious mental activity related to self-image. Neither do they quiet the internal emotional eruptions that manifest physically as bingeing. Even if a procedure stops us from eating, the addiction to food as a means of self-medication, sedation, and control is transferred to other behaviors. For a while we may look good, but our thoughts still get tangled in negativity. No matter how much fat is removed, surgically or otherwise, beneath the surface we don't *feel* good. The long-term outcome is proof of this.

The consequence of making drastic physical changes is that such changes exaggerate our mental and emotional condition. The more we cover up our suffering by resorting to primarily physical procedures, the less efficiently we function mentally and emotionally.

The illusory bubble of a surgically beautiful body inevitably bursts into mental chaos and emotional catastrophe. It may take a while, but it happens. The moment the newly improved physique doesn't have an external admiring fan club, it becomes infected with rumblings of internal despair. Making primarily physical adjustments in an attempt to remove discomfort from the quality of our experience is to set an emotional time bomb ticking. One day it detonates.

As a result of repeated failure with a primarily physical approach, we may arrive at a point where we attempt to approach our condition mentally. We may change our thinking about the food we are eating and the image we have of ourselves. Gaining enough insight to identify self-defeating thought patterns that don't serve us, we perhaps enlist in a "mind power" or "positive thinking" seminar. Such an attempt at a change of thought makes a difference, although the adjustment we are able to make to our physical condition is slower than resorting to primarily physical procedures. Nevertheless, by consistently working at the "mind over matter" approach, we start losing weight – but only to a point.

Unfortunately, any change achieved through mental reconditioning isn't only limited, but it's also temporary because we are still fiddling with *effects:* our thoughts. We aren't yet making an authentic causal adjustment.

We may lose weight, but we don't tend to achieve the optimal weight for our physique – and even if we do, we struggle to maintain it. This is because even though we may have adjusted our conscious thoughts, we are unable to protect the quality of our experience from the impact of our unconscious thoughts.

Integrating unconscious thought patterns is only possible when we address the condition of our emotional body, which is the root from which thoughts sprout. The extent to which our unconscious mental commotion continues is therefore the extent to which our body holds onto excess weight.

The consequence is that we continually run the risk of "going off the rails" every now and then. When this occurs, we again eat too much of the wrong foods, and as a result think poorly of our undisciplined behavior. This happens even though we've convinced the thinking aspect of our mind that such activity isn't beneficial. We are still unable to stop our unconscious thoughts from manifesting as self-sabotage. We may look a bit lighter physically and think a bit better of ourselves mentally. But underneath it all, we don't *feel* any better.

When we don't feel better emotionally, we are forever in danger of resorting to eating for consolation, along with other activities that are a catalyst to gaining weight. The changes made in our conscious mental processes also have consequences for our emotional condition, because changing the nature of our conscious thoughts without attending to our unconscious thoughts is mental control. Sooner or later, this control is lost as we are deluged by tides of emotional disarray.

When we finally discover we are unable to have any authentic and lasting impact on our condition physically and mentally, we may at last choose to tackle our weight emotionally. For many this is challenging because it requires authenticity, which is why it's usually the last approach we consider. Making changes to the emotional body requires gradual and consistent "process work," which isn't a quick fix. As challenging as it is, any amount of emotional work offers deeply rewarding consequences because it's *causal*.

If we have been overweight and resolve our emotional baggage, we immediately feel improved, and this feeling filters along the pathway of awareness into not just our awareness but also our physical circumstances. Our eating habits and our approach to our physical interaction with the world adjust. Thus our weight effortlessly regains its natural balance. We don't diet, but instead eat in a manner that's healthy. Because we no longer use food to suppress unintegrated emotion, we eat less. Because we now seek to enjoy our world by physically participating in it, we don't need to engage in extreme exercise. Because we initiate causal change in the quality of our experience, we are no longer anxious that our weight might return.

An integrative approach to adjusting the quality of our experience is built on the realization that our physical, mental, and emotional bodies are reflections of each other, and that the experiences that occur in each are interlinked. An integrative approach is also founded on the understanding that when we are authentic in making changes in the quality of our experience, we don't need to waste time and energy focusing on the effects of our unintegrated childhood experience. Our intent is to initiate change at the causal point.

The gentlest approach involves an integrated approach, which is a holistic approach. This entails working simultaneously with our physical, mental, *and* emotional bodies, with the intent to gradually move into and integrate the condition at the causal point within the emotional body.

An integrative approach takes into account that an uncomfortable emotional cycle that has been unconsciously repeating itself in our experience since childhood isn't deactivated overnight. The Presence Process therefore makes its approach gently, methodically, consistently, moving deliberately along the pathway of awareness, utilizing physical, mental, and emotional procedures with the overall intent to restore harmony to the condition of the emotional body. The art of an integrative approach is that it moves gently through the layers of the effect until it touches on and adjusts the cause.

Applying an integrative approach to restoring harmony to the quality of our experience is both simple and deeply complex, involving both common sense and paradox. It accomplishes its intent "in the moment," but also allows the passage of time for these consequences to filter through and manifest in our experience. Observable on the surface of things, it's simultaneously active beneath the surface.

An integrative approach is "process work," which means it unfolds organically. It calls upon the stamina of patience and *consistency* to flow as a conscious current throughout all our endeavors. An integrative approach works with all the parts of the whole but keeps its eye on the causal point. It knows with certainty that when change is activated from the causal point of anything, the effect manifests in the entirety.

An integrative approach also knows and therefore trusts that this ripple effect unfolds at a pace most suited to the wellbeing of the whole. There is therefore no purpose in hurrying, for each experience activated needs to be fully digested for absorption of its nutritional benefits. Hurrying causes indigestion and constipation. Hurrying is drama.

When we "live in time," whenever we complete anything, we wish to enjoy the benefits, outcomes, and consequences *right now*. When we finish an assignment for someone, we expect to be paid immediately. When we achieve something significant, we want to receive acknowledgement for it instantly. This is our fast-food, fast-paced mentality. We don't save up to buy our first car but go to the bank and they buy it for us. Teenagers expect to become adults overnight, and adults expect to be able to attain a four-year degree in a one-year part-time program. Many modern mothers and fathers no longer wait for their babies to birth naturally. Even vegetable and fruit produce is genetically engineered to grow bigger and faster. When we can't have what we desire now, we are annoyed and seek it elsewhere.

Though we are addicted to instant gratification, we are seldom gratified because, although we are making everything possible *now*, we are *seldom present to enjoy it now*. The moment we attain our desire, our attention jumps out of the present and into planning our next acquisition. This creates a world that's comfortable with living in debt, on borrowed time, and on somebody else's energy. We no longer own our houses, cars, and clothes – the bank does. We have robbed ourselves of the satisfaction of organic accomplishment. There's no more "rite of passage," only the fast lane. Young children want to be teenagers, teenagers want to be adults, and adults want to accomplish a lifetime's work before turning thirty. We spend each moment running ahead of ourselves, believing there's a destination we are supposed to arrive at that's saturated with endless happiness, acknowledgement, ease, and luxury. We are forever running away from something and toward something – and because everyone is behaving in this manner, we accept it as normal. We mentally leapfrog over the eternal present moment in everything we do, ignoring the flow of life.

The Presence Process – including the consequences inherent in completing it – moves at a different pace. This journey isn't about getting something done "as quickly as possible." It's about *process*, not instant gratification. The consequences we activate by completing this journey are made possible because of its gently unfolding integrative approach. By following the instructions carefully, taking one step at a time, being consistent and committed to completing the task at hand no matter what, we experience a rite of passage that reminds us of what "process" means.

Realizing what "process" involves isn't just a mental realization, but requires an integrated emotional, mental, and physical experience. Awakening to the value of process work is rare in a world of instant gratification. It powerfully impacts the quality of our experience because life in the present is an ongoing organic process. Realizing the power within the rhythm of process work may not necessarily impact our ability to earn a living, but it enhances our ability to open ourselves to the heartbeat of life.

An experience that flows from present moment awareness flows in cycles and tides. Because it's integrated and causal, it's simultaneously in a continual state of rest. It rests calmly and peacefully in the knowing that when causality is impacted, effects are inevitable. There is no need for hurry. Such a journey surpasses any mental destination we limit ourselves to in time-based consciousness.

LEVEL OF ENTRY

The Presence Process is a one-size-fits-all process because the causality of all unbalanced physical, mental, and emotional experience is the same: the unintegrated condition of the emotional body. However, because we come to this journey with varied intensities in our emotional body, the process has two levels of entry: introductory, and experiential. To compensate for our unique experiences, each varies in intensity.

A choice about which level to enter this process is taken using common sense and insight. When we take on too much too soon, we lay a foundation for the possibility of experiencing unexpected internal resistance reflected as a sudden increase in confusion and chaos. Overwhelming resistance sets us up to run from this experience, so that we fail to complete the journey.

We are therefore not to hurry into the process entertaining the illusion that if we "just get it done" and "get it over with as soon as possible," everything will be all right. The Presence Process isn't only about the next few weeks of our experience, but about *the rest of our experience*. It's about discovering how to live each moment responsibly for as long as we are given moments to experience.

INTRODUCTORY APPROACH

The introductory approach is simple. We continue reading this text as though it were a novel. We don't concern ourselves with repeating the conscious responses, and neither do we commence the breathing practice or apply the assigned perceptual tools. We read through the text for each week as though it were chapters in a book. We move through it all primarily mentally, abstaining from any conscious experiential participation.

We still receive significant insight and benefit from the introductory approach. This text is saturated with insight. Reading and comprehending it automatically transforms the way we interact with our experience. It gifts us with insight into the fabric of a relationship with Presence and the consequent radiance of present moment awareness.

Once we have completed the introductory approach, we may return to the beginning and commence the experiential approach. Having already read the course materials doesn't lessen the experience for us. On the contrary, it enhances it!

EXPERIENTIAL APPROACH

The experiential approach guides us into entering the process physically, mentally, and emotionally. It incorporates a gradual introduction to the breathing technique, the conscious responses, and the perceptual tools.

In order that we might gain as much as possible from our journey, it's recommended we complete the experiential approach three times, regardless of how we perceive the current state of our emotional well-being. This is only a recommendation. After each completion of the experiential approach, it's wise to take at least three weeks' break from deliberate session work to allow for physical, mental, and emotional integration.

During the break between completing the experiential approach and re-entering it, even though we engage no conscious mental processing, it's crucial we continue our 15-minute breathing routine twice a day. It's recommended we continue to attend to this daily breathing practice for up to six months after completing The Presence Process.

When we have completed the experiential approach for the first time, have taken an integration break, and are ready to re-enter the process, we make a discovery: re-entry is like entering a whole new experience. Because of our accumulated present moment awareness, we re-enter the process from an adjusted level of awareness – an altered "point of you." Consequently, the reading materials and the conscious responses greet us at a different place of awareness. On occasion, it appears as though we are reading the text for the first time. This is normal. Everyone who enters this process more than once experiences this. Because the process itself is neutral, it always meets us wherever we are, thereby reflecting and engaging the processing requirements of our current situation.

It may help us to think of The Presence Process as a manual that instructs us how to drive our moment-by-moment experience consciously and responsibly. The introductory approach is a theoretical overview of the task at hand. The experiential approach is actual practical instruction.

Once we have trained ourselves to consciously and responsibly drive the physical, mental, and emotional aspects of our experience, we are encouraged to take our newfound perceptions out onto the freeway of life to realize the possibilities. In each facet of life, comprehending and perfecting *the basics* establishes a thorough foundation for excellence. This is also the case with The Presence Process. This is why we are encouraged to complete the experiential approach more than once.

Don't be in a hurry to "get somewhere." Being in a hurry is to miss the point. Hurrying is drama. Think journey, not destination. The imprints that distract us from the present may seem all-pervasive, yet when we gently move ourselves through the experiential approach more than once, we gradually rise above these imprints and receive great insight. One such insight is that our personal imprints are intentionally placed before us, and by consciously resolving them we have an opportunity to discover the tools and capacities required for becoming conscious, responsible drivers of the experience we call "life."

By completing the experiential approach more than once, we gain enough present moment awareness to be able to take our attention off our personal imprints and place it on the world with the intent on being useful. Becoming available and useful is the responsibility of those who choose to walk awake among those still tossed unconsciously by the dreamy sleep of time.

This is the invitation: to embrace the art of living life consciously.

This is the journey: to awaken from time and become present now, in this world.

This is the promise: to become available and useful.

This is the gift: experiential awareness of Presence through present moment awareness.

NAVIGATIONAL GUIDANCE

Navigational guidance assists us in remaining steadfast in our intent. It contains insights to questions that arise as a consequence of entering The Presence Process experientially. It also contains explanations for many of the experiences encountered. Navigational guidance is worth reviewing whenever we feel unclear, confused, or wonder "what is happening to me?" or "is this supposed to be happening?" **Bookmark this page.**

1   Before entering week one, it's self-facilitating to establish an overall intent for this journey, preferably writable as one simple sentence. If we aren't certain of our intent, we ask without answering, then remain open to receiving insight unexpectedly. Our intent is realized because The Presence Process is an intention-driven journey. However, our journey toward this realization may not unfold as anticipated. Inner growth comes from *what we don't know* and unfolds in a manner we seldom foresee. Intention setting initiates movement, but it doesn't define what this movement will be. We also accept that our initial intent for entering this journey changes and even drops away as the process unfolds. This is because we all enter this process in a state of wanting, driven

by our desire to feed our unintegrated emotional charge. As we progress, this wanting dissipates. These desires become redundant, enabling us to experience this process unconditionally. Intent initiates movement, but it doesn't determine how the process unfolds or the consequences.

2   Circumstances may arise throughout our procedural experience that cause some of our breathing sessions to be unavoidably postponed or cancelled. We don't turn these occurrences into drama. We only realize why this happens in hindsight. Once we set our intent and commit to completing this experience, we make the most of each moment *as it unfolds.* Our experience of this process is valid, and our task is to respond to what unfolds instead of reacting to it.

3   This process unfolds to our benefit. However, it's useful to realize that what benefits us isn't necessarily in line with our personal agenda. Under no circumstances are we to "push the river" by assuming we know what's supposed to happen and how it's supposed to unfold. If we truly knew what we require and how to bring it about, we would have achieved this by now. Our responsibility the first time through is to follow the instructions without tampering with the procedural mechanics. If the text says "do this for one week," then we do it for one week. We don't add days or weeks because we don't feel our personal agenda is being met. If we miss a breathing session, or even both sessions in a day, we don't postpone our processing by adding an extra day. Remember, this is not about perfection, but about participation. Judgment is drama, so we don't judge what we have accomplished.

4   This process requires no "trying." No added effort beyond the current instructions is needed. There's no one "out

there" to acknowledge us, to impress, or to judge our progress. There are also no reference points by which to compare our progress. Comparing our journey to someone else's is drama. Our experience of this process is unique to us. Whatever happens is required and valid. By following the instructions to the best of our capacity, we effortlessly receive the required experience as and when we require it. Our experience is valid even when we don't think it is.

5   We dress comfortably in loosely fitting clothing whenever we are engaged in our breathing practice. If possible, we attend to this practice in the same place every day, and we do so in privacy. This process is inner work and not to be used for "show and tell." When we attend to our breathing practice in front of another, we are showing off. Such behavior is drama and achieves nothing. Of course, if the presence of another in the room is unavoidable, it's unavoidable.

6   Because entering the process experientially stimulates detoxification, it's recommended we drink at least three pints, or one-and-a-half liters, of pure water each day. However, we don't drink too much liquid in the hour prior to breathing.

7   Where possible, we abstain from ingesting medications that may cause drowsiness prior to breathing. We are aware that as we move through this journey and impact our emotional charge, our physical, mental, and emotional experience adjusts. *We don't react to these adjustments as though something is wrong.* Our physical body may at times feel uncomfortable, our stomach may flush toxins from our system, and we may experience aches and pains from past injuries that are resurfacing for integration. Integration occurs from "being with," not "doing to." Because integration requires

our felt-awareness of surfacing discomfort, we avoid taking a pill for minor discomforts, together with the drama of unnecessarily running to doctors and other healthcare practitioners. However, when a condition persists and requires relief so we may continue our processing, consulting a relevant healthcare practitioner is recommended.

8   For the duration of the process, we don't consume alcohol. In the context of this work, alcohol even in small quantities sedates authenticity and exaggerates drama. This becomes obvious once we gain present moment awareness. However, if we enter this process believing we are severely addicted to alcohol, we are wise to heed the guidance given in the section *Beyond Addiction and Affliction*.

9   We don't smoke marijuana or take any mind-altering substances during the entire process. Within the context of this work, these substances – marijuana in particular – prevent conscious access to, and hence awareness of, the authentic condition of our emotional body. It's therefore counterproductive to use marijuana during The Presence Process. It inhibits successful integration of suppressed trauma, masks the causality of addiction, and muffles the emotional charge. Attending to our breathing practice when not in an altered state is the most efficient and responsible approach. *Sobriety is a prerequisite for reawakening authenticity.*

10   We cannot enter and fully benefit from this experience if we are doing it to please someone else. This point can't be overemphasized. When we enter this process to please or manipulate someone else, we experience the journey as challenging. In the same light, we can't integrate an addiction because someone else asks us to. We can't succeed in inner work to satisfy someone else's demands. Individuals

who are unable to complete this journey often discover they entered it with an agenda other than to sincerely make a change in the quality of their experience *for themselves.*

11   Even when we willingly enter a process like this, we still at times resist the prescribed tasks, just like children when given homework they don't like. This process isn't homework. It is however "the work required to get us home." Each facet and element of the process is deliberately designed from years of personal and observed experience. Because we only comprehend the value of its structural integrity in hindsight, when we commit to this process, we do so as fully as possible. We may encounter moments in which we experience levels of intense resistance to what's happening. It's normal for this to occur when deeply unconscious imprints surface. During breathing sessions, this manifests as a desire to sleep rather than breathe. Resistance may also cause us to avoid mentally repeating our conscious responses. This is the time to "show up" and be as present as possible. The way out is through. Resistance may also manifest as delaying breathing sessions, as anger and irritation toward the process itself, and as emotional states of depression and hopelessness. Resistance may even manifest physically as cold and flu-like symptoms or various chest maladies that seemingly justify our canceling and postponing breathing sessions. We are to attend to our daily sessions *especially when we don't feel like it.* The way out is through.

12   As deeply unconscious and long-suppressed memories start surfacing, we may feel resistance to every aspect of this experience. When this happens, we don't allow ourselves to become concerned. We have spent much of our time keeping these unintegrated conditions hidden from our awareness. By entering this process, we intend them to surface

because we are now equipped to consciously integrate them. However, as they surface, our programmed instincts lead us to believe that what's happening to us is wrong, uncomfortable, or to be feared, and that it means we are "out of control." This is the voice of the mental body. Naturally, as this occurs, we feel resistance toward whatever is facilitating this change of circumstance. We therefore feel resistance toward everything about The Presence Process. Instead of reacting by backing away from commitment, we embrace these emotional states of resistance as positive indicators that the process is having a causal impact. Through perseverance, we break through to the other side of the resistance and feel the release of this unconsciousness. The way out is through.

13　Like any endeavor, the more we give of ourselves unconditionally, the more we receive. Often we don't do what we are invited to even when we know it's in our best interest because this is the only way we feel we have control over the seemingly ongoing chaos in our current experience. Once we enter The Presence Process, we don't consciously or unconsciously resist doing what's instructed as a means to feel some control over what's happening. This journey is an opportunity to realize what surrender is. In The Presence Process, the word "surrender" doesn't mean "to give up." It means we *surrender to the process* and hence *don't* give up, no matter what. To complete The Presence Process is therefore an act of surrender. The mental body may decide to make changes to the way the process is constructed. For example, it may decide to change the wording in a particular conscious response or not to read particular aspects of the text because it disagrees with the content. The mental body may decide we don't need to wield certain perceptual tools because we have already "done processes like this in the past." When we feel compelled to alter any aspect of this process, there are two facts worth considering. The first is that only a controlling mental body attempts to make adjustments to this process. The second is that the mental body lives in the dark. It may think and believe it understands everything, yet it "knows" nothing. We cannot control the consequences of doing this process, although we may attempt to. We cannot control our entry into present moment awareness. We can only lay a foundation that enables us to consciously reawaken into it. Because the mental body is a time-based identity, it's allergic to being present. Hence we are wary of entertaining its reasoning for bailing out in the midst of discovery. The way out is through.

14   We may only comprehend this in hindsight, but it's worth planting the insight now: *Everything that happens in our life experience from the moment we commence reading this text is part of The Presence Process journey.* Everything! We are facilitated by Presence twenty-four hours a day and well beyond the tenth week. The mechanics of how and why this facilitation works are explained during the course of the process. Throughout The Presence Process, unconscious memories surface so we can consciously integrate the energy we have invested in them. Because our capacity for suppressing memories is a fine art form, these unconscious memories don't surface as pictures and images in our mental body, but as unfolding external circumstances, such as the way people around us behave. We are going to become increasingly aware that the behavior of people around us and the circumstances we are experiencing are *deliberately* reminding us of our unintegrated past. We are taught how to consciously integrate these reflected memories so that their uncomfortable impact on the quality of our experience is integrated.

15   We keep in mind that this is "a process." It begins when we commit to it, but it doesn't reach a noticeable point of completion until we take the entire ride. Even then, it's still just the beginning of something ongoing. While we are in the middle of the process, we may feel we are getting nowhere. This is because *we are in the middle of the process*. By completing this process, we realize we are shown a door and taught how to open it, and that the rest of our unfolding experience is an opportunity to enter into present moment awareness. The Presence Process is therefore not an end to anything, but a continuation of something already in motion.

16   People may start behaving differently around us. When this happens, we pay attention *because something is changing in us* and being reflected in our perception of others.

17   Our body may develop aches and pains for no apparent reason, but we don't become concerned. Pain is one of the ways our physical vehicle draws our awareness into the present. Through developing containment – by placing our attention on the discomfort without judgment, concern, or complaint – we experience increased present moment awareness and integration.

18   Symptomatic conditions we are already experiencing may be heightened. This occurs because, as our attention increasingly re-enters our physical body, our awareness of our bodily *condition* increases. This increase of awareness may initially manifest as an apparent worsening of symptoms. However, it isn't. On the contrary, it's often the first step toward integration.

19   Old injuries may resurface. They do so because we are now willing and able to attend to them unconditionally through

present moment awareness, instead of suppressing, sedating, and controlling their symptoms.

20　We may have moments or even whole days when we feel distracted and confused. This occurs because we gain a new awareness of where we aren't present in our experience. These states of distraction and confusion already occur throughout our experience. However, as our present moment awareness increases, we become acutely aware of them. Our unconditional felt-awareness of them facilitates their integration.

21　We may discover we no longer care about circumstances over which we previously enforced control. When this happens, we go with the flow because this is a beneficial development. It occurs because many of our priorities are established for the benefit of others, not ourselves. As we become increasingly present, we realize we are all responsible for the quality of our personal experience and that we cannot therefore be responsible for the quality of another's. We may at times believe we are, or assume we are supposed to be, but this is an illusion. As we become increasingly present, this illusion crumbles. We cease using our energy to control the world and its inhabitants.

22　We may speak our mind in situations in which we would normally have kept quiet. This happens when our authenticity reawakens and is a necessary development, although at first it may feel uncomfortable. Through this process, we discover our ability to say "no" when we mean "no" and "yes" when we mean "yes." Initially, wielding our authenticity may cause us to feel we are doing something wrong. We are to honor ourselves. "No" is a complete sentence.

23   Our financial situation may shift. It may appear as though our resources are diminishing. For the most part this is temporary. Money is a metaphor for our personal flow of energy and therefore for movement in our experience. When we deliberately approach our emotional charge, we are inwardly examining disturbances in our personal energy flow. This inner examination is sometimes reflected as a disturbance in our financial resources. This especially occurs when we have attachment to money and judge our self-worth by financial indicators. Once we integrate the related emotional charge, we realize authentic abundance.

24   Our family members, partner, and close companions may start discouraging us from attending to our processing by claiming we are being self-centered. This is because we may be taking steps to nurture ourselves for the first time in our life, as opposed to "helping" others all the time. Others may not feel comfortable with our attention being taken off them. This is no reason to be concerned: they will survive. Some of them may even awaken to the necessity for emotional growth themselves.

25   We may feel sleepy for no reason. This is because our attention is on our suppressed unconsciousness. As we place attention on unconsciousness, it's often reflected as sleepiness. This is beneficial. We do best to rest when we are able, and to persevere when not.

26   We may experience occasional difficulty sleeping. This is because our increasing level of present moment awareness, and the processing that accompanies this experience, energizes us. It doesn't help to toss and turn in bed all night. It's more beneficial to arise and be constructive – to sit up and digest our alertness by being present with it. These

moments of late night and early morning alertness contain gifts of heightened awareness, insight, and inspiration.

27 We may experience vivid dreams, some of them disturbing. Often they are revealing in terms of the nature of our processing. Increased awareness of our dreamtime is due to emotional processing taking place while we are asleep. We don't take any of these dreams to be "true," especially when they feature people we know. For the purpose of The Presence Process, all dreams are metaphoric. In dreams, men who are older than us represent our relationship with our father and therefore what we need to learn about inner guidance. Women who are older than us represent our relationship with our mother and therefore what we need to learn about nurturing ourselves. Women the same age as us represent our feminine side and therefore our relationship with our emotions and the integration process. Men the same age as us represent our masculine side and therefore the condition of mental activities and the lessons we are currently learning. Individuals who are younger than us represent our male and female sides at these ages. We embrace the images we perceive symbolically. They are messengers who bear insight. To interpret them, we ask what the symbols mean to us. The language of dreams is seldom literal, but metaphoric.

28 We may become grumpy and irritable for no conceivable reason. This is because we have most likely been inwardly grumpy and irritable for much of our life. We now allow these suppressed emotional states to surface. We are allowed to feel grumpy and irritable as long as we don't take it out on others. The Presence Process teaches perceptual tools that facilitate us in integrating these emotional states without reacting outwardly.

29   If we don't feel like being in the company of our regular social companions, we honor this because it's an opportunity to discover how to say "yes" when we mean "yes" and, often more importantly, "no" when we mean "no." It's an invitation to be authentic.

30   People from our past and family members we haven't heard from for a while may contact us. Even though this process is an individual journey, it impacts our whole family and all with whom we are energetically connected. Our relationship with anyone is based on how we perceive them. As our perceptions alter, so does the nature of our relationships. These unanticipated contacts from people are a positive sign we are accomplishing something. When we impact the condition of our charged emotions, our world shifts. Often these unanticipated communications are invitations extended by the unified field to make amends, to take responsibility for the quality of past experiences, and to witness the profound accomplishments of integrative work.

31   We may feel melancholy and perhaps start missing people from the past. These are memories stirring so our attachment to them may be integrated. As memories stir, the images we associate with them come into mental body focus. We aren't actually "missing" these people and images, but are integrating our memories of them.

32   For a while we may find it challenging to be around our parents and immediate family members. *This has nothing to do with them and will pass.* These emotional states arise because those closest to us are the clearest mirrors in terms of reflecting imprints we prefer to hide from ourselves. The Presence Process instructs us how to perceive these reflections in a manner that empowers us to grow emotionally.

33   Our children may start behaving differently. They may behave
      exactly as we did when we were their age. They also act as
      mirrors so we may perceive through their Presence the unin-
      tegrated childhood imprints we are suppressing. This is an
      invitation to *watch* and *not react*. The behavior we are see-
      ing isn't authentic, but a reflection – a memory. As we inte-
      grate our childhood memories, we release our children from
      having to carry this baggage. Their behavior then transforms.
      Each time we complete the process, we notice how our chil-
      dren become lighter, more joyful, and authentic.

34   Our children may feel ill and experience cold or flu-like
      symptoms. What we don't integrate from our past is ener-
      getically carried by our children through imprinting. As we
      enter this journey, our children are already carrying uninte-
      grated imprints in their emotional body. Therefore, as we
      integrate our emotional body, our children simultaneously
      experience a shift within theirs. They may experience this
      through bodily symptoms, mental confusion, or emotional
      displays. As we complete the process and gain a new level
      of emotional equilibrium, they also accomplish integration.
      This doesn't only apply to our children. When we enter this
      process, everyone in energetic proximity to us also
      processes. However, unlike us, they move through this expe-
      rience unconsciously. For this reason we are compassionate
      with those closest to us. We are also unconcerned as they
      go through their emotional, and thus mental and physical,
      integration. They are mirroring us. Whenever we feel com-
      pelled to "do" anything, we make sure that whatever it is,
      we "do it unto ourselves." We also use common sense.

35   We may feel weepy for no apparent reason. When this occurs,
      we consciously intend for a quiet, uninterrupted moment to
      open up so we can be with these emotional states. Then we

cry, and cry, and cry some more! Crying for no reason at all, when it takes place when we are alone, detoxifies the emotional body like no other human activity. However, we don't use crying as a tool to gain attention and sympathy. Despite what many therapists tell us, crying alone when involved in emotional processing is more beneficial than crying on another's shoulder because then it's pure and authentic. It doesn't become a superficial drama and a tool in the hands of the mental body.

36   Old imprints we *think* are already resolved may resurface. This is because, in the past, we didn't unconditionally integrate them, but instead controlled and sedated them out of our awareness, believing this to be "healing." As we regain present moment awareness, these old imprints surface for integration, providing us with an opportunity to be *with* them without condition.

37   Our eating habits may change. As we gain present moment awareness, we become more conscious of the sensations in our physical body. The more present we become, the more aware we are of how food impacts our physical body. Entering present moment awareness often causes a change in our eating behavior, as we move from "dead and heavy foods" to "living and light foods." It may also cause the opposite, such as causing a vegetarian to start eating meat.

38   We may feel cravings for foodstuffs we enjoyed in the past. This is because we are activating memories from these time periods. Since this is often a temporary experience, we allow ourselves to enjoy.

39   We may go through moments of feeling overwhelmed, though such moments pass. They are caused by a buildup of

energy in our emotional body. We aren't required to deal with more than we are able, but we are often not required to deal with less. The key is to be strong, patient, and consistent.

40   We may experience emotions we can't describe or even recognize. This occurs when memories surface from experiences that occurred before we had a grasp of language. These memories move through our field of awareness as emotional states and sensations for which we have no explanation or means of description. We allow ourselves to feel them without condition.

41   It may become exceedingly difficult to explain to others what we are going through. Our course of action isn't to attempt to explain the mechanics of this process to them, but to simply introduce them to the book and invite them to investigate it for themselves. Because The Presence Process is a personal journey, there aren't always tangible points of reference for what we are going through that we can share with others. Everything we are experiencing is greeting us within the context of experience as a whole, and this makes its mechanics easily comprehensible to us. However, when we attempt to explain isolated aspects of this process to others, they struggle to grasp the individual pieces because they don't have a context in which to contain them. Remember how much text we were required to read and digest before we entered this process. The pre-process journey in this book is an "attunement." It creates a multi-dimensional perceptual pathway that enables us to navigate through complex terrain in a simpler and gentler way.

42   Even if we choose not to repeat this process, it still benefits us to reread the entire text at some point. As we journey through The Presence Process, we gather an ever-increasing

amount of present moment awareness. Consequently, we reread the text from a different point of awareness. We gain an adjusted "point of you," enabling us to enjoy many insights we didn't receive during our initial reading. We also definitely enjoy a few "Aha's," together with a few chuckles at the extent of our drama.

43   By completing this process, we are trained in a practical art form that equips us with the insight, experience, perceptual tools, and physical practice to enable us to process and integrate our charged emotions. Having this capacity removes anxiety from our experience. By continuing responsibly along the path this process initiates, we place increasing deposits of present moment awareness in the bank account of our current experience. The more present moment awareness we accumulate, the more conscious we become.

44   Before we actually complete the process, it's unlikely we will feel complete. We therefore complete the process in order to feel complete.

45   *Trust the process.* These three words become a life raft in moments of doubt and confusion. We all experience moments of doubt and confusion during this journey because there are aspects of this experience we cannot navigate, control, or even comprehend with the thinking aspect of mind. Once we commit to this journey, we do best to trust the process *no matter what.*

46   The way out is through.

PART III

THE PRESENCE PROCESS

WE ARE NOW MENTALLY PREPARED for The Presence Process. As we embark upon this journey, let us be comforted and encouraged by the following:

- There are no qualifications for entering The Presence Process other than our willingness to do so.

- There is no particular way we are supposed to move through this experience other than by following the instructions to the best of our ability.

- There are no correct or incorrect experiences. There is only our experience. Our experience – exactly as it unfolds – is valid. We succeed by following the instructions and completing the process. Completion is its own success.

INSIGHT AND FELT-PERCEPTION

As we begin The Presence Process, we are encouraged to consciously set our intent to be receptive to Presence, which is our facilitator. By reading the text up to this point, an awareness of Presence is gradually acti-vated. Whether we are aware of it or not, we are already familiar with its medium of communication. Within the context of The Presence Process, we call this medium of communication "insight."

Through reading the text up to this point, a transformative per-ceptual framework has been constructed. This framework enables a deeper comprehension of the conscious responses, the weekly reading, and the perceptual tools. This framework also enables us to under-take intricate and sensitive energetic procedures with greater gentle-ness and ease.

The voice of Presence communicates primarily through insight – *in sight*. This insight communicates what we need to know at the time we need to know it. First, though, we have to consciously develop our capacity for insight. This is accomplished organically through our conscious integration of charged emotion. As we feel our emotional charge without condition, we naturally develop felt-perception.

Our insight communicates to us primarily through felt-percep-tion. We *feel* something to be true for us. Developing this feeling capac-ity empowers us to comprehend insight that comes directly through Presence, and this in turn assists us in transcending the necessity for reliance on the mental body and its addiction to understanding.

We develop the ability to listen to the voice of Presence through trial and error, as we both ignore and obey felt-insights, then witness the consequences. When we go against our insight, we stumble – and in stumbling, we realize we ought to listen. When we obey our insight, whether we understand why or not, we progress. Accordingly, we gradually embrace insights brought to us through Presence without being suspicious of motives. Along the way, we discover how to trust felt-perception implicitly. Through personal experience, we realize Presence always has our most noble interests at heart. We *feel* this.

Presence doesn't mentally manipulate or emotionally sway us. This is one way of recognizing insight. It doesn't interfere (enter fear), doesn't punish us for not paying attention, and doesn't withdraw from us because we don't accept its guidance. Neither does Presence entertain drama. Its expression is pure, communicating only what's required, when it's required. It doesn't compete with or shout above the voice of the mental body. Instead of long drawn-out understanding, it provides instant "knowing."

The instructions that come from Presence often don't make sense. They are completely self-contained "knowing." Presence speaks from beyond our time-based mentality and therefore knows ahead of time what's going to occur. For this reason, its communication often doesn't appear to be in sync with where our conscious attention is anchored in time. We therefore learn to trust our insight, especially when we appear to have no logical reasoning to back up what's being shown to us. Listening to Presence is the key to unlocking the door to present moment awareness.

The Presence Process deliberately sets out to dismantle the energetic barriers manufactured by the endless chatter of the mental body so that we may once again reawaken our inner ear to the voice of Presence. It intends this because to establish insight is to accomplish everything.

NOW, WE BEGIN...

WEEK 1

Our Conscious Response for the Next Seven Days is:

"THIS MOMENT MATTERS"

ACTIVATION AND MAINTENANCE

ACTIVATION

We are now ready to enter week one and to activate our journey through The Presence Process. **Bookmark this page so it may be reviewed if any confusion arises about how we daily and weekly follow the process.**

Activation of The Presence Process is simple:

1   We memorize the given conscious response.

2   We page through the reading material for the week to see

how much reading is required. We then either read it all in one sitting or section it off into seven parts to read over the next seven days. In any event, we read or review some of the material each of the seven days.

3   We connect our breathing for at least 15 minutes. This initial breathing session serves as the experiential moment of procedural activation.

MAINTENANCE

During the seven days between activating each new weekly session, we are required to:

1   Attend to the 15 minutes breathing practice twice daily as soon after waking as is practical and as one of the last activities of our day when possible. For some of us, breathing as the last activity before bed may not be practical. It may energize us too much or we may simply be too tired at this time of day. The practice can then be brought forward to earlier in the evening or late afternoon. However, repeating this practice twice during the course of each day is required to support efficient integration.

2   Repeat the conscious response for each week whenever not mentally engaged. Once we activate a new week and receive a new conscious response, we cease using the previous week's conscious response entirely.

3   Read or review sections of the allotted weekly text daily and apply the perceptual tools as instructed.

The instructions given throughout this process are for our benefit.

Entering this journey believing we will somehow find the time to attend to our procedural commitments as we go along is to invite self-sabotage. We therefore make a commitment to follow and stick to the instructions received throughout the journey *no matter what*. The capacity of The Presence Process is enhanced by *consistency*. Consistency is more productive than sporadic and drastic activity.

Inevitably, circumstances arise that prevent us from being as thorough as we may prefer to be. This is where we discover the experiential meaning of "surrender." If, against our best intent, the activities around us unfold in a manner that prevents us from fulfilling our week's commitments, we aren't to fight either the situation or ourselves. We surrender to it and continue. However, we don't confuse "surrendering" with *being in resistance* and *making excuses*.

The golden rule in discerning between surrender and resistance is that when we feel relieved that we have been prevented from attending to the process' commitments, we are in resistance and have unconsciously manufactured circumstances to sabotage our progress. When we are disappointed because we aren't able to meet the process' commitments, it's possible Presence is rearranging our routine because this is in our best interest. In hindsight, we are able to discern which is the case.

The mental body gives us many reasons we can't fulfill the process' commitments, especially when discomfort is surfacing for integration. This is where self-discipline and personal will are required. By recommitting daily to completing this process and attending consistently to its requirements, we strengthen our personal will and accumulate self-discipline.

We aren't to beat ourselves up mentally and emotionally should we fall along the way. Falling isn't failing when we get up and continue. Falling is only failing when we allow the fall to stop our momentum before we reach completion.

THE CONSCIOUSLY CONNECTED BREATHING PRACTICE

Throughout The Presence Process, we approach the breathing practice as follows:

1   We sit with our back comfortably straight and eyes closed. Cross-legged on a cushion or sitting conventionally on a chair are both recommended. *Preferably not in or on our bed* because of its strong association with sleep. The intent is to adopt a posture that encourages both alertness and the opportunity to forget our body.

2   We ensure we are comfortably warm.

3.   We connect our breathing naturally. We breathe in and out without pausing (no long breathless gaps between our breaths). We breathe in an alert manner, with our breathing loud enough for us to hear ourselves. We apply brisk effort to our in-breath, whereas the out-breath is automatic. It's useful to visualize the movement of water in a fountain: energy is only required to push the water upward, since gravity brings it down effortlessly. Our in-breath is the water being pushed upward, while our out-breath is the water effortlessly returning to earth. Even though we apply alert effort to our in-breath and allow our out-breath to be automatic, we ensure that both our in-breath and our out-breath are of an even duration. We intend to breathe in such a manner that our inhalation and exhalation are one continuous rhythmic pattern. (An audio demonstration of the breathing practice is provided on the audio page of The Presence Portal website: www.thepresenceportal.com.)

3. Nose breathing is preferable. When our nose is blocked, we use our mouth. However, we don't use both nose *and* mouth. In other words, we don't use our nose for inhaling and our mouth for exhaling, or vice versa. Using both nose and mouth causes an imbalance between the oxygen and carbon dioxide levels in the body.

4. Throughout the duration of The Presence Process, we synchronize our breathing with the following conscious response: I AM HERE NOW IN THIS. We synchronize our breathing and mental activity in this manner: "I" on the in-breath, "AM" on the out-breath, "HERE" on the in-breath, "NOW" on the out-breath, "IN on the in-breath, and "THIS" on the out-breath, using the same words for each cycle of in-breaths and out-breaths. This conscious response is for our breathing practice only.

5. By connecting our breathing, we approach present moment awareness, which means our concept of clock time alters. For this reason we may initially require a timepiece to assist us in keeping time.

6. After we complete our breathing session, we are encouraged to take our attention off our breathing, sit quietly, and be unconditionally with whatever we experience. All experiences are valid.

As we progress, we may feel inclined to breathe for longer than 15 minutes during our twice-daily sessions. This intent is valid. However, it's strongly recommended we don't breathe less than 15 minutes per session. The mental body provides many excuses to justify why we can't put this small amount of time aside for ourselves. Let its craftiness die from neglect.

Whatever happens physically, mentally, and emotionally during our breathing practice is valid. No matter what the nature of our experience – whether we perceive it as comfortable or uncomfortable – we keep our breathing connected, remain relaxed, and sit as still as possible. By keeping our breathing connected and remaining as relaxed as possible, discomfort that arises during our breathing sessions integrates. Tingling sensations may remain in the extremities of our body afterward. This is normal and beneficial.

Any discomfort we experience during a consciously connected breathing session is an indicator of charged emotion surfacing for integration. Discomfort experienced during breathing sessions is *the past coming to pass.* Trust the process and complete the session.

The Presence Process breathing practice is simple and gentle for what it accomplishes, as well as safe when we pay attention to these simple instructions. We don't let any discomfort experienced in these sessions steer our mentality into imaginary fears. Rather, we allow discomfort to serve as confirmation that we are energetically impacting the causality of the quality of our experience.

Trust the process. No one is hurt by breathing normally and naturally.

At times during breathing sessions, we may lapse into states of unconsciousness. This manifests as seemingly falling asleep without warning during our breathing session. We may also feel as if we are anesthetized. This experience is valid. It occurs when deeply unconscious memory becomes activated and surfaces. If we experience a reoccurring loop of unconsciousness, so that we lapse into sleep each time we sit to breathe, it's recommended we double the tempo of our breathing pattern until we again feel present. Even when we double the speed of our breathing pattern, we still keep our inhalation and exhalation evenly balanced.

Doubling our breathing pattern minimizes the occurrence of any pausing. Notice that the point at which we lapse into sleep is at the end of an out-breath. Doubling the tempo of our breathing helps minimize the possibility of this. Once we feel more alert, we return to the tempo of our regular breathing pattern. The more present we become, the less this surfacing unconsciousness overwhelms us. When we are feeling deeply unconscious, the only way out is to breathe our way through.

INTO THE BREATH

The experiential journey through The Presence Process is initiated when we first consciously connect our breathing.

Like many who have embarked on this journey, we may discover that at times it can be challenging to consistently attend to our twice-daily 15-minute breathing practice. We may discover there are moments in which we feel immense resistance to it. The first 15 minutes we sit alone and breathe may stretch out and become the longest 15 minutes we have ever experienced. (On the other hand, it may also fly by in what feel like a few short minutes.) Understanding why this occurs, and that it isn't unusual, assists and even motivates us to break through any mental barriers that may arise. All of these points of resistance are mental barriers that reflect underlying imprinted emotional charges. Everything we seek from this journey awaits us on the other side of this resistance.

The reason it may initially be challenging to sit down for a minimum of 15 minutes twice a day and connect our breathing isn't that this practice is difficult. When we follow the instructions for the breathing practice, we are simply breathing naturally. We are breathing *normally*. No over-exertion or special posture is required. We aren't invited to "do" anything other than what already happens naturally in our body. In fact, it's more accurate to state that we are invited to "undo" and enter an experience of "not doing." The physical effort required to consciously connect our breathing for 15 minutes twice a day is therefore not the issue.

One reason it may initially be challenging to attend to this practice consistently is if we are consciously or unconsciously entering The

Presence Process because someone else told us we "should" do it. Someone may have thought they were "helping us" by introducing us to this process, so we began it in order to please them.

We may also have other misguided motivations. For example, we may believe that by doing The Presence Process, we will gain something from someone or from the world. Perhaps we believe that by entering this process, our partner will return, since by doing the process we will have dealt with the issues that caused our separation. Or we may think that by completing this process, we will suddenly start making lots of money and become successful in the world.

These examples of misguided intent illustrate situations in which our entry into this process may be motivated by reaction instead of response. When this is the case, we may initially struggle with our breathing practice because, when we are doing this for anyone or anything other than ourselves, it's challenging to muster the willpower to attend to the practice consistently. It's uncomfortable to enter integration work for someone else and impossible to breathe for someone else.

The Presence Process may well be the first time we have done anything authentic for ourselves. To some extent, everyone who enters this process struggles with this. We all bear the scars of taking the cue for our behavior, our appearance, and our expectations of life from others.

As children, we enter the world of order, routine, and "appropriate behavior" through the guidance, encouragement, and insistence of our parents and peers. Our lack of personal willpower – the ability to source our intent from *insight* – is the consequence of our initial intimate relationship with our mother. We eat, dress, bathe, and behave in a manner determined by our mother. As we develop, we express ourselves according to what we perceive to be appropriate in the eyes of our mother and father. The consequence of this initial dependency is that on an unconscious level, our motivation for the way we eat, dress, bathe, and behave today is almost solely sourced from the reflected physical presence of others and hence is reactive. We unconsciously use these "others" as ongoing reflections of our mother and father. Through the physical presence of others, we still attempt to please and appease our mother and father as a means of gaining their approval and unconditional acceptance.

As we move through childhood, the teenage years, and into adulthood, this initial motivation to function according to mommy and daddy's intent is inevitably transformed and transferred. When we are young, this compulsion to act in a manner we believe enables us to gain our parents' love and approval is automatic. During our teenage years, this behavior is transformed into a desire to "fit in" with peer groups. By the time we enter adulthood, this need for external validation becomes cloaked as a desire "to appear responsible" and "to get ahead."

Let's call much of this behavior what it is: a desire to get a reaction, a drama staged for the purpose of gaining the attention and approval of others. For some of us, this desire manifests as its polar opposite: to not fit in and not get ahead. This resistance is also reactionary, an attempt to seek attention and approval, traced to our initial interaction with our parents or their substitutes.

No matter how we cloak our desire for attention and approval, and no matter how we justify it, deep introspection reveals the inauthenticity of this behavior. The tragedy is that we may go through a whole life experience and not accomplish anything authentically inspired. We ignore *in*sight (inside) and remain bedazzled by *out*sight (outside).

Even the notion of investing our time in self-oriented behavior may cause a stirring of emotional states such as guilt. We may also believe that taking care of ourselves is selfish. This is because, in the time-based experience of modern day society, we are expected to function like clockwork. Our current world is a drone-clone experience. We are expected to live as a dependent piece of the overall societal mechanism. Behavior that appears disconnected from the machinery – behavior by which we demonstrate nurturing of our individuality – is seldom encouraged. Its value for the whole can't be perceived by those who take their cue for the way they are conducting themselves from others.

The act of living for approval and acknowledgement is so part of our experience that it's challenging to grasp the implications of our lack of authentic willpower. We are seldom given the opportunity to develop the muscle that powers our will to act independently of what we perceive to be happening around us. We seldom realize just how little willpower we have. If many of us were taken out of our present environment and placed alone on an idyllic desert island, with all our heart's desire except the company of other humans and pets, we would likely become depressed and perish. If we didn't perish, we would undergo a profound internal transformation.

An indicator of our lack of personally motivated willpower is the way we say "yes" when we mean "no," and "no" when we mean "yes." This lack of emotional backbone is a consequence of the fact that our behavior is dictated by our reactivity. If we catch ourselves behaving in this manner just once, it's likely we are unconsciously behaving this way in many other aspects of our life experience.

When we say "yes" when we mean "no," and "no" when we mean "yes," we are living for the acknowledgement and approval of others. Accordingly, when we take our first step toward implementing any self-nurturing activity, such as attending to our daily 15-minute breathing practice, we may encounter a wall of resistance. Though the wall is invisible, it may seem impenetrable. However, it isn't.

Resistance to our daily breathing practice also increases when we tell others about our intent to enter this work. This is the risk we take when we talk about any work we enter specifically for ourselves. In most cases, we are only talking about it in an effort to gain outside support – to receive confirmation that our effort is worthy and appropriate.

When we enter The Presence Process, at first we may be inclined to tell others about it, disguising our desire for validation as casual conversation. When we behave in this way, we invariably discover that Presence has a sense of humor. Presence meets our instinctive desire for validation by placing people in our path who make comments such as: "You have been practicing your *breathing*? But surely you know how to breathe already, ha-ha." Other comments we might endure include: "Oh, I have done this before. It doesn't help." "I know this technique already. It doesn't work." "Why go into the past? Just get on with your life." "I'd love to do stuff like this too, but right now I have to deal with the *real* world." When nobody confirms the validity of our intent, and since we are unable to contain ourselves, we feel even more resistance to attending to our daily breathing.

On the other hand, if others tell us how great and noble an undertaking The Presence Process is, such comments initially make attending to our daily breathing practice easier, since we are then able to report back and receive accolades for our valiant effort. However, we gain nothing authentic. For instance, we don't develop willpower.

For anything we gain from this process to have substance, our intent must be sourced internally. It's likely that at some point we all make the mistake of seeking validation from others by telling them what we're doing. This is our shared, imprinted, habitual, reactive behavior. Hopefully we don't waste too much energy on such a pointless pursuit. In the end, our validation of ourselves is all we require for the process to have an authentic impact.

We therefore make a conscious effort to enter this journey for ourselves. Everything we accomplish internally inevitably benefits the world through which we move. But to begin with, we are the ones who must reap the rewards of our effort because *we cannot give away what we don't yet contain within ourselves.*

The first reward we intend for ourselves is that of building the muscle of personal willpower – the will to act on our insight in spite of what we perceive to be happening in the world. This capacity is one of the fruits we gradually enjoy when we consistently connect our breathing twice a day for a minimum of 15 minutes. When we breathe for ourselves and no "other," each added session steadily builds the muscle of personal willpower. *Consistency in any endeavor, despite external distraction, is the recipe for gathering personal willpower.*

It isn't necessary for anyone to understand why we are entering The Presence Process. Integrative work only makes sense to those who are ready to initiate authentic movement in their experience. At times, even we struggle to make sense of why *we* are doing the breathing practice – or any of this. This is normal. The paradox is that even when the mental body parades itself as godlike, it still can't comprehend the fact that we are responsible for the quality of our experience.

The mental body only understands blame. If our experience doesn't go according to our mentally devised plans and schedules, then someone or something else is to blame. Hence we apply ourselves to this course of action above and beyond the necessity of understanding why. We attend to our breathing each day no matter what. Our daily breathing practice is the seed of a plant that bears the fruit we seek: an intimate relationship with Presence through the perceptual experience of present moment awareness.

It's helpful to make our daily breathing practice special for ourselves, because in fact it is. It's *our* time. To assist us in this, we find preferably the same place and time each day to attend to this task. Familiarity tames the unruly mind and consistency strengthens willpower.

For the duration of this process, we make the entire experience gentler for ourselves when we choose to start and complete each day with our breathing practice. While remaining practical and sensible, we intend to let it be the opening and the closing song of our waking moments. By elevating our relationship with our breathing session to this status in our daily routine, we lay the foundation for a rebirth of personal willpower. This personal willpower, when authentic, isn't based on anything or anyone else. It arises from within us, and within it is the capacity to transform and elevate the quality of our current life experience – and so much more.

PRESENCE AND INDIVIDUAL EXPRESSION

From birth, we are taught our identity is that which makes us different from everybody else. We are told this identity has to do with our appearance, behavior, and life circumstances. Consequently, we mistakenly identify with our body, our behavior, and the circumstances we experience. While these individual expressions constitute the passing experience we are currently having, they don't readily inform us of what we *are*.

So, what are we? What about us is permanent and shared with everyone? What's common to all humanity?

The nature of experience is that it constantly changes in form and quality. The form of any given experience takes shape based on our previous emotional states, thoughts, words, and actions, while the quality of our experience depends on the interpretation we give these things. Although our experience comes and goes, ever changing, "we" remain – participating, observing, and witnessing. Ten years ago our experience was different, yet the part of us that was having this experience then is still here now, in this moment.

Realizing that all experience is in a constant state of change is a productive insight because it reveals that when we don't appreciate the quality of the experience we are having right now, there's a possibility of changing it. This realization goes to the heart of The Presence Process. This adventure isn't about attempting to change what we already are, have always been, and always will be. It's about making a change in *the quality of our experience.*

The Presence Process works from a standpoint that it's impossible to change what we are because we are eternal, unchanging Presence. For now, we are invited to accept our immortal quality as a concept. However, once we discover how to consciously detach from our ever-changing experience, we experientially perceive that even though our individual expression is constantly changing, we who are the expresser and experiencer remain unchanged. What remains unchanged is eternal.

Throughout this process, we are invited to realize what we already are by engaging in an intimate encounter with our shared Presence. Some call Presence "the observer." This is because it witnesses everything and therefore knows everything that has ever happened during our entire life experience. By entering into present moment awareness, we also discover that Presence also appears to know everything that is to occur.

As we develop a conscious relationship with Presence, we realize the following:

- **Presence knows no order of difficulty.** This means Presence has the capacity to bring into our experience the precise circumstances required to trigger in us an awareness of suppressed charged emotions that require conscious integration. Through responding to and integrating whatever Presence reveals, we accumulate present moment awareness.

- **Presence has our best interest at heart.** Because Presence knows itself, it knows us better than we presently know ourselves. It knows exactly what experience we require to restore present moment awareness. By surrendering to it, we are surrendering to our experience as it unfolds throughout this process. Because our experience is overseen by Presence, it's not only valid but also required.

- **The Presence within each of us is the same as the Presence within all living creatures.** Because Presence is a unified field of awareness that embraces all, our authentic identity is shared with all life. Presence is our shared connection with all life.

- **The Presence within us doesn't interfere.** Presence willingly attends to those aspects of our experience we consciously surrender to it. Learning to surrender is our ultimate challenge and one of the significant lessons offered through this process. Asking Presence for its assistance in any particular avenue of our experience, then simultaneously trying to figure out how to "get it done ourselves," is counterproductive.

At first the above realizations are delivered to us as mental concepts we may choose to accept or not. However, as we gather present moment awareness, which is the same as saying as we become more present within our current experience, we are given what we require to experientially realize these truths. These revelations, once acquired, stay with us. Present moment awareness, once consciously accumulated, seldom decays.

By developing an intimate relationship with Presence through the breathing practice, the conscious responses, and the perceptual tools, we gradually realize that what we have come to accept since childhood as our personal identity is inauthentic. In contrast to our authentic Presence, our adult identity is for the most part a manufactured pretence – a reaction to our unintegrated imprinting.

The Presence Process enables us to perceive that the aspect of us that makes us different from others – our beautifully individualized expression of the vibrational – when mistaken for our authentic identity leads to limitation, separation, and segregation. The process assists us in realizing that by identifying only with these outer individual expressions – our appearance, behavior, and life circumstances – we limit and separate ourselves from Presence, which is the unlimited, commonly shared, vibrant vitality that flows within all life.

When our identity is anchored solely to our expression, it's based on interpretation. This interpretation is manufactured from past circumstances, future projections, and the opinions and understandings of others.

We aren't our body or behavior, even as we aren't the circumstance of our current experience. Our outer expression is a temporary and constantly changing physical, mental, and emotional journey. Though it's awesome to behold, it passes and we remain. A more accurate definition of what we are is *that which we share with all life*. What is it that we share with all life?

EXPERIENCING PRESENCE

The simple breathing practice of The Presence Process facilitates an experiential awareness of Presence through activation of present moment awareness. However, the mental body is immune to such an experience, seeing no value in it. If it's allowed to have its way, it distracts us from making progress. By keeping the following in the forefront of our awareness while we attend to our practice, we train ourselves to bypass the antics of the mental body:

1 **WE BREATHE WITHOUT PAUSING, NO MATTER WHAT.** This point cannot be emphasized too strongly. *Our personal experience of Presence during a breathing session is cumulative based on the length of time we breathe without pausing.* We therefore keep our breathing rhythmically connected throughout our breathing practice, no matter what. Our experience of Presence builds exponentially with each moment our breathing remains connected. The moment we pause and our breath becomes disconnected, our growing awareness of Presence wanes. When this occurs, we may feel as if we have lost the present moment awareness accumulated during our session. *We do not lose the accumulated processing effect of a breathing session because we enter elongated pauses.* However, our awareness of "being within the Presence" may diminish. Therefore, during our breathing sessions, we intend not to pause, no matter what. If we need to go to the bathroom or place a blanket on ourselves, we attend to this without disconnecting our breathing. If we need to blow our nose, cough, yawn, or take a sip of water, we complete the task swiftly and return to our breathing. When suppressed emotion surfaces and we feel the urge to cry, we allow ourselves this experience. But as soon as it passes, we return to our connected breathing.

2   **WE REMAIN AS PHYSICALLY STILL AS POSSIBLE THROUGH-OUT THE SESSION.** Presence awareness isn't only generated by consciously connecting our breathing, but also by maintaining physical stillness throughout the session. Everything physical that occurs during our session, aside from our breathing, is either a releasing of charged emotion or the mental body's attempt to distract us from the experience in which Presence makes itself known. For this reason we ignore our desire to move about and instead keep our attention fixed on our conscious response ("I am here now in this") and our breathing. We avoid itching, fiddling, scratching, rocking, shifting our body, entertaining a sudden desire to do yoga postures, humming, or talking. This is all drama. Drama is an instant departure from present moment awareness. For the purpose of our journey through The Presence Process, no physical activity aside from the natural and balanced inhalation and exhalation of our breathing generates an experiential encounter with Presence. Other physical movements, no matter how relevant they may be to the mental body, are drama. For the purpose of this process, we are encouraged to keep the following in the forefront of our awareness: silence, stillness, consciously connected breathing, and a mental body focused on our conscious response, are our most accelerated pathway into present moment awareness. All else is interference.

ONWARD, INWARD, AND UPWARD

We can't force an experience of present moment awareness, but we can lay a foundation for it. An experiential encounter with Presence enters our awareness when least expected. This reveals the disadvantage of expectation.

Each moment of every day of this process counts. Every consciously connected breath makes this process gentler and simultaneously more impactful. We are therefore encouraged to make the most of every opportunity to connect intimately with Presence through application of this present moment awareness process. Once we accomplish this connection, everything is accomplished.

By applying ourselves to each aspect of this process, we enhance the quality of our entire experience. In essence, the opportunity presented by this process is for emotional rebirth into an experience we suspected existed, but that has remained unobtainable. The Presence Process is an opportunity to reach within and set in motion the causal events that enable us to reestablish authenticity, integrity, and intimacy in all our encounters. Nobody can accomplish this for us. Nobody ever did, and nobody ever will. We alone are responsible for the quality of our experience. It's our footprints that lead us into causally impacting the quality of our experience.

Each morning after our breathing practice, it's beneficial to set our intent to maintain our sense of present moment awareness throughout the day. To this end, the following technique is helpful. During the course of our day, when we become aware of our breathing, let it remind us to mentally repeat our allotted conscious response for the week. When we remember to mentally repeat our conscious response for the week, let it remind us to consciously connect our breathing for a few moments.

By remaining as physically and mentally present as possible throughout the day, we are more likely to respond than react to whatever we are currently integrating. We also bring more present moment awareness into our daily activities, imbuing them with Presence.

No matter how ardently we apply ourselves to this process, we still experience moments when we appear to be distracted and confused. This distractedness and confusion is an indication of a surfacing emotional charge. These charges surface because we are now ready to integrate them. We integrate them by "being with" them, without attempting to manipulate our experience in any way. We allow these uncomfortable felt-moments to serve as acknowledgement that the process is unfolding as required. Because The Presence Process is facilitated by Presence, we aren't given more than we are able to digest. We also realize we are not given any less.

THIS CONCLUDES WEEK ONE

WEEK **2**

Our Conscious Response for the Next Seven Days is:

"I RECOGNIZE MY REFLECTIONS AND PROJECTIONS"

IDENTIFYING MESSENGERS

By completing The Presence Process, one of the transformations we experience is an evolution from reactive to responsive behavior. This single adjustment to our perception of the world, and hence our interaction with it, benefits our entire experience. The consequences of consistently choosing response over reaction are eternal.

Whenever the consequences of our unintegrated emotional charge are significantly delayed by time, they appear to occur independently of any cause. Because of this, we assume the circumstances we encounter are happening *to* us, not *because of* or *through* us. This enables us to entertain a victim or victor mentality.

Behaving as a victim or victor means we either complain about our experiences with others or compete with them. Because of the time lag between cause and effect, it doesn't occur to us that *we are complaining about ourselves and the consequences of our own actions*. Neither do we recognize that we are competing with ourselves in the form of the obstacles we place in our own way. Victim and victor mentalities are like a dog chasing its tail.

Reactive behavior is based on a belief that the world is happening *to* us, and it's therefore our duty either to defend ourselves or to impose our will on what's happening. This charade appears authentic because of "living in time," which is a condition in which our attention is almost exclusively focused on a reflected past and a projected future. The gap between the reactive behavior that arises from charged emotional states and the physical, mental, and emotional consequences of this behavior is just long enough for us to convince ourselves we aren't the cause of our present circumstances.

While living in time, we can't discern the energetic connection between cause and effect. This is because this energetic connection unfolds in the present. The present, when we aren't conscious of it, becomes a blind spot in our awareness. This blind spot makes it impossible to perceive the energetic connection between all life. We simply don't see the continuity of everything.

To perceive the energetic connection and continuity of all life requires an experiential awareness of the intimate relationship between cause and effect. When we can't recognize this connection, our experience appears chaotic, random, and devoid of purpose.

When we live in time, we spend our days *seeking the meaning of life*. In contrast, when we are present, *we enjoy a life saturated with meaning*.

The perceptual framework we call "time" is an experience in which there appears to be a delay, a pause, an empty space between any emotion, thought, word, or deed and its consequences. This apparent delay allows the two events – a cause and its effect – to seem disconnected. As real as this delay appears to us, it's actually a perceptual slight of hand. Our reactive behavior and its consequences are energetically connected and therefore never separate.

For example, we may think poorly of another person. Within a matter of days, this individual behaves poorly toward us. When we live in time, we automatically assume their poor behavior toward us is validation of our victim or victor mentality, when in actuality it's the consequence of our poor thinking.

An obstacle to recognizing the energetic connection between cause and effect is that our attention is physically *trans*fixed. This means we are in a *trance, fixed* on the outer surface of things, as if they were solid. When we are physically transfixed by the world, everything "matters" to us. We also dwell in a story we tell ourselves about what we are seeing.

The consequence of this physically biased perceptual condition is that we can't see *into* anything and therefore have no awareness of the inner content of life forms. We can't recognize how everything interacts with everything else. This is because the causal point of authentic interaction between all life forms is located internally. When we are physically transfixed, the solid surface of whatever we focus on appears as a barrier, an outer skin of separation. The mental story we tell about what we are seeing sounds valid to us because we can't see what is really happening at the inner, causal level.

Rekindling our ability to perceive the connection between all life forms requires us to learn to perceive life as "energy in motion." We initiate this perceptual adjustment by consciously training ourselves to redirect our point of focus to the emotional content of our own experience. We first require an awareness of *our own* energies in motion, and this awareness is then reflected in the world around us.

The consequence of this gradual shift of awareness is that the distance between our emotions, thoughts, words, and deeds, and their physical, mental, and emotional consequences, appears to become shorter. It may feel like time is speeding up.

In reality we are becoming aware of the emotional undercurrent in our experience, the energetic chord that connects the causes and effects that flow throughout our experience. This energetic chord is always present, and our capacity to perceive it is the rebirthing of present moment awareness. However, it isn't discernable with our physical eyes or our mental understanding, but is discerned only by developing the eyes of the heart, which "see" with felt-perception.

When we enter present moment awareness, it becomes apparent that, whenever we live in time, the quality of the experience we are having is an effect. As we awaken further into present moment awareness, it becomes evident that the quality of our experience right now is a reoccurring effect of unintegrated emotional charges from our childhood. We realize that our unintegrated childhood emotions are the cause we normally can't perceive of the physical and mental circumstances unfolding as the quality of our adult experience.

Aside from the perceptual blind spot produced by our lack of present moment awareness, the reasons these points of causality – these emotionally-charged childhood experiences – are unconscious to our normal everyday physical and mental perception are twofold:

1   Most of them were imprinted in our emotional body before our awareness entered the mental realm. They are therefore not located within us as thoughts, words, and concepts, but as felt-sensations.

2   The core emotional experiences of the past that have an impact on our current experience are by their nature uncomfortable. Our automatic impulse is to push them out of our awareness so that we can "get on with our life." This is called "suppression," and it's achieved through sedation and control. We master hiding from ourselves that with which we don't know how to cope.

By entering The Presence Process experientially, our intent is that these suppressed childhood emotional charges surface into our awareness. A good illustration of the mechanics of this process is to visualize a clear glass jar containing oil and water. The water represents what we already are in our authentic being, while the oil represents the sum of uncomfortable physical, mental, and emotional experiences. When we live reactively in a victim or victor mentality, it's akin to shaking the jar endlessly in an attempt to change our circumstances. But all that happens is that the oil and water become so mixed up, it's impossible to tell one apart from the other. All our endless "doing" and "thinking" result in is a murky mixture. Reactivity is shaking the jar. Response is allowing the jar to come to stillness.

The Presence Process is about "not doing." It teaches us to put the jar of our ongoing experience down and leave it "be." This allows the oil to rise naturally and effortlessly to the surface, and consequently to separate from the water. This rising oil represents our unconscious childhood memories, which penetrate our awareness as uncomfortable charged emotional states.

While introducing us to "not doing," the Presence Process also instructs us to gently scoop the oil of our charged emotion off the surface of our experience. As we engage in this, the jar contains less and less oil. Simultaneously, the water – representing an awareness of our authentic nature – regains its clarity. By moving through The Presence Process, we become aware of what we already really are, in contrast to being endlessly distracted by the experiences we unconsciously manufacture as a reaction to our inner discomfort.

Fortunately, we don't need to re-experience, relive, or re-witness all the childhood experiences that were responsible for imprinting our emotional body with these uncomfortable charges. Mentally going over these in great detail is of no value. Many of these experiences re-enter and flow out of our awareness simply as felt-sensations that we can't seem to pin down to anything we even remember, let alone understand.

We only become mentally aware of the details of suppressed memories if we are meant to garner wisdom from them – that is, if the wisdom gained from recalling the details of these past experiences facilitates our current emotional development.

As these suppressed emotions *come to pass,* which is all that's occurring when we start re-experiencing them, we may at first perceive them as experiences that are unfolding for the first time. As we increase our present moment awareness, we realize these felt-discomforts are dated emotional states we have been unconsciously holding onto while simultaneously hiding from them! We are instructed how to wield our attention and intent to facilitate their integration.

Feeling them – without placing conditions on our experience of them – initiates integration.

Because these suppressed memories and their corresponding emotional signatures are so deeply imbedded within our unconscious that they are often only apparent to us, if at all, as nameless felt-sensations, it isn't either possible or necessary to recall them as mental body images in the way we do with the memory of a recent event. Hence this isn't the manner in which they surface into our awareness. When we intend them to surface in our experience so we may consciously integrate them, they do so as *reflections* and *projections.*

A *reflection* is the occurrence of an experience that reminds us of something, while a *projection* is the behavior we adopt when reacting to such a memory.

For example, when someone reminds us of one of our parents, this is a reflection. When we then start behaving around this person as we would around the parent they remind us of, this is a projection. A reflection occurs first, followed by a projection.

Most of the time, this process of reflecting and projecting happens unconsciously. In the context of The Presence Process, we call it being "triggered," "having our buttons pushed," and "getting upset." We see ghosts from our past (a reflection), then chase them (a projection).

Before accumulating present moment awareness, these reflections and projections appear as though they are events that are happening *to* us, independently of our behavior. They appear in the guise of seemingly random and chaotic external circumstances. They also appear as unprovoked behavior on the part of people around us, which we find emotionally upsetting.

However, as we accumulate present moment awareness, we also

attain the ability to perceive that whenever we are triggered in a manner that causes emotional discomfort, we are deliberately being "set up."

An *upset* is a *setup.*

Whenever we are upset, we are being visited by ghosts of the past, which furnish us with the opportunity to exorcise them so that they neither haunt our present nor infect our future.

To recognize the reflections of surfacing unconscious memories in the world around us, we are required to remember two insights:

> *Whenever anything happens that upsets us emotionally, whether it appears as an event or as another person's behavior, we are experiencing a reflection of our past.*

> *Whenever we react physically, mentally, and emotionally to such an experience, we are projecting as a consequence of this reflection.*

Unfortunately there is no exception to this rule. *Emotional upset = memory recall.*

When we are emotionally upset by anything, we are actively remembering something unconsciously hidden from us until this moment. We are energetically attached to this upsetting event, and therefore reactive to it, because it reflects unintegrated emotional circumstances from our past. We are haunted by it. This is why we react to it by projecting – by behaving as a victim or victor.

We have seen that one of the reasons we may not be able to recognize an upsetting situation as a surfacing emotional memory from the past is that, in "time," our tendency is to focus our attention on the physicality of the situation. Our attention is *trans*fixed by the physical event, circumstances, or behavior of the person who is upsetting us, instead of recognizing that the emotional reaction we are experiencing is a *consequence.*

This is key: The surfacing memory isn't something physical we look at or something we understand mentally, but something emotional we engage purely through felt-perception.

The memory is *an energetic echo we perceive through feeling.* This is why we don't say, "I do upset" or "I think upset." We say, "I *feel* upset."

Through The Presence Process, we learn not to focus on the physical event, the person's behavior, or the story we tell ourselves about these things. Instead, we train ourselves to experience the *felt-resonance* that arises during the upsetting situation *because it contains the emotional signature of the memory.*

Our earliest memories are only available as emotional signatures. To gain the capacity required to recognize and consciously integrate them requires us to become aware of felt-perception. Felt-perception empowers us to move beyond our current physical situation and the mental stories we attach to it, and to instead become aware of the emotional undercurrents flowing beneath the surface of life's events.

The physical world is in a constant state of change. Because the physical circumstances of our experience are forever changing, they appear to be brand new occurrences. For this reason, whenever we focus on the surface of an event, we are likely to assume that what is happening in any given moment is new.

However, the fact we are upset by certain circumstances but not by others – and that we then emotionally react to these specific circumstances – is evidence enough that whatever is occurring in the upsetting moment isn't in fact something new. It impacts us emotionally in an uncomfortable way *because it's reminding us of something uncomfortable from our past that is as yet unintegrated.* It triggers us emotionally because it's a reflection, usually of something we prefer not to remember. Hence our annoyance about it.

Throughout The Presence Process, we call the triggering event that upsets us "the messenger." During this experiential journey, Presence sets us up (upsets us) by deliberately sending "messengers" (reflections of our past) to assist us in recalling unintegrated childhood memories we have long since suppressed from our awareness.

Why does Presence do this? Because the use of reflections (messengers) is the only way to "see" our deeply suppressed past in a way that empowers us to integrate it. We are set up in this manner because unless these suppressed memories surface so we can consciously integrate them, they continue to impact our current circumstances. The nature of these deliberate setup experiences is that they are almost always uncomfortable. However, they occur to liberate us, not humiliate us.

To encourage our conscious embrace of this setup procedure, it's recommended we not approach this journey with the intent that it be easy or that it makes us feel good. Such an intent causes us to steer away from experiences that are occurring to facilitate our emotional development. These experiences – and our conscious feeling of them – develop our capacity for felt-perception. The Presence Process therefore asks that we don't use our energy to "try to feel better," but to "get better at feeling."

How is Presence able to send us "messengers" and thus initiate opportunities to become aware of our suppressed past so that we have an opportunity to integrate it?

It's simple. Week one of this process introduced us to the attributes of Presence, one of which is that the Presence we authentically are is intimately and continuously connected with the Presence found in all life forms. This omnipresent attribute enables Presence to activate the people and circumstances in our experience so that they replicate behavior and situations that remind us of interactions and incidents we have long since suppressed. It enables Presence to "set us up" whenever, wherever, however, and with whoever it sees fit. Each upsetting incident only occurs because it's required for facilitation of our emotional development.

Unconscious memory activation through the use of messengers is an integral part of The Presence Process. It enables us to accomplish that which is impossible through conventional physical and verbal therapeutic procedures. By the time we complete this experiential journey, we experience enough of these setups to eliminate any doubt about whether this "triggering" is deliberate. By the end of our ten weeks, we know through personal experience that each time we are emotionally upset, we are being set up to become aware of our charged emotional states.

Knowing this doesn't make being upset easier. Unfortunately, the humorous aspect of being set up is usually available only in hindsight!

When we are upset, it's authentic to feel upset. *Feeling* upset is required so we can develop our capacity for felt-perception. However, our awareness of this deliberate use of messengers empowers us to increasingly choose response over reaction.

The realization that Presence acts through anything and anyone to facilitate emotional awareness may be somewhat daunting because we then realize this awesome omnipresence pays close and personal attention to us in each and every moment. However, this realization is comforting when it becomes evident we cannot ever be – nor have we ever been – alone, lost, or without assistance.

Being unaware of Presence is a symptom of being asleep and in the dream of time. As long as we are wandering mentally through the haunted corridors of time, we render our awareness numb to this direct experience of Presence.

The ongoing circumstances of our life are akin to a play that's being staged for our benefit. This play is a reflection out in the world of what we have suppressed within. Because we have limited capacity for *in*sight, we are facilitated by what we perceive outside – *out*sight.

Along the way, we also have the opportunity to realize that the reflections that cause us to project and hence react are personally suppressed memories that only have meaning *to us*.

We realize this when we approach "the messenger" – someone who is activated by Presence to emotionally upset us – and ask them why they are behaving like this toward us. They most likely look at us in confusion or as if we are crazy. "I don't know what you are talking about," they might respond. "I'm not trying to make you feel this way at all." This is because the whole setup and its implications are happening unconsciously for the person our unintegrated memories are being reflected off. They are being unwittingly activated by Presence to facilitate us.

The chief players in this staged drama of ongoing setups are our immediate family, our intimate relationships, and our work relationships. However, anyone and anything in the world may be used by Presence to direct our attention to an unintegrated emotional condition.

Another significant realization to digest throughout these setup experiences is that *the reflections are not real.*

Having said this, it's crucial we are aware that *our projections have a real impact and thus have consequences.*

This means that although the memory we perceive through felt-perception is a shadow cast by the past across the present, when we react to it emotionally, mentally, or physically, we add substance to its effect on the present.

For this reason, for the remainder of this journey through The Presence Process, we are wise to sit back and watch our experience as we would a play in a theater. When watching a live play, we don't get up from our seat and confront the actors because they utter lines and exhibit behavior that upset us. We remain in our seat because we accept that what's unfolding in front of us is a play, and that the actors are only emotionally triggering us because they are reflecting something close to our heart.

This is exactly how we experience the surfacing of unconscious emotional memories during the course of The Presence Process and beyond. In fact, this is how it always occurs, quite apart from The Presence Process. It's just that we can't perceive this set up procedure as long as we are caught up in the dream state of time. Being able to recognize a surfacing memory through felt-perception is a barometer of increasing present moment awareness.

When we grasp how this procedure of being set up works, we laugh at how well and how often we get set up. On one level, our entire life experience is a setup. This is the so-called "cosmic joke." When we discover how to laugh at how well and how often we get set up, and at how we react unconsciously to these experiences, we have access to endless laughter.

To react to the people and circumstances that are emotionally triggering us – to project onto them – is to shoot the messengers sent by Presence. Instead of reacting, we instruct ourselves in the perceptual steps that empower us to respond. The core difference between a reaction and a response is:

A *reaction* is unconscious behavior in which our energy is directed outward into the world in an attempt to defend ourselves or attack another. A reaction is a drama played out in an effort to sedate and control the cause of our upsetting experience. The theme of all reactive behavior is blame and revenge. When we react we "do something about what we perceive is happening to us."

A *response* is a conscious choice to contain and constructively internalize this surfacing energy with the intent of using it to integrate unconsciousness. The theme of responsive behavior is responsibility. We respond by "unconditionally feeling the emotional state unfolding within us, without projecting it outward onto others."

From this point onward, certain circumstances will unfold in our daily experience that magnetically attract our attention. These are the circumstances we pay attention to so we may integrate them. This magnetic pull on our attention occurs because these specific situations are energetically connected to our suppressed past.

These situations isolate themselves from all the other circumstances we experience in that we emotionally react to them.

We continue to react unconsciously to these setups until we gain the present moment awareness to behave consciously and responsibly. It's therefore vital to keep in the forefront of our awareness how suppressed memories surface: not as stories and images in our mental body, but as unfolding circumstances and the ways people behave that upset us.

Our task for this week is to identify the messengers that reflect our unintegrated memories as they appear in our experience, together with our projections and reactionary behavior as it's triggered. We are required to feel this triggering without attempting to manipulate what we are feeling so we feel better.

By setting out on this task, we awaken a quality of "seeing" – of felt-perception – that enables us to perceive that which is energetically flowing beneath the surface of our physical circumstances. This skill is essential because it enables us to differentiate *what is actually happening* from *a reflected memory*. It also empowers us to discern what's reactionary and what's responsive.

By assigning ourselves this task, we ready ourselves to exorcise the ghosts of our past. By being able to identify messengers, and to discern between response and reaction, we become ghostbusters. As ghostbusters, we consciously steer our awareness out of experiences reactively manufactured by the dream state of time.

THIS CONCLUDES WEEK TWO

WEEK 3

Our Conscious Response for the Next Seven Days is:

"I CHOOSE TO RESPOND"

RECEIVING INSIGHT

The Presence Process invites us not to react to our experiences, but to observe them as though watching a play. This isn't as easy as it sounds because, while "living in time," we are addicted to reacting.

Being reactive appears as normal behavior because our planetary population currently lives in a state of continual reaction. For this reason, not reacting may initially feel like abnormal behavior.

In week two of The Presence Process, we were invited to acknowledge the reflection of our unconscious memories in the world by watching our experience with the intent to identify "messengers" sent by Presence. These messengers are easy to identify because they materialize as any event or person's behavior that upsets us. We were invited to do our best not to "shoot the messenger." Accordingly, we "dismiss the messenger" and in the same breath acknowledge that the value of the upsetting experience is in *the message,* not its carrier.

We don't blame the mail carrier for bills that are delivered, just as we don't blame a mirror for what it reflects. Likewise, it's pointless reacting to reflections of our unintegrated emotional charge. Reacting to reflections of our unintegrated emotional charge by behaving as if it's something real is a perceptual dysfunction. Psychologically, it's insanity.

Having said this, there are definitely instances when we are called to action, as opposed to simply dismissing the messenger. But it's important we consult common sense prior to taking any action, and that we ensure we aren't simply taking action to make ourselves feel better. Remember, this work is not about behaving in a manner that will make us feel better, but about getting better at feeling.

If we remain true to our intent of responding to our experiences by keeping our unconditional attention on the felt-aspect of our encounters, any action that arises is likely to be responsive rather than reactive. It's the nature of this work – work in which we experience all types of challenges designed to develop our emotional capacity – that sometimes we are called to "speak our truth" or verbally "draw our line in the sand." Sometimes we are called to do this to know that we can – and that, when we do, the world doesn't end. There are no rules as to when such behavior is appropriate or not.

If we are being true to our experience by honoring the felt-aspect of any encounter, the consequences of any activity we take are likely to be beneficial for all involved. The bottom line is to use common sense, trust our inner knowing, and ensure we aren't behaving in a manner that's a deliberate attempt to be hurtful to another. Only we know what our authentic intent is when we choose to engage others in the world.

During this third week, we take this process one step further. Having dismissed the messenger, it's essential we now receive the intended message – the *insight.*

Initially this may be challenging because, up to this point, we are probably used to reacting whenever we are emotionally triggered. However, because we are consciously connecting our breathing twice each day, and thereby consistently accumulating present moment awareness, we are becoming increasingly more aware. Present moment awareness enables us to become aware that anything we find emotionally upsetting in our experience is a tool wielded by Presence to reflect our unconscious emotional charges.

Presence accomplishes this by transforming our world experience into a mirror-effect, by means of which we perceive reflected – seemingly outside of us – the physically manifest shadows cast by our deeply suppressed emotional charges. To succeed at the task of receiving the message from a messenger requires:

1   Taking our attention off the messenger (the physical event or person's behavior that is triggering us).

2   Stepping away from the story that urges us into reaction (in other words, detaching from the mental event).

3   Placing our attention on how we are feeling as a consequence of the triggered upset (the emotional event).

We accomplish this task by asking ourselves the following question each time we are emotionally triggered:

> *"How does this triggering event impact*
> *me on the level of felt-perception?"*

The answer to this question isn't a *mental description* of our perceived emotional state, but our *felt-experience as encountered through felt-perception* – that is, an emotional state we *feel*.

In other words, the answer is neither verbal nor mental, but an experience of direct felt-perception. Direct felt-perception turns our attention inward on causality, whereas a verbal description of our experience turns our attention outward toward effect. Grasping this application of felt-perception reveals where and why traditional verbal therapy fails to impact causality efficiently.

When a therapist asks their client, "How does this make you feel?" the therapist is asking the correct question. However, from this point onward, many therapists mistakenly channel their client's attention away from causality and outward into the mental by encouraging them to respond to the question verbally – that is, by asking them to describe their perceived emotional state as an "understanding."

The correct answer to the therapist's question is *an experience of direct, non-verbalized felt-perception.* The client *feels the answer,* without projecting it outward as a mental concept – without turning their experience of direct felt-perception into a story.

By insisting that the client verbalize their response to this question, the therapist prevents the client from accessing causal memory that was imprinted before the development of mental capacity. This mentally driven path of examination is valued when the process of mental understanding is regarded as curative. Mental understanding is only lauded as curative when the mental body is perceived as causal, and hence godlike. This mistaken approach is the consequence of the "I think, therefore I am" consciousness.

To access the messenger's message, The Presence Process asks us:

"How does this triggering event impact me on the level of felt-perception?"

We know we have received the messenger's message *when we feel something,* usually something perceived by us as uncomfortable. We may be able to verbalize the energetic state we are feeling as a recognizable emotional condition, though such verbalization isn't required. Feeling the energetic state is in and of itself the answer.

Through our capacity to feel, we peer inwardly at the point of causality, which is to activate *in*sight. Our body confirms the receipt of the message by *resonating* – by communicating this message to us as a tangible physical sensation. This resonance may manifest as our hands buzzing, solar plexus tightening, heartbeat increasing, face flushing, or any number of other bodily indicators. Once we access this felt-resonance within (or around) our body, we have received the message.

Once we have received the message, we are ready to take the next step, which is to access added insight. We are ready to perceive, through felt-perception, that this particular emotional reaction triggered by the messenger isn't new, but that it's a charged emotional condition that occurs repeatedly. To access this insight we ask:

"When last did I experience this same felt-resonance?"

By asking this question, we intend to unearth an experience from our past in which we were triggered into feeling the exact same emotional discomfort as that which arose from our current setup. By asking this question, our awareness is automatically directed toward a previous incident of upset. When there is no immediate felt-recall, we remain open and allow the answer to be given by Presence when required.

Without getting mentally hooked into the physical details of the previously revealed triggering event, or becoming involved in a mental conversation with ourselves about it, we acknowledge the occurrence of the identical emotional signature – the same uncomfortable felt-resonance – and continue to probe further into our past using our felt-perception. We accomplish this by asking:

"When prior to this setup did I experience the same uncomfortable felt-resonance?"

By continuing to ask this question each time we unearth a previously triggered upset, we gradually uncover a reoccurring felt-pattern extending all the way back into our childhood.

When it feels challenging to trace this emotional pathway, it's often because our mental body is too focused on the physical aspect of the trail. The physical circumstances trailing back into our past that trigger these same reoccurring emotional reactions may not resemble each other at all. For this reason, we make sure that our intent during this questioning is to focus our attention specifically on recalling *similar emotional reactions,* as opposed to scanning the past for the appearance of *similar messengers.*

A useful insight for tracing a specific reoccurring emotional signature is the realization that core emotional charges repeat approximately every seven years. When we have difficulty retracing the pathway of emotional reactions, it can be helpful to skip back about seven years from the most current occurrence and ask how our emotional charge surfaced during that period. By applying this technique, we are able to journey back to a point close to or within our childhood experience.

It's normal to struggle to access the initial causal event because it most likely occurred before we developed the mental capacity with which to form a concept of the experience. The core event may have occurred at our birth or in the first year or two of our life experience, which was a time when we interacted with the world primarily through felt-perception. As such, it's recorded as a felt-resonance without an attached mental concept.

To some extent, everyone lives in continual reaction. While we "live in time," the events of this world play out as an unconscious drama in which our past and our projected future write the script for our ongoing experience. The Presence Process is an opportunity to awaken from this pre-written drama.

The first step in awakening is to learn how to take the cue for our behavior from what's unfolding *now,* and not reactively from what happened in the past or what we imagine might happen in the future.

Being able to discern the resonance of the present from the ghosts of the past and phantoms of the future requires a capacity to distinguish reflections and projections in contrast to authentic occurrences. This is why we now train ourselves to distance ourselves from engaging with the "messengers" and instead redirect our focus toward accessing "the messages" they bring.

By inwardly asking the series of questions below whenever we are emotionally triggered, instead of reactively projecting our attention outward, we gain profound insight into the source of our repetitive emotional behavior.

1 "How does this triggering event impact me on the level of felt-perception?" We answer this by engaging in the arising discomfort through felt-perception.

2 "When, prior to this present setup, did I experience the same uncomfortable felt-resonance?"

3 "When, prior to this earlier setup, did I experience the same uncomfortable felt-resonance?" We keep asking this over and over until, to the best of our ability, we approach causality.

Throughout The Presence Process, accessing information from the messenger by using the above questions is called "getting the message." We may also regard it as opening ourselves to receive insight. By choosing to take our focus off the physically upsetting event, which is the reflection of our emotional charge in the form of the messenger, and instead placing it on the felt-resonance of the emotional reaction we are experiencing, we get the message and thereby take a perceptual leap away from a victim or victor mentality.

Our choice to respond instead of react gradually neutralizes our unconscious automatic impulse to react. Also, what we initially perceived as events that happen randomly and chaotically become gems of insight into our behavioral patterns. These insights are the raw material for our emotional development.

By applying this questioning technique, we become increasingly aware that the physical, mental, and emotional discomfort in our experience right now isn't at all random. By "getting the message," we are able to receive the insight that everything that impacts us emotionally in a charged, uncomfortable way is part of a recurring pattern anchored in the past and perpetuated unconsciously by the unintegrated emotional charge of our childhood experience.

Until we experientially perceive this for ourselves through the conscious wielding of our felt-resonance, we are unable to commence integration of these reoccurring patterns. Perceiving them experientially through felt-perception changes everything because it elevates what was unconscious, and therefore unseen, into conscious visibility.

For a while we may still continue to impulsively act out these learned dramas, but we are no longer able to do so completely unconsciously. We realize we are reacting *while we are reacting,* or soon thereafter. Eventually we are able to identify a messenger approaching a mile away and thereby catch ourselves *before* reacting.

Getting the message and receiving its insights changes everything because, by doing so, we realize that the emotional reactions we feel as a consequence of being triggered have nothing to do with our adult experience. They are the consequence of the unintegrated emotional charge we've been suppressing for years.

They are our childhood leaking unconsciously into our adult experience.

These emotional triggers now purposefully surface into our awareness as external circumstances, such as the behavior of others, so we have an opportunity to perceive, acknowledge, and integrate them. Until we consciously integrate them through the wielding of unconditional felt-perception, they diligently recur in our adult experience in some form or other, often in a manner that seemingly sets out to sabotage our best intent.

The Presence Process invites us to mature emotionally. This means that instead of reacting, we choose to respond. We choose to take a deep breath, then gracefully move out of the triggering situation. By so doing, we keep ourselves from adding fuel to the fire.

If we are ever so mentally occupied by our circumstances that it isn't possible or appropriate to attend to our emotional processing, we bank the incident. We then intend a quiet time to open up later in our day so we can spend time alone asking the relevant internal questions. When such an opportunity arises, we recall the "setup" and, by applying felt-perception, the emotional reaction triggered by it.

Remember, it's *the asking of the question* that's important. Mental information about past triggering events related to our current setup is of secondary significance. The answers we seek by asking these questions are the experiential felt-resonances that correspond in content to our current upset. If these aren't immediately accessible, thinking about them only leads us away from causality.

There is absolutely nothing to think about or to analyze. For this reason we avoid all such mental pursuit. The answers come as felt-resonance, and they will come at the most auspicious time, right on schedule.

Even though the asking of these questions appears to direct our attention into the past, this isn't what's occurring. Our past no longer exists as something "behind us" that we can "go back to." The past is past. However, these unintegrated emotional charges continue to exist as energetic conditions imprinted *within* our emotional body. In essence, we aren't "going back" but "going in." The answers are all within us *now*. Trust them to surface when required.

THIS CONCLUDES WEEK THREE

WEEK 4

Our Conscious Response for the Next Seven Days is:

"I FEEL UNCONDITIONALLY"

FEELING UNCONDITIONALLY INTEGRATES

The consequence of "living in time" is that we experience pain and discomfort. Throughout The Presence Process, when we refer to "pain and discomfort," we include all discomfort, whether it manifests physically, mentally, or emotionally.

Pain and discomfort are words we use to describe an energetic condition within our emotional body. This energetic condition contains an unintegrated charge, which we perceive physically and emotionally as uncomfortable. Mentally, it feels "wrong," unpleasant, unproductive, against us, harmful, and unnatural.

Due to our conditioned mental and physical perception of this emotional condition, our automatic reaction to it is usually founded on fear, and therefore fueled with resistance. From the moment we enter this world, we are taught by example to fear and therefore resist pain and discomfort by controlling them, sedating them, distracting ourselves from them, numbing them, and drugging them. We are led to believe that pain and discomfort are our enemies, and that when they manifest, we are to escape from or conquer them at all cost. We consequently assume pain and discomfort are indicators that *something is wrong*.

In contrast, The Presence Process invites us to respond to our experiences of pain and discomfort by listening to them instead of running from or attacking them. We are asked to consider the possibility that any experience of pain and discomfort is purposeful – that it's occurring *intentionally*.

In other words, when pain and discomfort arise, it's because they are required. They are valid because they are forms of communication that have a necessary and valuable function.

This insight invites us to alter our perception of pain and discomfort. We now entertain the possibility that pain and discomfort are our friends, not our enemies, and that they have come to assist us, not hurt us. The way they assist us is by focusing our attention on a specific aspect of our physical, mental, and emotional experience. Why is this required?

Consider how we impulsively react to pain and discomfort, running in the opposite direction by pulling our attention away from the area in which we are experiencing the pain or discomfort. We do our best to annihilate our awareness of this experience with tablets, alcohol, and various medical procedures.

Our reactive behavior doesn't integrate the pain and discomfort, but merely suppresses and postpones it for a time. Inevitably, the pain and discomfort reappear at a later date or show up in another form as they continue their attempt to gain our attention.

Consider this possibility: *One of the most uncomfortable aspects of our pain and discomfort may well be our resistance to them.*

During The Presence Process, our suppressed memories surface so they may be integrated by the wielding of our felt-perception. As these memories surface, they often do so as physical pain and discomfort. This is our body's way of calling our scattered attention inward so we can attend to our predicament.

Our reactive and programmed impulse is either to run away or find someone to attend to us. To depend on the attention of another, when the entire force of the unified field is accessible within us, is futile. Hence we are now invited to transform this tendency to run to others entirely, choosing instead to unconditionally *feel* the physical, mental, and emotional sensations we have long avoided.

No matter how qualified and experienced another human may be, they aren't able to feel our discomfort on our behalf. They may be able to take physical action or even go through mental processes on our behalf, but no one can *feel* for us.

To see this clearly, imagine we have a friend who informs us they are going away for three weeks and invites us to housesit. We agree and move in. While our friend is away, we take care of physical activities in their home, such as feeding pets and tending the garden. We even take care of mental activities on their behalf, like delivering information to people who want to visit them during the period of their absence. But it would be ridiculous for our friend, upon departure, to request of us, "While I'm away, please feel on my behalf."

We are invited to consider that our limited success in integrating pain and discomfort in the past is because *it isn't possible for someone else's attention to integrate our experiences on our behalf.* Since it's *our* experience that's in a state of discomfort, it's *our* wielding of *our* attention that's required to accomplish integration.

All who have mastered their journey through the human experience report that a direct link to the creative principle, which we regard as our shared source, resides within each of us. If on some level we are able to accept this, even if initially only as a concept, we open ourselves to the possibility that *our* direct link to the intimate Presence, and the unlimited integrative capacity of this shared creative principle, is found in *our own consciously wielded attention.*

However, the possibilities contained in this realization remain mental gymnastics until they are explored experientially. The way we go about this exploration is by determining to integrate our experiences of pain and discomfort by giving them our conscious attention.

In other words, our moment-by-moment experience becomes the laboratory for our investigation.

During The Presence Process, we deliberately use our 15-minute breathing practice as a tool to bring our attention back into our body and anchor it in *this-here-now*. One of the consequences of this practice is that we become aware of pain and discomfort that have been with us since childhood, but that we have successfully suppressed from our awareness.

The analogy of being asked by a friend to housesit for three weeks reveals how suppressed pain and discomfort may come to our attention as the consequence of increasing our present moment awareness. Imagine we have been accustomed to visiting our friend once a week for tea. Each time we visit them, we spend an hour or so in their home. After a few years of visiting them once a week, we assume we are familiar with their home. But after only one full day in their home, something unexpected starts occurring: We notice things about the interior of their home we didn't notice before. It may be a crack in the ceiling or a picture in the hallway that somehow escaped our attention all these years. As the days pass, we notice even more details that had somehow escaped our attention during our many previous visits.

A similar scenario unfolds when we choose to consciously connect our breathing. Instead of mentally flitting in and out of the perceptual paradigm called "time," we now deliberately anchor our awareness in our body. Consequently, physical, mental, and emotional experiences come to our attention that may appear new to us. However, they have actually been going on for most of our life experience, though we haven't been aware of them because we haven't been physically present long enough to perceive them.

If we now choose to run from these surfacing experiences, we defeat the intent of choosing to become aware of them. This is a "no pain, no gain" predicament. Instead of resisting our pain and discomfort, we resist our automatic reflex to suppress or hand this experience over to someone else and willingly explore the experience through choosing to feel it. To do so, we step beyond any masking behavior that allows us to go on pretending we are "fine," "all right," and "okay." Bravely answering the call of the body to embrace that which is arising as a necessary part of our integrative journey, we overcome our reactive reflex to instinctively run from discomfort, choosing to gaze into it as deeply as possible with unconditional felt-perception. As we embrace and willingly seek out its center, we open ourselves to *in*sight.

Integrating pain and discomfort is a simple procedure. We choose to "be" with our pain and discomfort *unconditionally*, which means we have no agenda aside from *being with it*. We aren't trying to fix, change, understand, visualize, transform, heal, or manipulate the discomfort in any way. We watch it with our felt-perception as deeply as we are able, allowing the charged emotion to respond *as required*, which means that whatever happens as a consequence of our *being with it* unconditionally is valid.

This approach gradually transforms our relationship with pain and discomfort. Instead of treating these occurrences like an invading enemy, we approach them like a mother gently comforting a distraught child with her unconditional Presence. This releases within us energetically integrative capacities instead of the armor and weaponry of war.

War within ourselves cannot realize inner peace. However, the integrative capacity inherent in unconditional attention does. This integrative capacity is in all humans, and indeed is our birthright. We come into the world equipped with the felt-perception required to integrate the discomfort within our experience. All that's needed is for us to develop this capacity, which we do by wielding it.

Just as no one can feel on our behalf, neither can another person integrate on our behalf. Having another perform such a feat on our behalf is called "magic." Magic is an illusion in the mental body of a believer in magic and a delusion in the hands of someone who professes to be such a practitioner.

These "magical" illusions, though they may initially appear to have validity, inevitably collapse with the passage of time. Time reveals they have no authentic causal impact. Authentic and lasting causal impact is only accomplished through our own conscious focusing of our unconditional felt-perception on any aspect of our experience that requires integration.

We feel it to integrate it.

Integrating any experience requires us to gauge exactly how out of harmony the experience is. Such gauging isn't possible unless the experience in question is consciously felt. Feeling is the gauge. Machines, tools, and qualified practitioners can't feel on our behalf and therefore don't have the capacity to achieve this feat. Feeling and integration are two halves that make whole the procedure for resolving our unintegrated emotional charge. Until we accept and act on this insight, we remain unable to restore harmony to the quality of our experience.

Harnessing our capacity to integrate pain and discomfort requires one specific ingredient: feeling without condition, which can be applied wherever we are. When we place unconditional attention on our pain and discomfort, we notice how the sensations we are experiencing change. We witness these changes without judgment. We don't expect the changes to be favorable, or even to be an end to our discomfort. We are *open to any outcome,* but we don't *intend* any preconceived outcome. We acknowledge whatever changes occur as required and therefore valid.

Sometimes when we apply our unconditional attention to our pain and discomfort, the condition appears to become amplified. *This amplification doesn't mean it's worsening. It means we are becoming more aware of it.* Sometimes it changes form. Sometimes it appears to move within the body. Sometimes it subsides and dissolves. Any outcome is valid and therefore required.

When we in any way make up our mind what outcome we want, we energetically bind and restrict the motion of the underlying point of causality, and this in turn adds to our discomfort.

Once we are consciously playing our part with our attention and intention, we allow the sensations of pain and discomfort to take their required course. Any other approach is a return to the hostile behaviors of sedation and control. Remember, Presence knows no order of difficulty, which means Presence knows precisely what's required to accomplish integration. Therefore, let it determine the outcome, and let all outcomes be received and perceived as deliberately administered by Presence.

We have ignored and suppressed this pain and discomfort during most of our life experience. We have treated it as an enemy and not as the facilitating messenger it is. Patience is therefore required as we now consciously approach it. A child ignored by its parents for years doesn't immediately soften toward them because they suddenly open their arms affectionately. There's hesitation as the child first watches for consistency. Similarly, we aren't to hurry by expecting immediate consequences.

Any integrative approach isn't about a "quick fix." It requires gradual perceptual transformation of a lifelong hostility toward what we perceive as pain and discomfort. Whenever we nurture ourselves in this way, we initiate integrative consequences.

THIS CONCLUDES WEEK FOUR

WEEK 5

Our Conscious Response for the Next Seven Days is:

"I AM INNOCENT"

INTEGRATING OUR CHILDHOOD

Dormant within us is the trinity of father (guidance), mother (nurturing), and child (innocence, joy, and creativity). Setting our intent to re-establish a relationship with our child self by integrating our charged emotional states activates this trinity. It also allows us the opportunity to actively give ourselves the quality of unconditional attention we required as children but didn't receive.

The intent to re-establish an unconditionally attentive relationship with our child self awakens the emotional capacities required for us to become our own parent. Connecting with our child self calls us to step onto the pathway of self-nurturing and inner guidance – a pathway paved by displaying compassion toward ourselves. This pathway enables us to overcome the unintegrated imprints we still unconsciously share with our parents. Each effort we make to re-establish an unconditionally attentive relationship with our child self is rewarded with increased Presence and present moment awareness.

The child within us is born innocent and simultaneously help-less. Because of its helplessness, it trustingly gives its allegiance to its parents. As a consequence, the vulnerable child becomes imprinted with experiences that are less than loving – not because the parents are intentionally unloving, but because *parents are only able to offer the same quality of unconditional attention to a child that they received during their childhood.*

As the child becomes an adult, it's confronted daily with mani-festations of the uncomfortable energetic imprinting it received through interaction with its parents. As an adult, it identifies with the outer physical, mental, and emotional manifestations of these uncom-fortable experiences to the point that it comes to believe "I *am* fear-ful, angry, and sad," as opposed to "this is a manifestation of fear, anger, and grief received through imprinting. *It isn't what I am.*"

Our identification with the *manifestation* of uncomfortable imprinting causes us to forget that we entered our life experience in a state of innocence. By identifying with our experience – with our imprinted state, instead of with the Presence we authentically are – we lose awareness of our innocence.

By identifying with our outer projections – with the manifestation in our current adult experience of the imprinting we received in child-hood – we mistakenly base our identity on what we perceive as "our faults." By aligning ourselves with these outwardly manifesting "faults," we lose our awareness of and capacity for inner sensibility – our capacity for *inner sense,* or innocence. We aren't the faults that manifest through our experience. We were born innocent because Presence, which is our inner sense, is innocent.

As adults, many of us then attempt to overcome our perceived faultiness through being *helpful to others.* However, when it comes to knowing how to *nurture ourselves,* we are at a loss. We may even feel a sense of guilt whenever we attempt to do anything authentic and loving for ourselves. Because of our perceived faultiness, we feel *we* aren't deserving of our own unconditional attention. We may even be prepared to sacrifice our own wellbeing in the name of helping another. We don't yet realize that it's our unconscious sense of faultiness – and our feeling of helplessness to do anything about it – that drives us to sacrifice ourselves in the name of helping others.

Assisting others to the detriment of our own wellbeing is fueled by the reflection of our own plight in the world around us. When we behave in this manner, our helpful behavior may for a moment allow us to feel better, but it eventually debilitates those we profess to be helping by rendering them dependent. This dependence reinforces their own belief that they are unable to tend to their unintegrated emotions and the manifestations of apparent "faultiness" that originate from these unintegrated emotions.

Helping others as a means of making ourselves feel better isn't beneficial to either party because we can't give away what we don't have. When we behave as if we can, our actions are proven by the passage of time to lack substance.

Only when we discover how to nurture ourselves with our own unconditional attention do we develop the capacity for attending to others unconditionally in an authentic way. The first step in learning to accomplish this is to recognize which aspect of our being feels broken, or at fault, and requires our unconditional attention.

As adults, we experience varying physical, mental, and emotional states of discomfort, which we usually do everything we can to numb or distract ourselves from. Or we run to another for attention. When we live in a time-based paradigm, we are unable to perceive that *none of our current physical, mental, and emotional discomfort arises from what's happening now, even though it's clearly reflected in what's happening now.*

During Week Four, we are encouraged to feel our discomfort unconditionally. Through this approach, the realization we invite is that all discomfort carries an emotional signature. The emotional signature is the felt-resonance that accompanies our discomfort, identifiable as an emotional state. This emotional signature is one of the many emotions that arise from within the trinity of fear, anger, and grief.

Accessing our emotional signature is simple. For example, if we have a persistent backache, we ask ourselves:

"How does this backache make me feel?"

Our reply will likely be that it irritates us, annoys us, frustrates us, or the like. Whatever word we come up with when we ask ourselves this question points toward an emotional state that's arising either from fear, anger, grief, or a combination of these. By arriving at this description of the emotional state that's being triggered by our discomfort, we access a mental description of our emotional signature.

To access an emotional signature directly requires felt-perception. *The emotional signature is therefore not something we think about or mentally describe, but the direct felt-texture of the emotional state we experience when confronted with our discomfort.* Throughout The Presence Process, we call this emotional signature "the emotional charge."

As we progress through The Presence Process, it becomes increasingly apparent that it's the charged emotion crouched behind our discomfort that fuels our compulsion to run from the present into self-distracting mental and physical activities. By reacting to an emotional charge instead of responding to it, we move from Presence into pretence. We sidestep authenticity and enter into drama. All human drama is an outwardly projected manifestation of our individual and collective reaction toward our unintegrated emotional charge.

We also know by now where this charged emotion is anchored. In Week Three, we were instructed how to track it to its experiential origin. To recap: When we look back over our life experience, if we choose to perceive our past as a reoccurrence of emotional signatures instead of viewing it as a series of physical circumstances, we are able to identify a pathway of similar emotional signatures extending back into our childhood. This pathway reveals that the discomfort we feel today – be it physical, mental, or emotional – has nothing to do with our present adult experience, but is merely *reflected* in it. One of the biggest insights we may receive at this point is that it isn't our adult experience that requires integration, but the unintegrated aspects of our childhood.

From the moment we turn our back on our childhood in order to become acceptable to the adult world, our child self uses physical, mental, and emotional states of discomfort in an attempt to regain our attention. It does this so we can attend to the unintegrated emotional predicament in which it still resides. Until we consciously attend to this unintegrated experience of childhood, our adult experience continues to manifest the consequences.

In other words, while "living in time," our adult experience is an echo of our childhood – a seemingly chaotic and disconnected experience sewn together with what appears to be randomly occurring physical, mental, and emotional discomfort.

It's crucial at this juncture in The Presence Process that we recognize the manifesting discomfort of our adult experience as an effect, not as the cause of anything. This is crucial because it's futile to tamper with an effect. Only by impacting the point of causality is authentic change initiated. The value of any adult discomfort is to use it as a pointer to its childhood cause. Until this is clear, our attempts at integration remain ineffectual.

The pursuit of happiness – as in the drive to control and sedate our external circumstances so we feel at ease in ourselves – is nothing more than a behavior that stems from fiddling with an effect in an attempt to adjust the cause. Since this is impossible, such behavior leads us further and further away from the joy already available in our child self. Our child self is our harbor of innocence, joy, and creativity. When we ignore its unintegrated state, we diminish our capacity for innocence, joy, and creativity, and instead invest our energy in attempting "to be happy" by "making something out of ourselves."

So we arrive at another major insight: Unless we reach back through time and space to rescue the stranded aspects of our child self and bring them into the resonance of the present, where we provide them with the unconditional attention they require, we can't fully realize peace.

The intent to reach back and rescue the stranded aspects of our child self may be perceived as a form of time travel. However, this form of time travel isn't science fiction. It doesn't take place "out there," and its purpose isn't to visit far-off places. It takes place *within us*, and its "soul" purpose is energetic reconnection with an aspect of our being from which we are currently separated and alienated.

In other words, this is an inside job that consciously integrates our unintegrated past into our present. This intent invites unconscious behavior triggered by unintegrated past experiences to the surface *now* so we may attend to it unconditionally. When approached with consistency, this inner work releases our child self from its unintegrated trauma.

The consequence of "rescuing the unintegrated aspects of our child self" is that our present adult self is released from the charged emotions that currently manifest as physical, mental, and emotional discomfort. *The identity of the unintegrated aspects of our child self, and the sum of our unintegrated emotional charge, are one and the same.*

Emotionally, our unintegrated childhood is in "the charge." Until we integrate this emotional charge, *we* are not in charge of the quality of our experience. As an adult, we are either *driven by a charge,* or *in charge.*

To be driven by a charge means our adult experience is being run by the unintegrated aspects of our child self. In this light, it isn't the whole of our child self that requires rescue, just those parts that are currently unintegrated.

Like any innocent child, our child self perceives everything it's exposed to as true, real, and possible. It doesn't know the difference between the validity of what it sees on television through our adult eyes and what it experiences through us in our daily activity. It also doesn't know the difference between what we visualize in our imagination and what it experiences through us each day of our adult life. This means that it's both gullible and vulnerable.

Our child self listens to everything we think and say. It also watches everything we do, such as how we behave toward others, and learns by our example. When we say "no" when we mean "yes," or "yes" when we mean "no," it becomes mistrustful of our ability to take care of its requirements. Because it's a child, it doesn't view our present adult self as part of who it is. Instead, it perceives our adult self as a parent-figure separate from itself.

For this reason, our intent in approaching our child self requires impeccability. This is why we attend to it *unconditionally* and *consistently*. When we attend to it conditionally and inconsistently, we intensify its current unintegrated states of fear, anger, and grief.

If we haven't consciously interacted with our child self before, then our current relationship with it is similar to that of a parent who has for many years abandoned their child. At about the age of seven, our childhood experience is deliberately redirected in preparation to enter the adult world. This requires a willingness to turn around and walk away from our childhood. As the years unfold, it's unlikely we will choose to look back and consider the state of the child we once were. We lay a blanket of forgetfulness over this aspect of our experience and openly admit we can't remember much of what happened when we were children. For this reason, we may no longer be aware of our child self even though it continually watches everything. We seemingly no longer feel the unintegrated aspects of its condition, despite the fact our adult discomfort is a mirror of this unintegrated charge. We are so out of touch with how our child self affects us in the present that we may ask, "Why now go back and face the past? Why not leave the past alone and carry on with our life?"

Our unfortunate predicament is that the discomfort of our unintegrated childhood follows us as an emotional trail that pollutes our adult experiences through manifesting ongoing patterns of discomfort as regularly and punctually as a timepiece.

Furthermore, this timepiece isn't neutral as are the mechanical watches we wear on our wrist. The ticking of this childhood timepiece, and the effect it has on our current experience, could be called "emotional time." Wearing a watch, and using it as an instrument to navigate through the present moment, are quite different experiences.

To use it to navigate is a conscious experience. We may choose to remove the watch and no longer be exposed to its influence, but until the debris of "emotional time" is consciously integrated, it constantly distracts us from being present.

We may successfully sedate and control the effects of the unintegrated childhood debris that leaks into our adult experiences for many years, but sooner or later this energetic charge rears up and we find ourselves in a crisis.

Thankfully it isn't necessary to manifest a crisis before we agree to attend to our unintegrated childhood debris – although sometimes a crisis is exactly what's required for the unintegrated aspect of our child self to gain our attention. Nevertheless, the moment we turn inward and attend to our child self, our physical, mental, and emotional states of discomfort begin to be integrated.

Once our child self comes to peace, so do we. It's this simple and powerful. If we aren't experiencing peace right now, it's because an aspect of our child self is still unintegrated. There's nowhere else to look, and there's no other response but to consistently and unconditionally feel the resonance of this unintegrated aspect of our experience.

INTEGRATION OF THE CHILD SELF

On our journey through The Presence Process, there have already been, and are still going to be, numerous moments when we feel anything but present.

During these moments of distraction, we may feel irritable, annoyed, anxious, and confused—in other words, full of fear, anger, and grief. These are moments in which we are being called upon to attend to the unintegrated aspects of our child self.

When we are in such an uncomfortable moment, we strive to remind our adult self that the discomfort we are feeling has nothing to do with what's happening *now*, although it's clearly reflected in the felt-resonance of this moment. This discomfort is *a call for assistance from an unintegrated childlike aspect of our self that's still struggling with experiences it can't digest.*

How do we respond to this call? The answer is simple. It requires unconditional, continuously wielded felt-perception. We direct our capacity for feeling to the felt-resonance of our uncomfortable emotional state and be with it without condition.

Symptoms of discomfort are echoes. Phonetically, the word "symptom," when spoken aloud, may be heard as "some time." This is what a symptom is: a piece of our unintegrated past manifesting as discomfort.

Depending on where our awareness is anchored, symptoms appear to us on three levels: physical, mental, emotional, or a combination of the three. As we have already discovered, the physical and mental aspects of our discomfort are an effect – a consequence – of the point of causality, which is the initial unintegrated experience. The actual resonance of this point of causality is purely energetic and contained within our energy body, or what we also call our emotional (energy in motion) body. We either find our emotional body peaceful, which is the consequence of energy that's freely and harmoniously in motion, or we find our emotional body uncomfortable due to an emotional charge that arises because our energy can't move freely.

When we encounter the causal points of energy that isn't freely in motion – which we may conceptually call emotional states such as fear, anger, and grief – our intent to be with these by wielding felt-perception is akin to taking the unintegrated aspect of our child self in our arms and unconditionally loving and comforting it.

Because some of us are wired slightly differently, we may find it beneficial to actually imagine such a scenario. For example, when we experience an emotional state such as anger, it can be self-facilitating to close our eyes and imagine our self as a child of seven years or younger standing in front of us as we are now, feeling the way we feel. We may then visualize ourselves picking this child up and being with it as it moves through its anger. We don't attempt to alter the child's experience in any way because its experience is valid and required. We simply be with it *unconditionally*. Through this visualized nurturing of our child self, we activate the qualities of our inner parent. A comforting resonance of consistency arises whenever we commit to attending to our child self in this way.

This visualized approach isn't for everyone, and not even necessary, though some may find it helpful. For many of us, it's enough to place our felt-perception on the felt-resonance of a surfacing charge – the emotional signature – and be with it as a non-visualized, non-conceptualized, felt-experience. It's not our imagination but our unconditional and consistent intent, combined with our applied felt-perception, that contains the "no order of difficulty" integrative capacity of Presence.

One of the ways we know our intent to integrate this aspect of our child self is working is an emotional response like crying. Such crying doesn't have to occur in the moment we are attending to our discomfort. It may occur randomly, when we least expect it. Crying on our own for no apparent reason is the commencement of the integration of charged emotion. Tears shed in this manner aren't adult tears, but the tears we couldn't cry as a child. These tears represent blocked and stagnant energy that has unconsciously polluted our life with discomfort. When we let these tears flow, we increasingly re-enter the flow of the present. Such an emotional response means an energetic pathway is being restored between our adult and child self.

There's no reason to be concerned if we don't initially experience any emotional response. Often the unintegrated aspects of our child self are numb and energetically calloused from neglect. Our task is to persevere. Our intent to integrate this aspect of our experience is unconditional. Tears of release and relief flow when least expected.

Once integration of this aspect of our experience commences, we receive the fruits: increasing awareness of peace, joy, and creativity. Aspects of our daily experience that once annoyed and irritated us no longer seem to matter. We spontaneously enjoy playfulness with others and appreciate an ongoing decrease of physical, mental, and emotional discomfort. We trade a life of walking around and carrying a charge for a life in which we feel confidently in charge. Our drama and states of pretence are gradually replaced by a growing radiance of Presence and present moment awareness.

Reaping the rewards of rescuing the unintegrated aspects of our child self takes consistent application of unconditional felt-perception. It requires awareness that the emotional signatures that flow beneath our current discomforts are valid. Nobody gives up attempting to drive a car just because they can't achieve high speed during their first lesson. We are also encouraged not to give up on the unintegrated aspect of our child self, or on our ability to achieve integration, just because the consequences of our attempts aren't experienced immediately.

As we approach the unintegrated aspects of our child self, which are our unintegrated emotional charge, it's useful to remember how long we have ignored our child self's cries for assistance by sedating and controlling its attempts to gain our attention.

When we keep in the forefront of our adult awareness that any uncomfortable experience we are now manifesting is the call for assistance from our unintegrated past, and when we commit to responding to this call whenever possible with consistent, unconditional felt-perception, we set in motion an energetic process that restores harmony to the quality of our experience and liberates a precious aspect of our human expression from the conceptual prison of our past.

THIS CONCLUDES WEEK FIVE

WEEK **6**

Our Conscious Response for the Next Seven Days is:

"I INTEGRATE CHARGED EMOTION"

INTEGRATING CHARGED EMOTION

We are now at a point in The Presence Process where we have familiarized ourselves with the various aspects of a perceptual tool designed to integrate charged emotion. This tool is called "the emotional integration procedure." The beauty of this perceptual tool is that we apply it simply by being familiar with its mechanism. Its application isn't "a doing," but a state of being.

Before we explore the emotional integration procedure, let's examine the nature of the emotional body in and out of time, and the origin of what we call "charged emotion."

In the present, the highest application of our physical body is as a focal point for consciously anchoring the full capacity of Presence in the world. Life in the body is an opportunity for us to achieve present moment awareness – to "show up" in this experience. To accomplish this, the mental and emotional bodies also require alignment with their highest application.

The highest application of the mental body is when it serves to navigate the focus of our *attention*, while the highest application of the emotional body is when it fuels the momentum of our *intent*.

The mental body is the navigation system of our capacity for *being*, and the emotional body is the fuel tank containing the various emotions, rather like different grades of fuel, intended to activate varying intensities of movement.

This means that our charged emotion doesn't require *healing*, as if it were broken. To imagine our imprinted emotional charge as something that requires healing or fixing, instead of integrating, would be no different from a can viewing a can opener as something that requires healing. The can opener simply needs to be put to use, as does our unintegrated energy-in-motion. In other words, dormant within our charged emotions is the potential to "open us up" to unrealized possibilities.

Charged emotion is like an untapped fuel cell, which through the process of integration empowers authentic movement. This movement manifests as irreversible perceptual shifts.

When we really grasp this, *we realize that our childhood imprinting is a means of endowing our body with fuel.*

When we are "living in time," we seldom fulfill the structural potential of our body, realize the power of its navigational system, or utilize its fuel capacity. Instead, we regard the body either as a vacant lot or as a pit stop between mental excursions into the non-existent past or future. We regard it as a place to pause between making plans.

We also use both our physical body and our mental body to distract ourselves by "doing a lot of stuff," engaging in endless physical doings and thought activity that seldom support our soul purpose. Thus we spend much of our life experience accumulating possessions we can't take with us on our journey beyond the borders of our present situation.

When we use the mental body as a tool for thinking, analyzing, understanding, and controlling our experiences, while we use the emotional body as a means of sedation, projection, and all manner of drama, we often feel like we are going nowhere. The fact is, more often than not, we aren't!

The Presence Process begins rectifying this predicament. It gets the motor running, assists us in reversing out of the garage, and places us on the road of life. It accomplishes this by:

1   Instructing us how to use our breath to consciously re-enter our body.

2   Providing us with conscious responses and text that activate and support ongoing mental navigation.

3   Assisting us to consciously tap into our dormant fuel supply by introducing us to the procedure for integrating charged emotion, which is to feel without condition.

While we live in time and are still attempting to have "a good time," or at least "an easy time," we are bouncing around between polarities. We attempt to have a good time because we feel bad, and we attempt to make things easy for ourselves because our experience feels hard.

The problem is that when we spend our time chasing one experience as we flee another, what we are "doing" is bouncing off the walls of a self-created perceptual prison. This commotion may trigger significant outer activity, and we may experience a variety of physical, mental, and emotional situations, but we accomplish zero authentic movement.

This is why we don't judge our progress through The Presence Process based on how good we feel or how easy it is. When it comes to initiating emotional growth – authentic movement – "good" and "easy" aren't barometers of success. They are usually indicators of avoidance, resistance, and denial.

To activate authentic movement requires an integrative approach

– one that elevates our perception to a point where it's no longer necessary to label our emotional experiences as either good or bad.

In present moment awareness, there are no good or bad emotions. There is only energy in motion or not in motion. In present moment awareness, all emotional states are considered varying grades of fuel for different intensities of movement. To achieve full throttle and thereby cover the maximum distance we can during our human experience, we use the entire range of fuels available to us. For this to happen requires us to become inclusive of all our emotions instead of excluding some of them.

For example, while "living in time" we confuse joy with the outer changing experience called "the pursuit of happiness." But experiencing authentic joy isn't just about feeling good. It's about *feeling everything*, which requires emotional inclusiveness. The good news is that we are able to integrate all our emotions so we are no longer unconsciously driven toward some experiences and away from others.

Since commencing The Presence Process, we've been training to consciously integrate our charged emotion by applying the emotional integration procedure. We are already familiar with the components of this tool because for the last four weeks we worked with each of its three components. It's designed to physically, mentally, and emotionally steer us away from reactivity and toward responsibility.

By applying the emotional integration procedure whenever and wherever possible, we gradually move from trying to "feel good" into a place where we are open to feeling everything. Diligent application of this tool transforms each challenging experience – each upsetting emotion – into an opportunity for emotional integration. Instead of being a catalyst for the buildup of heat, friction becomes an opportunity for movement. Mastering the emotional integration procedure ends anxiety because its consequences show us that each life situation we perceive as uncomfortable can be consciously integrated.

Up until this point in The Presence Process, we have explored three perceptual procedures:

1   We learned how to perceive the surfacing of unintegrated memories as reflections in the world. We call this identifying *the messenger.*

2   We learned how to access insight from the felt-content of these surfacing memories. We call this *getting the message.*

3   We learned how to unconditionally feel the pain and discomfort contained in these surfacing memories. We referred to this as *feeling unconditionally.*

The emotional integration procedure combines these three steps into one integrated perceptual tool. When used consistently, this tool charts a new pathway for our awareness that transforms us from reactive to responsive individuals.

With each application of this tool, we integrate charged emotion that was imprinted in our emotional body during childhood. As the heat – the discomfort in our emotional body – becomes integrated, those mentally entrenched belief systems that arise out of our emotional charge are dismantled. In turn, this decreases our need to gain attention and hence reduces the drama we manifest. It also unplugs the cause of self-medicating behavior. The consequence of this is that the quality of our experience is transformed.

Through consistent application of the emotional integration procedure, we achieve authentic movement. This confirms that the quality of our experience is determined by the quality of our emotional condition. The moment we integrate our emotional condition is the moment we regain our freedom, because we then *know* through direct experience that we are responsible for the quality of our experience.

Consistently applying the emotional integration procedure requires a willingness to be responsible. We are already trained for this. All we now require is initiative, consistency, and patience.

Despite its simplicity, learning to wield this tool efficiently is like learning to walk again. We don't discover how to walk in a single step.

It involves learning how to get up and stand on our own two emotional feet, perhaps for the first time in our life experience.

THE MECHANICS OF REACTIVITY

Before introducing the mechanics of the emotional integration procedure, it's helpful to explore the mechanics of reactivity.

Charged emotion that's surfacing for integration is identifiable as specific circumstances and behavior that upset us. Whenever we are upset, our behavior follows a predictable pathway, leading to physical, mental, and emotional states we call reactivity, or drama.

During childhood, we master these reactionary approaches by witnessing how our parents interact with us, with others, and with their obstacles and issues. In other words, the mechanics of reactive behavior are passed along as part of the imprinting process. If we don't at some stage consciously choose to unplug ourselves from this reactive behavior and instead replace it with responsiveness, we automatically pass it on to our children.

The difference between reactive and responsive behavior is that reactive behavior adds fuel to the fire, whereas responsive behavior throws water on the flames. Again, it's about "heat." So, how do we behave when we are engaged in an unconscious reaction to our experience?

First, when something doesn't go our way – and therefore seemingly insults our sensibilities – we become upset. We have then reacted. A reaction is any upsetting physical, mental, or emotional behavior for which we attribute the cause – and therefore the responsibility – to factors other than ourselves.

Reactive behavior either directly or indirectly involves blame. In the final analysis, the consequence of blame, whether we admit it or not, is guilt, regret, and shame. We have all experienced becoming upset, resorting to blame, then – as we return to our senses – feeling ashamed of our behavior. Reactive behavior is wasted energy and avoidable.

The trinity of the mechanics of reactive behavior is getting upset, blaming, and feeling guilt, regret, or shame. Let's examine each of these aspects in more depth:

1   To begin with, we examine the behavior we call "getting upset." The perceptual shift The Presence Process invites is this: that we aren't so much "getting upset" as "being set up."

When we view the upsetting experience through the gauge of felt-perception, it's also evident that whenever we are upset, this isn't the first appearance in our life experience of the emotional charge that underlies this particular setup. That it's a repeated experience is validated by the word "reaction." Examine this word visually: A reaction is by its visual definition a repetition of a particular action. It's a *re*-action, a repeated act. The structure of this word tells us that the event that sets us up doesn't lead to any new behavior pattern on our part. It evokes a habitual and predictable behavior pattern that surfaces over and over again each time a similar situation occurs.

The first stage in the trinity of reactive behavior is therefore that we become upset. The upset entails acting out a calculated, habitual, and hence predictable physical, mental, and emotional drama – our *act*. The charge that's the cause of this particular repetitive drama is imprinted in the emotional body during childhood.

2   The second stage in the trinity of reactive behavior is that whenever we are set up, we resort to a specific type of drama that has at its core the same intent: blame. The drama is a repeated act that attributes responsibility for what's happening to someone or something other than ourselves.

Blaming is one of those unique behaviors in which drama is used not only to gain attention, particularly sympathy, but also to direct attention away from us and place it on someone or something else. We resort to blame as long as we aren't ready to take responsibility for the quality of our experience. Blame is accusing the mirror for the content of its reflection.

However, blame has consequences. Examining this word visually also reveals the inauthentic nature of our behavior when we resort to this tactic. To blame is to "b-lame" – to *be lame*. Blame disempowers because, whenever we blame, we declare that our perception of ourselves is that we are a victim and therefore the powerless prey of others.

3   Out of this sense of disempowerment, we arrive at the third stage of reactive behavior: guilt, regret, and shame. Consciously, we likely feel guilty, regretful, and shameful because of the reactive behavior we project when we are upset, but this isn't all that's transpiring. Unconsciously, we also feel guilt, regret, and shame because, by blaming another, we betray ourselves. We betray and disempower ourselves by inadvertently declaring we are enslaved by circumstances beyond our control.

Through an allegiance with blame, we dismiss the existence and consequences of cause and effect. To do this invalidates that which makes us all equal and free.

Reactive behavior doesn't serve us on any level. Fortunately, it's easily unlearned by charting a new course for our behavior. This is why we apply the emotional integration procedure whenever we are emotionally triggered.

THE EMOTIONAL INTEGRATION PROCEDURE

STEP ONE: DISMISS THE MESSENGER. Whenever we become emotionally upset, the first step is to acknowledge that the person or event setting us up has nothing to do with what's happening. They are "the messenger" (mess-ender). The messenger reflects a memory that's currently surfacing from within our unintegrated past.

"Shooting the messenger" is futile because Presence has an unlimited supply of such messengers! The first step in the emotional integration procedure is therefore to *dismiss the messenger*. Internally, we may thank them for their service and let them be on their way. Instead of reacting to and venting at them, we might say, "I could use a little time alone right now." In the beginning, this step of gracefully sidestepping our urge to react takes courage because it requires dismantling our lifelong habit of knee-jerking into drama.

STEP TWO: RECEIVE THE MESSAGE (insight). The second step is to *get the message*. To accomplish this, we turn our attention inward and, through wielding felt-perception, encounter the underlying energetic resonance of the emotional reaction we experience through the setup.

We know we are succeeding when our body resonates. When we engage the felt-aspect of our upset, our face may flush, our hands may buzz, or we may feel a downward movement in our solar plexus. Whatever we feel as a consequence of our intent to feel is valid.

STEP THREE: FEELING UNCONDITIONALLY. Instead of externalizing our discomfort by resorting to blame, we now consciously contain and digest the uncomfortable resonance of the upsetting experience. We feel it as it is, without agenda, without manipulating it, and without trying to fix, heal, or understand it.

Through this particular step, we trade projection for integration, which we accomplish through unconditional containment. Containment isn't to be confused with suppression. Suppression is the act of "pretending it didn't happen" or doing whatever it takes to wipe our awareness clean of the experience. Containment is a declaration that "this *is* happening," and that what was initially perceived as happening "out there" finds its cause within our energy field.

Containment is a responsive mode through which we accept complete responsibility for the quality of our experience. It's an active realization that the emotionally triggered discomfort we feel as adults is a cry for help from our child self. Containment is our way of answering this call. It's our response to our child self – a response in which, through our unconditional felt-perception, we declare: "I know you're hurting. I know you're feeling fear, anger, and grief. I'm now choosing to acknowledge this. I'm choosing to give you my unconditional attention by consciously feeling this discomfort, and to consistently respond this way for as long as it takes for the awareness of peace to be restored." Through feeling without condition at the causal point of our discomfort, we initiate integration. Integration is the conscious digestion of the unintegrated aspects of our childhood.

We may apply this three-step technique to integrate disagreements, physical ailments, and any conflict that arises to cause us emotional discomfort.

Each time we apply this technique, we experientially approach the realization that we can transform the quality of any uncomfortable experience we perceive as "out there" by moving consciously into ourselves and making internal adjustments through unconditional felt-perception.

Consistent application of this technique confirms that the quality of everything we experience in the world is a reflection of our current emotional condition. It proves experientially that realizing peace has nothing to do with "the other party." An unbalanced adult is an unattended child, and feeling unconditionally integrates our discomfort.

THIS CONCLUDES WEEK SIX

INTO THE WATER

Read Before Commencing Week Seven

We activate weeks seven, eight, and nine by submerging ourselves in a bathtub of comfortably warm (not too hot) water for 15 minutes. If a bathtub isn't available, we may enter a comfortably warm shower for 15 minutes.

While in the water, we aren't to focus on consciously connecting our breathing. Instead, we place our attention on the felt-aspect of any experience that surfaces in our awareness as a consequence of being in the warm water.

As soon as we exit the water, we dry ourselves off, then attend to our regular 15-minute breathing practice. This water session is only necessary for the first breathing session of each of these three weeks. However, during these weeks, it may be repeated as often as we choose.

We may discover as a consequence of being in the warm water prior to attending to our breathing that during our breathing practice, deeper physical, mental, and emotional experiences are activated. No matter what these are, or even if nothing seems to happen, the experience is valid.

Whenever we perceive an experience to be uncomfortable, we keep our breathing connected, remain relaxed, and focus our attention unconditionally on the felt-aspect of the experience. We dismiss all stories that arise concerning "what this discomfort means or is about." All mental stories are irrelevant. Only our unconditional felt-perception, applied to the point of any perceived discomfort, has integrative power.

The following guidance ensures that our water sessions are efficient:

1   We drink plenty of pure water during the 24-hour period before a water session and afterward.

2   We ensure that the bathwater is comfortably warm. The ideal temperature for this procedure is body temperature.

3   We lie back in the water so that our entire torso is submerged and our head, particularly our face, is out of the water. It's useful to have the water over the heart area (chest) for as much of the session as possible, though not essential. Obviously, if we use a shower, this doesn't apply. However, we may choose to sit on the floor of the shower and allow the water to flow onto our heart area.

4   If for any reason the water session becomes challenging, we relax by reminding ourselves that whatever we experience is valid. Any discomfort is the sign of charged emotion surfacing. We feel the discomfort as the emotional charge passes through and out of our field of awareness. The way out is through.

5   In the case of those of us who are elderly or whose health is fragile, for safety reasons it's recommended we have someone sit with us through the water sessions. When there is *any doubt* about the safety of engaging in a water session, we first consult a medical practitioner.

6   If the felt-aspect of an experience is occurring when our 15 minutes is up, we may choose to either remain in the water a bit longer, or to exit while remaining fully aware of what

we are feeling, dry ourselves off, then attend to our regular 15-minute breathing practice. Remember, there are occasions when discomfort is not fully integrated within a water or breathing session. This is because sometimes full integration requires encounters out in the world. The main thing is not to try to force any experience we are having to completion. If we choose to remain in the water longer, but then after a while feel we have been in the water too long, we get out, dry off, and breathe for a while. We trust our common sense.

WEEK 7

Our Conscious Response for the Next Seven Days is:

"I FEEL SAFE NOW"

EMBRACING PHYSICAL PRESENCE

Embracing physical presence is the first step we take toward accomplishing a permanent shift from reactive to responsive behavior.

Unless we are physically present, we don't make responsible choices. Responsive behavior is causal and therefore leads to integration of discomfort stemming from our surfacing emotional charge.

When we aren't present within our body, we are adrift in the mental plane. This means our awareness is floating in some conceptual place we call the past or future. We then make decisions based on what we perceive within these illusory mental places. This can't benefit us in any way.

Our reactivity toward ongoing manifestations of unintegrated fear, anger, and grief is self-destructive. This is because we are engaging effects, not causality. This is why emphasis is placed on attending to our daily breathing practice. Consciously connected breathing is an

accelerated procedure for extracting awareness from our mental preoccupation with "living in time," enabling us to accumulate and
maintain physical presence.

During childhood, we began the habit of mentally leaving our
physical body and departing full awareness of our current surroundings to enter the illusory mental experience called "time." We did this
as a fearful reaction to what was happening in the present. It's this
simple: we lost our awareness of Presence through fear. Fear causes
evacuation from the body. Through fear, we trade Presence for the
mental armor of pretence.

We all had fearful experiences, and because we couldn't integrate
them, we mentally escaped into the illusory corridors of time. In this
mentally manufactured dream world, we pretend that "everything is,
or will at some point be, all right." There's a case to be made that, for
many, this mental evacuation served as a saving grace. However,
because of the insights received through The Presence Process, such
reactivity is no longer useful or necessary.

During the past six weeks, we have gained deeper insight into the
causality of physical, mental, and emotional discomfort. We have also
been introduced to perceptual procedures that assist us in laying the
foundation for our return to present moment awareness. Through
consistent application of the emotional integration procedure, we are
already changing our approach from reactive to responsive.

It's now not so difficult to embrace the possibility that the challenging, fearful experiences that have shadowed us from the past are all dis-
guised opportunities for growth and gain. They are emotional fuel cells
yet to be tapped. We may not have the capacity to perceive this while still
perceptually bound by the effects of these causal experiences, but this
possibility becomes available as we enter present moment awareness.

As we experientially integrate charged emotion and realize the
gifts that come with integration, we then perceive all the bumps in the
road of life as growth opportunities. Arriving at this realization
requires *experiencing it to be so,* which is very different from wishing,
hoping, or being willing to believe it's so.

This revelation is available to all who consistently apply the emotional integration procedure. With each charged emotion we integrate, we gain access to an emotional fuel cell whose energetic capacity injects our experience with authentic movement. Once we realize this, our past doesn't trail us as something to be afraid of or to resent, but rather as an opportunity for personal evolution.

At some point, it becomes hard not to accept that the entire experience is a brilliantly manufactured setup. Once we recognize this, the only thing standing between our fear of the past and the realization of present moment awareness is our allegiance to the stories we have told about why things happened and what these events mean. To extract ourselves from the maze of the mental plane requires that we choose to "drop the story" and instead pay attention to feeling its causal emotional charge unconditionally. As long as we cling to our stories, we choose the past over this moment.

As we become proficient at responding to surfacing charged emotions, a sense of safety gradually seeps into our overall human experience. This means that as we step into the role of taking responsibility for the quality of our experiences, our child self starts feeling safe again. It's becomes safe to depart this illusory mental experience called "living in time" and re-enter our body, which is our authentic home while we journey through our current experience. By intending a conscious return into our body, we simultaneously choose to become physically present in each aspect of our experience. As we do so, we discover that a safe child is a spontaneously joyful and creative child.

Our regained physical presence is a gift because it empowers us to redirect our intent, which enables us to consciously steer ourselves into experiences that serve us. This is the moment in The Presence Process when we embrace the task of taking charge of our experience.

We have two tools we use to navigate toward, through, and out of all our experiences: *attention* and *intent*. Attention is the tool of the mental body and is the "what" of our focus. Intent is the tool of the emotional body and is the "why" of our focus. The quality of our experience in any given moment is determined by how consciously we wield attention and intent. It's this simple. However, we are required to be physically present in order to wield these two perceptual tools consciously.

Whether we recognize it or not, in each moment of our experience, we wield both attention and intent. Mostly we wield them unconsciously, driven by our unintegrated emotional charge. Because we are adrift in the mental plane, we don't realize our life experience is a vessel that's being driven by the continual surfacing of unintegrated discomfort.

In view of our physically and mentally transfixed condition, we tend to perceive ourselves as being *forced*, moved along against our will by seemingly unexpected and unpleasant physical events. We then tell ourselves stories about these events. Based on the stories we tell, we take reactive countermeasures. But as we are discovering, these unexpected and uncomfortable physical events are all messengers – outer reflections of our surfacing unintegrated emotional charge.

The stories we tell ourselves, which we began telling once we started developing our mental capacity, established our current library of core beliefs. Because much of the charge that drives these beliefs was imprinted in our energy system before we had mental and hence conceptual capacity, none of these stories are valid. They are all effects, which means our beliefs form an illusory mental passageway we mistakenly walk along as a desperate means of making sense of the apparent chaos and unpredictability of our circumstances. To direct our attention and intent according to them is self-defeating. On a psychological level, it's insanity. We appropriately call it "being mental."

Because our stories are rooted in what we believe happened in the past and what we suspect this means for the future, it means that until recently we have been designing the quality of our human experience based on fearful "guesstimations." Actually, it may be more accurate to state we have allowed the unintegrated aspects of our child self to be in charge of determining what's best for us based on its undeveloped interpretation of the world!

Since none of these stories are valid as a means of interpreting our current human experience – and definitely not of any use for integrating – it's self-defeating to continue allowing these unconscious core beliefs to function as the parameters by which the quality of our current experience is determined. For this reason, we now become conscious navigators of our life experience.

The first step in this new direction is to *drop the story.*

Even if we believe our stories have the validity to stand up in a court of law, they are still mental interpretations of charged emotional predicaments. Clinging to any story is clinging to the past. No story has the capacity to free us from the past.

Only *feeling what is, without condition,* empowers a return to an awareness of Presence and the radiance of present moment awareness that emanates from us whenever we identify with this authentic expression of our being.

FEELING OUR WAY THROUGH

When we enter The Presence Process, we are deliberately "set up" to traverse a pathway that reawakens an awareness of our authentic inner condition. To accomplish this, we wield a variety of tools. The breathing practice assists reactivation of physical presence, while the conscious responses, text, and perceptual tools team up to reactivate mental clarity.

As we move through the next three weeks, we consciously reactivate *emotional body awareness* by adding the procedure of submerging our body in warm water. Accordingly, we now consciously enter the emotional leg of our journey. For many of us, this entry into and movement through the emotional realm is challenging because we can't *think* our way through it. We are required to *feel* our way through it. During this phase of the process, it's beneficial to remind ourselves that we don't need to know "why" in order to accept what we are feeling and what Presence is communicating as valid.

Feeling unconditionally – as opposed to thinking, understanding, and analyzing what we are feeling – is what it takes to enter an experiential relationship with Presence. To integrate the reason this is so, visually examine the word "presence," and also listen carefully to its audible vibration: presence = pre-sense.

To activate an authentic relationship with Presence requires us to stop trying to make sense of everything. Trying to make sense of everything causes us to become mentally fixated. Whenever we are mentally fixated, we struggle to accept an experience as valid unless we first "understand" it. This puts us at a disadvantage because Presence "knows" as opposed to "understands." Presence doesn't think, ponder, and reflect. For example, as we move through the water sessions, it isn't necessary to understand what's happening for the experience to be valid.

An experience we have is valid because we are having it – because we are feeling it – not because of what we think about it. Our stories and their apparent understandings have no purpose in the validation of our experience.

We now intend restoration of emotional body awareness. Emotional body awareness is *our capacity to be fully aware, through direct felt-perception, of the authentic condition of our emotional body.*

Emotional body awareness enables us to perceive all emotional states as "energy in motion." It empowers us to engage our emotional body without having to translate the felt-experiences that emanate from within it into stories so we can "understand" what's happening.

The danger of this mental habit of constantly turning our felt-encounters with energy-in-motion into stories is that when we believe these stories, we are likely to act on them. Such activity is reactivity, which is akin to taking one step forward and two steps back. In other words, it's wasted energy, and we can't achieve authentic movement by wasting our energy.

Once we can feel without telling stories about what we are feeling, why we are feeling it, and what this means about our human experience, our capacity to integrate charged emotion accelerates. This acceleration is mirrored by an equal amount of transformation in the quality of our experience, as well as through evolutionary adjustments in our perceptual capacity.

Developing the capacity to feel without telling stories simultaneously empowers us to consciously enter and contain vibrational awareness. Understanding doesn't endow us with vibrational awareness because *vibrational awareness can't be understood,* only experienced directly.

It's to be expected that as we move through this next stage of our journey into present moment awareness, we will continue to *try to think our way through* what's happening to us. It's natural for us to "try to understand." However, our habitual impulse to try to mentally grasp and categorize what's happening causes us to experience varying degrees of confusion.

As we proceed from week seven toward week ten, it's useful to hold the following "knowing" in the forefront of our awareness: *Right now, as we move deeper into an awareness of the authentic condition of our emotional body, experiencing a sense of mental confusion is beneficial.* It's a sign of progress and an indication that the mental body has taken us as far as it can go. The mental body has, figuratively speaking, hit the wall!

Confusion serves us. It prevents us from attempting to barge our way into the emotional realm mentally. By giving ourselves permission not to have to understand an experience for it to be valid, we ensure a gentler and less frustrating ride through this part of our journey.

By being at ease with inner mental confusion, accepting it as a temporary necessity – and as a sign of progress – we avoid indulging in unnecessary drama. There's nothing wrong when we feel confused. We are to feel confused without placing any conditions on the experience.

As we commence week seven with our first water session, we are called upon to feel our way through to week ten. By feeling our way through the emotional realm, we are bringing added awareness and dexterity into the emotional body. We are reawakening it and awakening to it. This added awareness decreases reactivity to charged emotion because it brings Presence to bear on any situation.

By submerging ourselves in warm water, we are deliberately bringing the heat manifested in our resistance to feeling charged emotion head-to-head with the warmth of the water, albeit subtly at first. The one is authentic (the water) and the other pretence (our emotional resistance). These two states of heat combine, and unless one of them gives way, we feel a growing state of *dis-ease* and claustrophobia – and the type of story we tell is, "Something terrible is going to happen." What we are feeling is our charged emotional content surfacing to be integrated by our unconditional attention.

As we exit the water and enter our breathing session, this heated exchange remains just beneath the surface of our awareness. By staying present with the felt-aspect of this experience, we bring Presence to it and integration commences.

This integrative experience manifests physically through bodily sensations, mentally through thought processes, and emotionally through expressions of fear, anger, and grief. Through feeling whatever is unfolding without condition, this charge is gradually released from our emotional body. We may experience this as a buildup of heat in our body accompanied by perspiration, followed by a sudden discharge and a consequential coolness. In this moment of cooling, an aspect of our outer drama also peels away as pretence is replaced by increased Presence.

This integrative process also occurs through our daily breathing practice, during which we may experience rising waves of heat that then subside, leaving us feeling a little cooler than usual. This is the surfacing and releasing of charged emotion. This exchange of heat also occurs when we simply allow ourselves to feel "what is" without conditions, especially when we feel deeply uncomfortable emotional states and don't react.

Doing a session in warm water is akin to having the opportunity to allow some of the weight of our past emotional baggage to pour down the drain. We know when we have consciously released a portion of charged emotion because we feel as if we have room to breathe. We stand up straighter, are able to take deeper breaths, and scan the horizon of our experience as it is right here, right now. Our perception adjusts accordingly, so that we see our life as it really is instead of through the distorted lens of an unintegrated past and a projected future.

With the completion of each additional water and breathing session, charged emotion continues to be integrated, and evidence of our liberation from the past continues to manifest in many ways.

For instance, after releasing charged emotion, we may feel a sense of emptiness. This is natural. Something from the past we have carried unconsciously and mistakenly presumed to be part of what we are is now integrated, so that we no longer perceive it as something separate from us that requires "fixing." Often the release of charged emotion is followed by the feeling that our overall body temperature is cooler than we are accustomed to. This is because we have released something we were resisting, along with its associated friction, and therefore our overall body heat decreases. Our body quickly adjusts and adopts a new equilibrium.

As we journey through the next three weeks, it's important to keep the following in the forefront of our awareness. With each water and breathing session, we gather increasing emotional body awareness. By submerging our body in water for 15 minutes, then attending to our breathing immediately afterward, we activate accelerated present moment awareness. This means the distance between our emotions, thoughts, words, deeds and their consequences appears to become shorter. This is because we are now perceiving the connection between causality and its effect. This improved perception makes it feel as if time is speeding up. Rather than being threatening, the experience is enjoyable.

From this point within the process until we commence week ten, we are welcome to submerge our body in warm water, immediately followed by our breathing practice, as often as we are inclined. The more we submerge our body in warm water with the intent to activate emotional body awareness, the more efficiently our charged emotion surfaces for integration. However, we aren't to force anything. We don't need to push the river.

NOTE: For the purposes of The Presence Process, we are to submerge our body in warm water for 15 minutes, then immediately exit the bathtub, dry off, and attend to our 15-minute breathing session without delay. When, as a consequence, we experience emotional, mental, and physical discomfort during breathing sessions, we keep our breath connected and be with the felt-aspect of the experience without condition. Following these simple instructions ensures gentle processing.

We are now well on our way to re-establishing an open channel with Presence. This is no ordinary accomplishment. The pathway of awareness we moved through as we entered this world – from vibrational (womb), through emotional (childhood), through mental (teenage), and into physical (adult) – enabled us to arrive here and to anchor our awareness in a body. However, this is only a starting point for the journey.

The Presence Process automatically activates continuation of this journey, taking us from physical presence (breathing), into mental clarity (conscious responses, text, and perceptual tools), and on into emotional body awareness (water sessions). This perceptual movement represents a conscious return along the pathway of awareness, allowing us to develop the felt-perception required for conscious re-entry into vibrational awareness while still in the physical.

This "closing of the circle" within the journey of our awareness initiates wholeness and thus restores holiness. In this light, The Presence Process enables us to consciously anchor our awareness in the physical world, and to simultaneously retrace our steps and re-establish a conscious connection with Presence, which is the vibrational state of being from which we emerged.

The consequence of accomplishing this is that we establish an open line of communication that enables us to be in this conditional world and simultaneously consciously connected to the unconditional source that brings each aspect of this experience into being.

The possibilities that flow from achieving this are as yet unexplored. This is the new, uncharted frontier of the evolving human experience. It elevates us into a state of being in which we are "in the world but not of it." It enables us to stand in a place in which we touch this world deeply through our shared Presence, but also remain untouched by it. It transforms us from victims and victors into vehicles complete with a navigational system and a fuel supply, piloted by Presence.

Are we ready to take the ride?

THIS CONCLUDES WEEK SEVEN

WEEK **8**

(Activate with Second Water Session)

Our Conscious Response for the Next Seven Days is:

"I FORGIVE MYSELF"

PEACE IS A VIBRATION WE FEEL

One of our greatest misconceptions is that if we seek peace, we have to "make it." We even say, "Let's *make* peace." This assumes peace doesn't exist unless we manufacture it.

This misunderstanding arises from being mentally and physically transfixed. It stems from the belief we are to rearrange the physical and mental aspect of our experience in order to moderate the quality of our experience.

To see that this approach is a misconception, we only have to observe how we behave when we claim we seek peace. Because of our misconception about what peace is, we predictably take one of two approaches: we either attempt to rearrange our circumstances *physically*, or we attempt to arrange them *mentally*. Observing our world and community leaders demonstrates these two ineffectual approaches (in-*effect*-you-all: they are an effect, not causal).

Our leaders demand that for there to be peace, people must be moved and removed, borders redrawn, and population behavior controlled. This is born of a belief that peace is established through rearranging physical circumstance. This approach never achieves peace. Any appearance of peace gained from rearranging physical circumstances is always short-lived because it's born of control and sedation. Though peace may be expressed physically, its existence isn't determined by physical circumstances.

Our leaders also insist on approaches such as "peace talks," in which governments and peace organizations present treaties, make compromises with each other, and declare after long discussion and debate that peace has been agreed. This approach mistakenly believes peace is something mental. It too has never realized authentic peace, and any appearance of peace gained from mental discussion and debate, leading to agreement between opposing parties, is always short-lived because it also is born of control and sedation. Just as peace isn't a physical circumstance, it's also not a mental agreement.

Peace is a vibration that's recognized through felt-perception. We don't "do peace" or "think peace." We *feel* peace. Peace *is*. It doesn't need to be manufactured. Peace is everywhere, whether we are aware of it or not. The entire planet is blanketed in peace.

In fact, it's easy to realize this experientially. If we enter any wartorn environment – any experience of conflict – and remove all human beings, what becomes immediately self-evident is the resonance of peace. Peace is in the midst of all chaos and conflict. Nothing we do or think adds or takes away from this actuality.

In each moment of our individual experience, we are immersed in the vibrational resonance of peace. However, due to our imprinted charged emotion, which emanates as fear, anger, and grief – coupled with the mental stories told by these emotional states and the physical activities born of believing such stories – we remain unaware of the peace that has already been given to us.

We aren't required to "make peace," but simply to realize it – to *real eyes* it, perceiving it with the eyes of the heart.

When we are unable to feel peaceful, it's because our current experience of peace is obscured by physical, mental, and emotional reactions to our discomfort. By sedating and controlling our current states of imprinted felt-discomfort, we simultaneously shut down the perceptual mechanism required to realize peace, which is our feeling capacity. The road to realizing peace is therefore intimately interwoven with the intent to integrate our emotional charge.

We are all personally in charge of our capacity for peacefulness, all personally responsible for whether we experience peace. No other can feel on our behalf, and therefore no other has the capacity to grant us the experience we call peace. Peace is available to us right now through a decision to feel peaceful.

Once we truly feel the vibrational resonance called peace, this resonance automatically radiates into our mentality and physicality. Peace therefore begins within us, individually. Realizing peace individually is a prerequisite to realizing it collectively. Hence the saying, "Peace *be* with you."

REALIZING PEACE THROUGH FORGIVENESS

We are angry because, instead of being loved unconditionally as children, we were conditionally loved. This isn't an accusation, but simply the predicament of being born into a world of constantly changing conditions.

Since childhood, we have spent huge amounts of energy attempting to live up to the conditions we imagined would earn us unconditional love. This manifests as the endless physical, mental, and emotional "doings" (drama) we perform to gain attention and acceptance.

Unconditional love isn't something we persuade others to channel in our direction through drama. Attention we attract through drama is *by its nature conditional.*

We fail in each attempt to obtain the unconditional attention we seek because unconditional love isn't like money – isn't something we *earn.* Love isn't something achieved through merit. We don't qualify for love. Love just is. Love is our birthright. Love is what we *already are.*

During childhood, the example of love set by our parents' inter-action with us, with each other, and with others becomes our primary definition of love. This is the automatic consequence of emotional imprinting. For this reason, whenever we seek to manifest an experi-ence of love for ourselves as adults, we unconsciously manufacture a physical, mental, and emotional scenario designed to recreate the emotional resonance we experienced during our childhood interac-tions with our parents. This resonance doesn't have to be comfortable or in any way pleasant, only similar and hence familiar.

For example, if as a child we received abuse when we required love, then the felt-resonance associated with abuse became part of our childhood definition of love. Consequently, whenever we feel a need for love as adults, we manifest an experience that unfolds in such a manner as to at some point include this abusive felt-resonance. This happens unconsciously, automatically. Why? Because this is the only way we know how to get what our imprinted condition leads us to assume love is. However, because of its conditions, the love we end up receiving hurts.

On a conscious level, we may then ask, "Why does this keep hap-pening to me?" The reason we keep manifesting the same hurtful experiences is that we don't know any better. This is the predicament emotional imprinting perpetuates. This is the open wound in the col-lective heart of humanity. This is why many of us assume love hurts. But hurting is a condition, whereas love isn't – it's a state.

Throughout The Presence Process, we are gradually taught how to perceive beyond the limitations of our imprint-driven interpretations. We are taught how to grow up emotionally. The consequence of this emotional development is that we begin lifting the conditions set in place by our childhood experience. As these conditions lift, we entertain a different perception of our experience. This different perception isn't fueled by our unintegrated emotional charge, but is accessed through present moment awareness.

Confirmation we are awakening into present moment awareness comes in the insights we receive about the predicament of our shared human condition. One of these is that *without exception, everyone we encounter, no matter what their behavior, is seeking the experience of unconditional love.* Even if they are being hateful, what we are witnessing is a misguided cry for love.

Until we reawaken into present moment awareness, it isn't apparent to us that the behavior we use in an attempt to manifest the experience of unconditional love for ourselves seldom reflects the unconditional love we seek. We can't recognize how our behavior is designed to "get" love from others and how we place conditions on the unconditional love we seek to get. In other words, we are unaware of how our behavior is a contradiction of the very experience we seek!

As we become aware, we realize (real eyes) that everyone is attempting to "get" something from us. The feeling that the world is constantly attempting to get something from us is the automatic reflection of *our own getting behavior.* We appropriated this getting behavior in childhood by parroting our parents' management of their own emotional predicament. They appropriated it by parroting their parents, and so on. But unconditional love is never experienced in "the getting," only in "the giving and receiving."

When we gain enough present moment awareness to perceive that we unconsciously manifest conditional love experiences based on our imprinted condition, we accept the comic tragedy of our predicament. We laugh at how we blindly follow an example set by our parents. How could our predicament possibly have turned out differently based on their initial input?

It's valid to state that *we are our parents until we integrate the imprinted energetic condition received through our childhood encounters with them.* It's a case of the blind leading the blind.

Recognizing this cyclic situation empowers us to forgive ourselves for our misguided behavior in the past. We look for love in all the wrong places and in all the wrong ways. This insight enables us to realize why we manifest the poor quality of experience we manifest.

We embark on the journey into authenticity by admitting we don't know what unconditional love is. Not having a clue what unconditional love is has nothing to do with our level of intelligence. In a world of constantly changing conditions, the experience of unconditional love is the rarest of gems. Awakening into unconditional love is like attempting to find a breath of fresh air in the depths of the ocean.

And herein is the clue to awakening into unconditional love while in this world: When we intend to experience a breath of fresh air in the depths of the ocean, it's recommended we *place it there ourselves*.

As we come to comprehend our predicament, we may laugh at ourselves for the drama we manifest. Laughter is the medicine we are after. Being able to laugh at our drama is evidence our self-forgiveness is authentic.

Once we accept this about ourselves, we accept this about everyone. No matter how anyone's behavior appears, they are looking for the experience of unconditional love based on the felt-resonance of the emotional charge with which they were imprinted when they sought to be loved unconditionally as children. No matter how we perceive the quality of their behavior, the appearance they project, or the life circumstances they manifest, *we are all doing the best we can in light of the imprinting of our emotional body*.

Despite understanding this predicament at a mental level, it may still be challenging to forgive others for the hurt they have caused us due to their imprinted condition. Initially, we may be able to accept this seemingly tragic and misguided state of affairs as far as our own situation is concerned. We may be able to accept that because we don't know what unconditional love is, we hurt ourselves and others. Still, we may be unwilling to accept that this is also the plight of others, especially when it comes to our parents or anyone who continues to hurt us. Why?

Because there is an aspect of our experience that's still clouded by – and fractured by – anger. There is an aspect of our experience that feels the need and right to blame. There is an aspect of our experience that seeks revenge for not receiving what we believe we deserved.

The part of us that has difficulty accepting how others hurt us is the needy and unattended aspect of our child self – the emotional charge related to being loved conditionally as a child.

We know we are regressing into this needy and unattended aspect of our child self when we hear ourselves say: "They are my parents. They should have known better." Or, "They brought me into this world and it was their responsibility to keep me safe." This is drama. This is the voice of a child who doesn't yet comprehend the complexity of the human predicament that envelops us all.

Integrating anger, the need to blame, and our insidious desire for revenge requires facing one of the greatest obstacles set before us on the path of emotional evolution: *arrogance. Arrogance prevents us from being able to recognize our plight flowing through the experience of another.*

Once we experientially comprehend the mechanics and consequences of emotional imprinting, only arrogance stifles our capacity to forgive both ourselves and others.

The consequence of arrogance is that we may easily be able to accept the fact we didn't know any better, but we are still angered by how others behave. Unless we choose to integrate this anger, it will prevent us from accepting that others, especially our parents, did the best they could with the hand dealt them through their parents.

Neutralizing arrogance and the anger it breeds requires the following simple insight: *All behaviors we witness during our interactions with others that aren't acts of unconditional love are unconscious pleas for unconditional love.*

On the surface, this may not be apparent because we adults are masters at hiding our internal condition. As adults, we become professionals at pretending "everything is all right." We know how to act as if we intend one thing, while we actually intend something else entirely.

In the adult world, everything is "fine," "nice," "okay," and "not too bad." However, the emotional condition hidden beneath the surface of the adult world is that the people we meet who aren't peaceful contain children within them who are afraid, angry, and heartbroken because they didn't receive unconditional love.

This insight is the key to our perceptual liberation. This insight is the doorway to establishing our own peace of mind. This insight is the foundation for all authentic forgiveness.

When we make an unkind assumption about another's behavior, we interpret a cry for love as something else. To come to this realization doesn't excuse us from the need to be discerning, but it does release us from being judgmental.

Judgment is the consequence of looking at the world in front of us and seeing our unintegrated past and fearfully projected future reflected in it, but instead of realizing this, blaming others for what we perceive.

As we approach present moment awareness, we perceive that the world in front of us right now is asking, in the only way it knows how, for unconditional love. So also are we. The world mirrors our plight.

Our parents were children once too. When we look at a parent through the eyes of present moment awareness, we see a child who, like us, was plunged fearfully into this conditional world. This child, like the hurting aspect of the child self within us, seeks to be loved unconditionally.

Are our parents responsible for energetically photocopying behavior that arises in them through their experience of childhood imprinting? How does holding onto anger benefit us more than making the compassionate choice to recognize the error in our perception? Judgment is a lack of clarity and a virus that infects our perception.

Judgment on all levels is arrogance.

Judgment is also a double standard. On the one hand it lifts us up to appear superior, while on the other it insists everyone behave exactly like us and admonishes those who don't.

However, the most damaging consequence of judgment is that

we identify ourselves and others by the experience we are having, instead of by the shared Presence we authentically are. The bottom line is that, through judgment, we blame others for a predicament we all share.

Therefore, let's intend to begin unraveling this perceptual mayhem by *forgiving our parents and blessing them with the unconditional love we wish we had received from them as children.*

Through this one act of love, we initiate the integration of a tragic cycle that has devastated countless generations before us. By setting ourselves free in this manner, we sow the possibility of a realization of what peace is in the experience of those who will come long after we have stepped beyond the borders of our current life experience.

Our journey into the arms of unconditional love commences with the act of *giving unto ourselves that which we are seeking from others.* Practically, what this entails is *feeling what we are experiencing in each moment without placing conditions on the experience.*

Practicing unconditional love toward ourselves is to realize that the ongoing felt-aspect of our human experience is not only valid but also required, and hence to be felt accordingly. No matter what the feeling that emanates from our emotional body, we give it unconditional attention through the medium of our felt-perception. No matter what, we give ourselves unconditional attention.

Unconditional love is *for giving.* Unconditional love is *forgiving.* We forgive ourselves through unconditional love.

Until we wield our felt-perception unconditionally on the uncomfortable resonances that emanate from our emotional body, our child self has no example of what unconditional love is. *We are to be the example* by the way we interact with it. Through setting such an example, we actively and energetically reveal to it what unconditional love is. Through this approach, we simultaneously develop the capacity to be this way with others.

Until we reveal unconditional love by example to the unintegrated aspects of our child self, *we will continue to entertain behavior founded energetically on the assumption that love is something we need to go out into the world and "get."*

Unless we place the example of unconditional love in our own experience through our unconditional behavior toward our own discomfort, the revengeful activity of our misguided child self continues to frustrate us. It frustrates us because whenever we seek to experience unconditional love, it sabotages our intent. It does this by manifesting a predicament designed to emanate the felt-resonance of its emotional imprinting.

There's no reason, excuse, or justification for treating ourselves with anything less than unconditional love. To do so is arrogant. We deserve to give and receive love unconditionally. It's our responsibility to discover what unconditional love is through practicing it toward ourselves, as this is the only way we gain the capacity to place this resonance in our experience of the world.

Loving unconditionally is the greatest service we render to humanity. Loving ourselves unconditionally is how we place a breath of fresh air in the depths of the ocean.

Our journey into uncovering the nature of this great mystery called love starts with being unconditional toward ourselves by feeling what we are authentically feeling without judging the experience in any way, and without trying to fix, change, understand, heal, or transform it. Being willing to integrate our own discomfort – to perceive it as valid and hence required, and behaving toward it accordingly – is the root of experiencing forgiveness and realizing peace.

By genuinely forgiving ourselves for the behavior that emanates from our imprinted predicament, we automatically forgive the world. Beyond the experience of forgiveness is our return to an awareness of what peace really is.

Realizing peace through forgiveness is in *our* hands. It has nothing to do with "the other."

PRAYING FOR FORGIVENESS

At this point in our journey through The Presence Process, it's beneficial to honestly ask ourselves: "How do we treat those in the world who ask us for unconditional love in the only way they know how?"

Let's remind ourselves that they use the only means at their disposal: The drive to recreate the resonance emitted by the emotional charge imprinted in them as children when they sought to be unconditionally loved by their parents.

Does our arrogance lead us to assume they should behave differently – that they should know better, even though we realize the impact of emotional imprinting on human behavior? Did *we* do any better?

This doesn't mean we are to allow others to walk all over us just because their destructive behavior is the consequence of imprinting. Being forgiving isn't the same as being nice to everyone. It's simply a perceptual approach in which we don't identify another by their behavior – by their imprinted condition.

Discernment requires us to say "no" to those who would, through the impact of their imprinting, hurt us. Discernment requires us to draw a line in the sand and make ourselves clearly heard if others disrespect our choices. However, even when saying "no" to another because of their destructive impulses, we still don't have to render judgment on them. We are able to take care of ourselves without confusing their behavior with their identity.

Saying "no" as a reaction is *the pushing away of another*. Saying "no" as a response is *a movement toward ourselves*.

It's useful to bring into our awareness those we feel are unforgivable, so that we may examine the felt-resonance that arises when we picture these individuals and allow ourselves to feel this felt-resonance without condition.

These people are the focus of our unintegrated child's revenge. They are the victims of our arrogance. These people are also the individuals who are assisting us in unlocking our peace of mind. Until we integrate the emotional signature that arises when we bring them into our awareness, we remain imprisoned by unintegrated emotional discomfort and its consequential mental confusion and physical reactivity.

Our ongoing anger toward them *is* our lack of clarity. It's the cause of our lack of awareness of the peace already given. By not allowing ourselves to integrate these uncomfortable resonances, an aspect of our felt-perception remains sedated and controlled – and therefore unavailable to feel the peace in which we are always immersed.

There is no awareness of peace without authentic forgiveness, and there is no authentic forgiveness until we integrate the resonance that arises in us when we place our attention on those who still anger us.

Prayer is the tool for neutralizing arrogance and regaining an awareness of peace. Arrogant people won't pray for help in this regard. Let's therefore pray for the strength, compassion, and emotional maturity to be able to truly perceive our predicament. Let's pray for the capacity to forgive ourselves, so we too may be forgiven for our hurting of others, and so we too may have the capacity to forgive others authentically. Let's pray to be shown the opposite of arrogance, which is humility.

Only through prayer do we realize that the people in our experience we have chosen to condemn and punish by withholding our forgiveness are our saviors in disguise.

Forgiveness can't be forced. Neither can it be accomplished mechanically because it's "the right thing to do." This is why we humbly get down on our knees and ask whatever we understand our source to be to assist us in this matter.

It doesn't matter what faith we hold: prayer is prayer. By asking for assistance in this humbling manner, we dismantle the fortress of arrogance and neutralize the venom of anger. Humility extinguishes arrogance. Only arrogance renders us unwilling to pray and ask for forgiveness.

THIS CONCLUDES WEEK EIGHT

WEEK **9**

(Activate with Third Water Session)

Our Conscious Response for the Next Seven Days is:

"I LOVE MYSELF UNCONDITIONALLY"

INTEGRATING OUR UNCONSCIOUS DEFINITION OF LOVE

We are now ready to make a causal impact on our unconscious definition of love. This unconscious definition of love is responsible for all the unpleasant circumstances we manifest whenever we "look for love," which is what we are doing most of our waking life.

Our unconscious definition of love manifests as conditions that make it impossible for us to experience unconditional love. This unconscious definition of love is the cause of our physical, mental, and emotional drama, as well as the causal point of all experience of lack.

All of us have one primary dramatic theme that has been repeating since we departed childhood. This is our tragedy, our mortal wound, our Achilles heel. Although it manifests as an array of emotional states, can be communicated as a mental story we tell, and is identifiable through the unfolding of uncomfortable physical circumstances, it isn't emotional, mental, or physical. At its core, it's *a resonance,* an energetic imprint received during childhood – energy trapped in a holding pattern of continual resistance.

As long as we are "living in time," our one obsession is with playing out this tragedy. But until we accumulate enough present moment awareness, the fact we are doing this remains hidden from us – though anyone who spends enough time in our company perceives it. (We are always the last to recognize it!)

To identify our unconscious definition of love is challenging because it's been with us since the beginning of this life experience. It's imprinted energetically in our emotional body through our relationship with our parents, through observing their relationship with each other, and through observing how they behave toward their life circumstances.

This observation begins as an energetic felt-perception, then becomes conceptual, and next circumstantial. We then identify with this uncomfortable resonance to the point we can't perceive it as something apart from us. As long as we mistakenly identify with our experience instead of with the Presence we are, we believe it's what we are.

Our *unconscious* definition of love isn't the same as our *adult* definition of love. As we move through our teenage years, the world gives us our adult definition of love. It tells us that love is wine and roses, getting married, having children together, and living "happily ever after." This worldly definition of love is conditional. In contrast, our unconscious definition of love is the dysfunctional definition of love our child self digested – one it relentlessly imposes on our adult life, seemingly against our best intentions. Whereas our adult definition of love is inherited mentally and is "a story" – a fairy tale – this childhood definition of love is emotionally imprinted and at its core is a felt energetic experience.

The conditionally loved child doesn't care what the world believes love is. If it feels love as hurt, then despite wine and roses, a wonderful marriage ceremony, and the life we attempt to build together with our children, until this unconscious definition of love is integrated, all of this leads only to hurt.

Although our unconscious definition of love seeps into every aspect of our adult life, it reveals itself most clearly through our intimate relationships. This is because our desire to be loved unconditionally and our desire for intimacy are joined at the hip, so to speak. For this reason, examining the fallout of failed intimate relationships is an effective laboratory in which to uncover our unconscious definition of love. We use the consequences of our attempts at intimate relationships to discover what our unconscious definition of love is.

When our primary intimate relationships – those we had with our parents – are dysfunctional, this dysfunction is repeated and reflected in all our intimate relationships with our lovers.

While we "live in time," no lover fulfills what we seek based on our "adult definition of love." *This is because they don't enter our experience to give us the unconditional love we want, but to reveal why we are incapable of manifesting an experience of unconditional love for ourselves.*

In other words, while "living in time," a lover comes to show us what love *isn't*. Only when living from present moment awareness is a lover a reflection of love's possibilities.

Our unconscious definition of love takes on a different face for each of us, but the mechanisms of its manifestation are identical. *Our unconscious definition of love is the resonance of the emotional signature we experienced as children whenever we needed to be loved.* Consequently, we unconsciously recreate the resonance of this emotional signature whenever we feel the need to be loved unconditionally and whenever we attempt to show unconditional love to a specific other.

Before we gain sufficient present moment awareness to perceive this in our own life experience, we tend to recognize it only in others. For this reason, whenever we attempt to have a loving relationship, it appears as though "the other keeps doing this unloving thing toward us." Through the messenger mirror-effect, our unconscious definition of love reveals itself in the conditions the other lays down for us in order to be loved.

The way our intimate relationships begin normally follows the dictates of our adult definition of love – with wine and roses, our best behavior, and a promise of living happily ever after. In contrast, our unconscious definition of love is evident in the *consequences* of our attempts at experiencing love. In other words, this definition reveals itself not in the way our intimate relationships *begin,* but in the way they *end.* If perchance our intimate relationships don't end, then this unconscious definition of love is revealed in the way they sour. Of course, we perceive these consequences as the other person's fault.

We can now see how the mirror-effect works. The person who "breaks our heart" is *the messenger.* How we emotionally react to this experience contains *the message.* By now we have the tools for integrating the charged emotion revealed through this message.

At this point in the process, we are ready to take another step toward a more direct integration of our unconscious definition of love. For a child, there is no greater cause of grief than opening itself to the experience of unconditional love and instead receiving hurt, rejection, and even humiliation. The resonance we call "grief" is amplified when the child enters adulthood and consistently has this unpleasant experience repeat over and over again. How do we integrate this unconscious, hurtful cycle, and all the physical, mental, and emotional consequences it seeds? We accomplish this by asking the correct questions, then allowing ourselves to engage the answers in a manner that impacts the causality of this ongoing drama, which is of course unconditional felt-perception.

Accessing this realization is simple to set in motion. We ask ourselves what we are left feeling when our intimate relationships end or sour. We ask ourselves: "What do *I feel* afterward?"

Asking this question requires us to shift our attention away from the physical circumstances that surround the way our intimate relationships have ended or soured. We take our attention off the physical behavior of our various partners, as well as ourselves. We seek only to *feel the consequences*.

Up until entering The Presence Process, it's likely that, when it comes to discomfort related to the fallout of our failed intimate relationships, the physical circumstances of the relationship were the focus of our attention. This is the reason the various relationships we have had in the past appear to have different outcomes. They are only different in physical circumstance and the content of the stories we tell about them. What we now do is place our attention on *what we were left feeling* after each relationship ended. Where is this feeling *now* within our body?

When we engage directly, through felt-perception, with the emotional charge related to our failed attempts at intimacy, we find ourselves face to face with our unconscious definition of love. To integrate it requires the same procedure used to integrate all emotional charges: feeling without condition. To feel without condition impacts causality, and the consequences are then spoken for.

How long this charge takes to integrate, and what our experience looks like as a consequence of our integrating it, isn't our concern. It takes as long as it takes. Feeling this charge without condition is also not supposed to be "the experience" or "an experience," but a tool we wield. Feeling this charge without condition has consequences. It initiates all manner of experiences that come into our daily life to reveal various necessary insights to us. It brings to us what we require in order to integrate this imprint.

One way we know we have commenced integration of our unconscious definition of love is *when we no longer seek someone out so we can feel loved*. The behavior of "looking for love" only occurs when we are driven by an unconscious definition of love. Once this charge is integrated, we allow love to come to us *as required*.

The love we unconditionally give to ourselves is enough. If anyone enters our space to share what we have to give, this is heavenly. *Love is then only about giving unconditionally – and in the unconditional giving lies the receiving.*

MANIPULATION

A boy is born. The first thing that happens is that his mother's nipple is thrust into his face. He sucks on it and through this experience receives all his nutrition. Then, after a relatively short period, the nipple is removed and forever hidden from him.

Poor little fellow! Without him consciously realizing it, he spends the rest of his life trying to see the nipple and suck on it again. Every woman he meets becomes a potential candidate for this desperately sought reunion. Because of this dilemma, he's constantly hungry and restless.

One day he meets a wise woman who says to him, "I'm not your mother. No woman is. Leave my breasts alone. Source is your only mother. Go find source's nipple and don't come back until you know what I am. Only then will I again lie naked in your arms."

This messes everything up for him. Up until this moment, he has lived his whole life assuming he knows what love is, and why he does what he does in the world. It's a shocking revelation: *man-nipple-nation – manipulation*!

With this revelation, he perceives clearly that while he treats women this way – while he treats anyone or anything this way – he's nothing more than an insatiable sucker.

Until we integrate our unconscious definition of love, we can't differentiate between a need, want, or requirement. Without realizing it, we therefore consciously and unconsciously manipulate every experience in an attempt to recreate the resonance of the emotional charge we mistakenly associate with our unconditional definition of love.

From the point of view of The Presence Process:

A need is that which is absolutely necessary to continue dwelling within the human experience – like food, water, oxygen, and so on.

A want is that which we seek to make us feel better about the uncomfortable condition of our imprinting. The intent of wanting is to diminish our awareness of the discomfort that arises from our charged emotion by sedating or controlling it. Because the causal point of this behavior is discomfort, the inevitable outcome is also discomfort.

A requirement is identifiable in that it's "what happens." Requirements are given whether we want them or not. They are all the aspects of our experience brought into play by Presence and intended to facilitate personal evolution. A requirement is seldom an experience we want, but when we respond to it, the consequence is personal growth.

When we are driven by our unconscious definition of love, we are only interested in wants. Because of this, we manipulate everything to get what it is we assume we want. But no matter how many of the objects of our wants we acquire, they are never enough. Our unconscious definition of love, since it's by nature *conditional*, can never bring about the unconditional experience we seek – and therefore it deprives us of ever feeling "we are enough." Only the resonance of "being unconditional" is able to initiate the experience of "enough."

As long as we are manipulating our experience, it's challenging for us to respond maturely to our needs, and it's almost impossible for us to gratefully receive what's required. What's required appears to continually interfere with us getting what we want!

By integrating our unconscious definition of love, we are able to discern between our needs, wants, and requirements – and to respond accordingly. Only when we are able to identify our "needs" as the primary nutrition for our body, and "requirements" as the primary nutrition for soul development, are we able to cease manipulating our experience.

It's only then that we recognize manipulation as *attempting to turn what's already happening into something else.* The intent to "be with *what is* without condition" integrates manipulative behavior by revealing the imprinted charge that drives it.

GIVING UNCONDITIONALLY IS RECEIVING

The consequence of our childhood imprinting is that we behave as if to receive something, we have to get it by taking it from another. The rule we adopt without question is that "getting by taking is receiving."

However, when we examine this behavior from a unified perspective, it doesn't make sense. Embracing a unified perspective requires the ability to picture ourselves as *a single cell in the body of all that is*. This simple visualization assists us in understanding how we are simultaneously individuals and interdependent. When we view our life experience as part of the unified field of shared Presence, one cell getting what it requires by taking it away from another means someone within the totality of experience is losing out. This initiates discomfort within the body as a whole.

When we attempt to get from this world by taking away from another, we initiate a reflection of lack in our experience of the world. How is it possible for the act of getting by taking ever to restore harmony? The mentality of getting by taking *only manifests lack*.

To commence integrating the fact that getting by taking manifests lack requires us to stand in front of a mirror and behave as though we are taking something away from our reflection. As we act out this "getting by taking" behavior, notice that the reflection simultaneously "takes to get" from *us*.

Even though this exercise may be visualized mentally without a mirror, it's necessary to demonstrate it for ourselves in front of a mirror so that our predicament can be grasped by our child self. It only takes a moment – a moment that, when integrated, alters the quality of our entire life experience.

Please go to a mirror, do this exercise, and observe. Stand in front of the mirror and behave as if you are trying to get something from the reflection by taking from it. You will see clearly that "getting by taking" is the cause of our experience of lack.

When we feel lack in any aspect of our experience, it's because somewhere or somehow we are attempting to get what we want by taking from others whatever we perceive to be lacking in ourselves.

Here is an important realization to digest: Our wanting, which is driven by our unintegrated emotional charge, leads us to believe that what we seek in order to feel satisfied is something solid and tangible – money, a car, a new house, a position in the workplace. But it isn't. It's never the "thing" that we are really after, but *the resonance associated with possessing the thing*.

We therefore ask ourselves: "What is the resonance associated with having what I want?" Then, instead of chasing this thing, we give ourselves this resonance by feeling it *now*. We feel this resonance without condition.

We perform this exercise whenever we realize we are again entering the experience of wanting. Learning how to feed ourselves the resonances we are seeking through our endless wanting gradually diminishes our "getting by taking" mentality.

Instead of attempting to get whatever we feel is missing in our experience by taking from others, if we first give it to ourselves unconditionally by feeling the resonance associated with it, our sense of lack noticeably decreases. Lack is a resonance that arises from not having the capacity to feed ourselves emotionally. The resonance then manifests as mental stories and physical circumstances.

For example, if we want a certain position someone in our workplace occupies, perhaps the resonance we believe we can gain by taking this position from this person is the feeling of being "successful." Our task is therefore to feed ourselves the resonance we associate with being successful by feeling it *in the present moment*.

To accomplish this, we ask ourselves, "How does it feel to be successful now?" We then allow the resonance associated with being successful to spontaneously arise within us, without placing any conditions on it. Because feeling this resonance without condition is causal, it has consequences for our unfolding life experience. These consequences bring us the experience we require for authentic success, which is so very different from trying to succeed by taking success from another.

Once we are able to feed ourselves the resonance we associate with success, we are able to interact with others in a way that empowers them to feel successful without placing any conditions on our intent to do so.

Then the magic really happens!

By feeding others this resonance, treating them as a success without placing any conditions on them, we awaken to another powerful realization – that *giving unconditionally is receiving.*

Using the mirror again, we can see how this works. Go to the mirror again and hand something to your reflection. Notice how your reflection hands the same thing to you. This demonstrates that giving is receiving. But it's vital to realize that the key to initiating this relationship of giving and receiving in the unified field is found in a single word: *unconditional.*

"Giving is receiving" is the energetic frequency with which the unified field we call the universe is aligned. However, *the point at which giving takes place isn't necessarily the point at which receiving has to happen.* Because we operate within a unified field, what we receive due to our unconditional giving may come to us from *anywhere.*

When we believe that receiving must happen at the exact same place we give, manipulation is always present in our giving. Such manipulation is what transforms giving into taking, and receiving into getting.

Learning how to give the resonance of what we are seeking to ourselves unconditionally, then developing the capacity to pass this felt-resonance on to others unconditionally, is the key to unlimited abundance.

Unlimited abundance is *the receiving of whatever we require in the moment we require it,* not the getting of what we want whenever we want it. It has nothing to do with satisfying our wants and their conditions. Our wants are all conditional. It's for this reason that the resonance of the emotional charge that drives our wanting has to be integrated before unlimited abundance can be experienced. Wanting – and the "getting by taking" behavior it provokes – causes lack, not abundance.

Releasing ourselves from lack and entering into unlimited abundance commences when we give unconditionally to ourselves that which we have been seeking from others: *unconditional attention*.

Love is everything. This is why integrating our unconscious definition of love is the key to unlocking both the awareness and the experience of what unlimited abundance truly is.

Our experience, exactly as it's unfolding – no matter how it may appear to us – is required. If it's happening, it's because it's required. Our task is to respond to what's happening to us as if it's valid, instead of reacting to it. Through unconditional response, we integrate. Through conditioned reaction, we disintegrate.

Responding unconditionally to our ongoing experience is simple. We engage with what's happening to us through felt-perception. We feel the resonance of what's happening to us from the point of view that it's required and hence valid. We therefore feel it *without placing conditions on it*.

We don't feel it to heal it, to understand it, to fix it, or even to transform it. We feel it unconditionally *because it's happening*. Our feeling of it isn't laced with any expectations.

Initially, this may be challenging. This is only because we are addicted to reacting to our experience by automatically manipulating it into becoming what we think we want from it – what we expect it to be. The moment we stop this manipulation – the moment we allow ourselves to receive what's happening to us as "required" by feeling without condition – we have initiated the integration of our unconscious definition of love. This is what it means to "love ourselves unconditionally" in practice.

Loving ourselves unconditionally at a causal level is embracing the felt-aspect of our experience in each given moment, recognizing that it's both valid and required, without judging what's happening through us and to us. Only when we are able to be this way with the felt-aspect of our experience are we able to be this way with others and the experiences they are required to go through.

There's nothing to "get" from this world. We came into it with nothing and we leave with nothing. This is a clue that *getting by taking* isn't part of our purpose for being here.

There is no love to "get" in the world either. The world is as neutral as a mirror. We perceive in it what we place before it. When we attempt to get love from this world by taking it, we steer our experience deeper and deeper into lack.

When we integrate, there's nothing to get in this world. Rather, *we have come here to place unconditional love in our experience of the world.* By so doing, we cross a bridge into an experience in which we consistently receive all we need and require.

Learning how to give to ourselves what we have been mistakenly seeking from others is *the message* our parents, family members, and those who bring any form of intimacy into our experience are attempting to convey to us. It was never their responsibility, and it never will be their responsibility, to place unconditional love in *our* experience. It's only their responsibility to reflect to us the conditions we place on our love for them. The energetic conditions imprinted in our emotional body during childhood are the conditions we have come into this life to overcome because they are what prevent us from experiencing unconditional love.

The moment we take steps to integrate the uncomfortable resonance that drives our unconscious definition of love, we begin to perceive our parents, family, and loved ones of the past in a new light. The veil our charged emotional state projects on them lifts, and we perceive them "in the light" of what they authentically are: the ones who loved us enough to take on the painful roles of reflecting our unintegrated emotional charge so we have the opportunity to perceive, unconditionally *feel,* and integrate it.

It's we who control and sedate this charge so deeply that the only way we can perceive it is when it's acted out as an external drama. The moment we take the responsive action required to integrate this emotional charge, this tragic play performed in front of us throughout "time" is no longer necessary.

It's we who can't see. The actors (the messengers), whether they are consciously aware of it or not, have our best interest at heart. For behind the surface appearance of their roles is the unconditionally loving energy of our shared Presence, which is doing everything in its power to awaken us as gently as possible without robbing us of our inherent responsibility. Presence knows that freedom without responsibility isn't freedom at all. For when we aren't able to respond consciously in each moment, how can we possibly be free?

Free will isn't about doing and getting exactly what we want, but about having the ability to respond consciously to what's required. Through the realization that we are to give to ourselves unconditionally the resonance of whatever we have been trying to get from everyone else, we receive everything we need and require.

When we struggle to let go of our imprinted conditions, the angels who come to free us appear as demons. But the moment we respond consciously, and so enter present moment awareness, these demons once again transform into the angels they are. They are our sisters and brothers, working with us to establish a conscious harmony in the whole. This conscious harmony is born of responsible awareness. The moment we experientially receive this awareness, our fear, anger, and grief commence integration.

One of the reasons we are given this life to live is so we may discover what it means to love unconditionally. When we engage in the felt-aspect of our human experience without placing any conditions on doing so, we are practicing unconditional love toward ourselves. By accomplishing this internally, we develop the capacity to be this way with everyone else.

THIS CONCLUDES WEEK NINE

WEEK 10

Our Conscious Response for the Next Seven Days is:

"I APPRECIATE WHAT I AM"

CONSCIOUSLY ENTERING THE UNIFIED FIELD

Cause and effect states that "what we seek, we find" and "what we ask for, we receive." The automatic and unfaltering consequence is that we always see exactly what we are looking for, and the experiences we have in each moment are precisely what we have asked for.

This means that our life and the way we experience it is an ongoing answer to questions we continually ask, and an ongoing revelation of what we are seeking. The reason this isn't readily apparent is that most of our seeking and asking takes place unconsciously, driven by the emotional charge imprinted in our energy field as children.

If we had the capacity to peer inwardly and feel the sum of the charge of our current imprinted condition, and if we had the capacity to then peer outwardly and feel the sum of the resonance emanated by the emotional, mental, and physical facets of our life experience, we would realize they are a precise match.

For this reason, whenever we don't feel in harmony with the quality of our life experience, it's our responsibility to integrate the imprinted condition that's the cause of this. No one can do this for us. Having the capacity to do this for ourselves is what free will is.

A key benefit of The Presence Process is that it gives us the opportunity *to live on purpose* within the unified field of the human experience. Let's explore how this can be practically applied in the context of our day-to-day life experience.

There's a gap between us and every other human being, the space we perceive between us. This gap appears real because of our physical body. In the gap between everyone else and us is where the world manifests. Our world is this gap.

Because our physical body leads us to believe this gap is real, we believe we can be separated from others. We believe our body is separate from the bodies of others and that we therefore have our own private physical sensations. We believe we have our own private mental body and therefore our own thoughts. We believe we have our own heart and therefore our own felt-states. We believe we have our own vibrational body and therefore our own vibrational insights and revelations.

This segregated perception leads us to believe that when we aren't in the company of another human being, we are completely on our own. Having a physical body allows us to believe we can be totally alone in the unified field.

However, we all have experiences that prove this isn't so. Let's call these "unified experiences." We have seen others physically hurt themselves and immediately felt their pain in our own physical body. We have thought about another, then shortly thereafter bumped into them or received a phone call from them. We have felt something behind us and turned around to discover someone watching us. We have found that as we are about to utter a thought, someone standing next to us expresses this thought exactly. We have been about to confide in someone about how we feel emotionally, when they have pre-empted us by revealing that they too are having the emotional experience we are having. We have also had vibrational insights and revelations we assumed were unique to us, only to hear others talking about their encounter with the same insight and revelation.

We may call these unified experiences "being psychic," "transference," "intuition," "empathy," "telepathy," or the consequence of "being sensitive." It doesn't matter what label we give them. What matters is that we adjust our perception of "reality" in accordance with the evidence continually placed before us by such unified experiences. The evidence inherent in these unified experiences reveals that:

- Our physical bodies, though they appear separate, aren't. They are intimately, energetically connected to each other's body.

- Our mental body isn't the physical brain in our head. Its capacities extend beyond the confines of our physical body to any distance we care to think about.

- Our emotional experiences aren't confined to us alone. They are shared by the world around us.

- Our ongoing and unfolding vibrational awareness isn't personal and exclusive. It's universal and inclusive.

In spite of these obvious unified experiences, which the mental body dismisses as quickly as possible, what keeps us believing we are having a separate experience from others is our inability to communicate what's happening to us clearly. We don't yet realize that when we explain ourselves to others, we are constantly verbalizing the same experience to each other. We don't realize this because we are focused on our personal interpretation of the experience we are having – our mental story – not on the resonance of the experience itself.

The moment we mentally interpret any experience, we personalize it, and in so doing turn it into an individual and therefore separate and seemingly segregated and isolated incident. When others can't comprehend or relate to what we attempt to communicate to them, we feel a sense of separation and alienation. This reinforces the illusion we are separate from others and can therefore have "our own experience."

Whenever we attempt to communicate our physical, mental, and emotional experience to each other, we are too focused on what our experience *means,* not on what's happening within us on the level of pure felt-perception.

Because of our differing belief systems, which are our mental stories about the nature of experience, a specific occurrence means different things to different people. Since our beliefs cause us to see what we are looking for, we bend the interpretation of what we experience to make it confirm that what we believe is true.

When what appears before us doesn't fit into our personal mental story of what's possible, we find a way to explain it away. This is the same as *not seeing at all.* The mental body continually explains away unified experiences because they don't fit in with our present collective story, which tells us that our physical body separates us from others.

There's no point entering a debate or even a discussion about whether we are unified or not, since – in accord with our personal stories – what "being unified" means to one person differs from what it means to another. It's therefore more productive to ignore what we *think* about being unified and focus on what the experiences we have of being unified are already revealing to us. Let our experience be the evidence. Let our experience be our teaching. Let our experience be embraced as valid.

If we think of someone and they immediately phone, why do we continue to behave as though we are separated from them? Isn't the evidence that we see in these experiences enough?

As we now consciously approach the unified experience, which is the intimate connectedness of Presence within each other and all life, we also remember to what extent we are still unconsciously and perceptually enslaved by ancient imprints that have been passed down through the generations. These imprints translate mentally into age-old beliefs that support a consciousness of separation. From the moment we entered our present experience, we inherited these ancient imprints through our parents – just as they inherited theirs through their parents.

Let's begin by acknowledging that by their nature, these ancient imprints and the beliefs they spawn about "how the world is" are out-dated. Even though they are familiar and hence comfortable to the mental body, they are ineffectual. We may acknowledge that they served us at one point in our evolution, but they no longer do. Now they limit us and maintain the illusion that we are separate from one another, that we may be alone, and that we have to "go out and get ours" or else we go without.

These imprints and the outdated belief systems they support are the foundations of much of our current suffering as a species. Through the separation, segregation, racism, nationalism, and class-conscious-ness they encourage, they are the foundations of eons of fear, anger, and grief. With the evidence of our current unified experiences before us, to maintain the perception that we are separate from each other on any level is madness. It's denial and delusion. It's the same as believing the Earth is flat, when we clearly perceive the curve of the open horizon.

An efficient and accelerated way to approach the updating of our perception, so that we may accommodate the actuality of being uni-fied, is to deliberately invite encounters with this unified paradigm to flood our awareness. We experientially initiate this updating of our perception by choosing from this moment onward *to behave as if we are one with all life around us.* In the same breath, we invite daily occurrences that support the unified paradigm's impact on our per-sonal experience.

Ask and receive. We activate this through cause and effect by con-sciously looking for experiential evidence that we are one unified body, one unified mental matrix, one unified heart, and one unified vibra-tional field. By consciously looking for evidence of it, we perceive it, because cause and effect states that we perceive what we are looking for.

Seek and find. All of this asking and seeking hinges on an agree-ment we make with ourselves that *when the experiential evidence is placed before us, we don't allow our mental body to explain it away.*

The best way to ensure this doesn't happen is to apply a procedure called *containment*. When experiential evidence of our unified paradigm is presented to us in our daily encounters, we aren't to reveal or explain it to others. By revealing or explaining these unified experiences to others, we are seeking acknowledgement that what's happening to us is valid. No one can ever confirm our personal experience of the unified field. This is because the act of explaining an experience of being unified is an immediate acknowledgement of separation. The moment we explain being unified to another, we go from being one to two! Explanation of a unified experience between two individuals requires and reinforces the consciousness of separation.

Another's agreement or disagreement with us has no bearing on the validity of what we experience.

When we don't attempt to explain these unified experiences to others, they can't be explained away. When we have a unified experience and instead contain it, we digest it. The nutritional benefit of holding these experiences within is that our faith in the unified paradigm grows into a "knowing." This knowing permeates our awareness and behavior in spite of what the world's ancient imprinting propagates. Faith doesn't require outer support, only belief does.

Anyone who informs us that "we are one" speaks from a point of segregated consciousness. An authentic feeling of "being unified" extends naturally into our behavior. It isn't something we have a conversation, discussion, or debate about as we seek validation.

After agreeing to contain and digest our experience, we can then accelerate the process of inviting this unified paradigm to flood our awareness. We achieve this by taking an active step toward having this paradigm confirmed. We choose to live this way on purpose. Accomplishing this is simple. Accomplishing this is what The Presence Process leads us toward. This is the invitation inherent in experiencing Presence. Being unified is the terrain of present moment awareness because experiencing unification with all life forms is only possible in the present. The present is the unified field.

Let's now bring our attention back into the gap we perceive exists between us – the gap in which the world exists. In this gap, there is stuff, plenty of it. We know what the stuff is in the gap between us because we agree on the names we give to the individual components.

For example, when we place a pen in the gap between us, we both know what it is because we agree on what we call this particular item and what its purpose is. Because of this agreement, we may then say "please pass me the pen" or "please refill the pen with ink." Because of our agreement on what a pen is, we understand each other without the need for a discussion. We understand each other because we aren't debating what the pen is and what its purpose is.

This is the nature of all the items found in the gap between us – they all have a name and a purpose. The names of the different items that appear in the gap between us are mostly agreed on. The names may change because the person using the item may speak a different language, but other than the translation, we generally agree a pen is a pen, a car is a car, and a house is a house.

Where a difference of opinion occurs – where the meaning of the item becomes relevant in the experience of the user, and discussion, debate, and possible misunderstanding may occur – is in the nature of its purpose. The pen itself, like all items in the gap between us, is neutral. Of itself, it has no purpose and hence no meaning. The user provides meaning and purpose, and it's at this point that the experience becomes shared or separated.

For example, a pen may be used to write a love letter or sign a declaration of war. The pen itself isn't fueled with love or hate, but is wielded by these things. Whether we support love or hate determines whether we share the experience of the person using the pen. The pen is there to facilitate experience.

To continue this line of inquiry, we are invited to suspend our beliefs about separation in order to consider the predicament this idea of separation places us in. We may easily accept that there's a gap between other human beings and ourselves. We may also accept that it's in this gap that the world as we know it exists. The Presence Process now invites us to consider that this gap between us – the one in which the world exists, which we have named and given purpose – is the thing that stands between us and our experience of what our shared Presence is.

In other words, we are asked to consider that the distance we perceive between any other human being or living creature and ourselves is the exact distance that lies between us and our experience of Presence. In the same breath, we are invited to consider that in any given moment, the significance we place on this gap is what prevents us from realizing that *it is always Presence looking directly back at us from the other side of the gap.*

It's beneficial to reread the above paragraph slowly with the intent of allowing our heart to feel and digest the words.

The Presence Process is inviting us to perceive that this gap between us – this world we have made – is a veil thinner than a butterfly's wing and more transparent than a breath of air. But because of the significance we place on the items in the gap and the meaning and purpose we assign to them, we forget how to perceive that which is authentic. We forget how to look across the gap and recognize that which never changes.

All the items in the gap keep changing. Therefore the gap and all it contains can't be defined as having any lasting reality to it. When, through developing felt-perception, we recall how to perceive that which is authentic and eternal, we realize that the Presence peering at us from the other side of the gap is always the same.

By engaging solely with what is inauthentic – with the gap and its contents – we focus on the expression of Presence, not on Presence itself.

To be able to look beyond the gap requires us to remember how to perceive beyond the trinity that makes up the structure of our transient human experience. We are required to train ourselves to place no overriding significance on the behavior, appearance, or circumstances of the expression of Presence before us at any given moment. Why? Because these aspects of Presence are constantly changing and therefore not authentic. They aren't causal, and hence aren't to be perceived as such. They are part of the veil of illusion between us and that which is forever unchanging. When we, through felt-perception, look across the gap and perceive that which is beyond these changing expressions, we realize it's always the same Presence that's before us. There's only one Presence. Presence is shared. It's *us*, unified.

Being able to "see" this takes the development of felt-perception. This felt-perception is developed by integrating the emotional charge imprinted in us during childhood. As long as our emotional charge remains unintegrated and our felt-perception therefore remains undeveloped, we automatically believe the mental story that our behavior, appearance, and life circumstances represent our authentic identity. We also mistakenly identify others in this way.

As long as we are unable to wield felt-perception to connect with Presence in ourselves, we struggle to connect with Presence in others. Consequently, we don't realize we are one body, one mental matrix, one heart, and one vibrational essence. Fortunately, choosing to dismantle this illusion only requires intent.

There are only two options before us in any given moment: *We are either opening the gap between us by living according to our ancient imprinting, or we are closing it by opening ourselves to the unlimited possibilities of being Presence unified.* We either value the gap and that which is in it, or we value Presence on the other side of the gap. It's this simple, this obvious, this easy. It's our choice to make.

For example, when we pay for our groceries, we either focus on the items we are purchasing or on the cashier who is ringing them up for us. We either fret about the price of the products or greet the cashier warmly. We either worry about whether we have purchased the correct ingredients for our dinner or ask the cashier about their weekend. We either open the gap by focusing on the items in it or close the gap by acknowledging Presence on the other side of it. It's this simple, this obvious, this easy. It's our choice to make.

When we only focus on the stuff of life – on the world we have built between us – the gap widens. When we focus on the Presence on the other side of the gap, the gap closes. Each human encounter is one in which we either open or close this gap.

Opening the gap is a reaction to life, while closing it is a response.

Each moment we live through is one in which we either support the veil of separation or consciously part it in the name of remembering our unified, shared Presence.

Opening and closing the gap isn't "a doing," but a state of being. There's no specific time, place, or job description that makes closing the gap possible or impossible. It's a point of view – one that recognizes "a sacred point of you." It's living from within the heart. It's a consciously chosen level of awareness that requires only present moment awareness.

Our interaction and relationship with the items in the gap also determines whether we are opening or closing the gap. We may use these items to serve either purpose because the items have no inherent purpose of their own. We may agree that everything in the gap we call "the world" is neutral, because it is. A bomb is a lump of stuff until we assign its purpose. A rose is just another flower until we give it to someone we love. We may agree the items are neutral because the user supplies the meaning and purpose of the items found in the gap. The user decides whether a pen writes love letters or hate mail. When we write love letters, we close the gap. When we write hate mail, we open the gap. The choice is ours, and our ongoing experience of life is a consequence of the choices we make and the intent we set. It's this simple, this obvious, this easy.

LIVING ON PURPOSE

When some of us enter The Presence Process, one of our intentions may be to discover what our life purpose is. We may believe that it's "something we do." We may believe that if we figure out what we are supposed to do – what our special calling and gift is – we will experience balance, harmony, and fulfillment. We may believe discovering our life purpose brings peace.

The idea that our purpose in being alive is found in something we are supposed to be doing is a misunderstanding that originates in childhood. It's a misunderstanding passed on as part of the ancient belief systems that are energetically imprinted in us from the generations before us.

The root cause of this misconception is simple. Because we aren't unconditionally loved for what we already are – each of us unique expressions of Presence – we attempt to figure out what we must do to become deserving of unconditional love.

Because we aren't unconditionally loved as children, we become uncomfortable within ourselves. We become uncomfortable with ourselves. This sets off a chain of consequences in which we begin seeking that which can enable us to be at peace with what we already are. Because we aren't accepted for what we already are, we turn our attention outward, away from our authentic Presence, and set out on a search for what we are supposed to be.

Our parents ask, "What are you going to be when you grow up?" This question denies the validity of everything we are already. Consequently, we behave as if manufacturing a life that supplies the correct answer to this question will bring us the unconditional love we didn't receive as children.

This quest sets in motion the endless "doings" that become our adult life experience. We try to prove we are worthy of being alive by succeeding or by not succeeding. Even though we are already alive, we go in search of a purpose through which we may "earn a living."

What we are attempting is to "earn a loving."

The consequence of this reactive behavior is discomfort, confusion, separation, lack, and the entire range of imbalances that stem from the trinity of fear, anger, and grief. Our life experience then becomes a poisonous quest to continually find meaning and purpose in all we "do."

Because we see no significance in being what we already are – a unique expression of our shared Presence – we attempt to manufacture significance through our doings. In addition, we place unwarranted significance on the stuff we do things with and the stuff we acquire through our doings. By believing our doings and the stuff we have enlisted to serve these doings are the source of our liberation, we build a wall between ourselves and that which is authentic. We manufacture an illusory gap between our inherent sense of wholeness and our manufactured expression within the world. This gap, and our belief in its validity, is a primal cause of all fear, anger, and grief. This gap isn't our purpose, and our purpose isn't found in it. This gap is something we do. It isn't truth, just a transient expression of truth.

If The Presence Process sets out to accomplish anything, it's this: It facilitates us in rescuing ourselves from an endless unconscious array of doings, and in the same breath invites us to return to an awareness of what we already are.

From the beginning, this procedure invites us to *stop* – to stop, connect our breathing, and respond to what we already are through the resonance of the present. We are already complete as we are. We are already perfect as we are. Nothing we do improves on what we already are. There's nothing "to become," other than being present in our current experience, just as it is – to be fully present in *this-here-now*.

The Presence Process invites us to stop so we may have the opportunity to discover our purpose, not as "a doing," but as *being*. We are human beings, not human doings. We realize this by bringing our reactive behavior to a point of stillness so that we contain it, feel the imprinted charge that unconsciously drives it, and through feeling it without condition – through "being" with it as it is – allow it to become integrated.

Until we experience integration of these ancient energetic imprints, we are forever lost in a world of unconscious reactivity, adrift in the gap. Until we discover how to stop, take a connected breath, and feel that which is without condition, we are marooned in an experience in which we mistakenly believe that when we uncover what we are supposed to *do,* everything will be made right.

By feeling the validity of the shared Presence we already are, we also feel the resonance of the peace that's already given. Then, no *matter* what, we go in peace.

APPRECIATING APPRECIATION

As we approach completion of this particular procedure, The Presence Process places one more task before us – a task we are invited to take beyond this ten-week journey into the entirety of the experience unfolding before us. Again, this task doesn't involve "a doing," but is a resonance of *being*.

We are invited to appreciate ourselves for what we already are and have always been, which is Presence – in fact, a unique expression of Presence unified. We are invited to look out upon the fabric of our life experience with awareness that this passing show isn't what we are, but that it is *an ever-changing radiant and unique expression* of what we are. We are invited to appreciate not only our eternally shared Presence, but also its unique and profoundly intricate, beautiful expression in this sphere of play we call "the world." However, let's not lose our awareness of that which is causal and that which isn't. Let's appreciate that which is causal: our shared Presence.

What does the word "appreciate" mean to us? On the surface, it means to admire, to value, to be grateful for, and so on. But there's another use of this word. When we have stocks and shares and they increase in value, we say they are "appreciating." When something appreciates, it increases in value. In other words, to appreciate something is also to increase its value – to make it more.

One of our creative abilities that we seldom consciously take full advantage of is that *whatever we give our felt-attention to unconditionally increases effortlessly.* In the context of The Presence Process, the word appreciation therefore also means *to lovingly make more of something by seeing and acknowledging the value of it through unconditional felt-attention.*

We are invited to appreciate our shared Presence so we may lovingly increase our awareness of it. We are also invited to appreciate all the facets of Presence's expressions. Through appreciation, we simultaneously increase our awareness of the attributes of our shared Presence: peace, innocence, unconditional love, and being consciously unified with all that is.

Appreciating Presence is something no other human can experience for us. Until we accomplish this for ourselves, we don't have the capacity to perceive beyond the illusion of the gap and thereby recognize and appreciate the familiar Presence watching us from and through all life forms.

Through appreciating Presence unconditionally, we restore our allegiance to what we already are instead of valuing only what we do. By intending this, we close the gap with each given breath. We also realize it's our choice as to how we utilize the items we encounter in the gap. By appreciating our shared Presence, we automatically use the items we encounter for the purpose of closing the gap.

By choosing to close the gap with the simple tool of appreciation, we discover something that propels our experience into unending awe. We discover that *the natural propensity of the unified field is to close the gap*.

The moment we sincerely commit to using our experience and "the stuff" of this world for the purpose of closing the gap, the entire resources of the unified field rally behind and support our every move. We then realize that our discomfort, confusion, and experience of lack, loneliness, fear, anger, and grief stem from the fact we feel, think, speak, and act as if we live in separation. The unified field doesn't support such behavior because the unified field doesn't support inauthenticity. We have had to support this illusion with our blood, sweat, and tears.

Living as if in separation is like attempting to push a river back to its source. It takes a lot of machinery, resources, and labor – and it's impossible to sustain indefinitely. If we have accomplished anything under the misconception that we live in separation, we have only done so with great effort. What's more, whatever we have accomplished from this point of view has no longevity. Meanwhile, it seeds endless expressions of discomfort.

When we appreciate our shared Presence as causal of *all* human experience, *no matter what* this experience may be, we discover a whole new way of being. We discover ease, clarity, spontaneous joy, comfort, safety, and an unlimited source of unconditional love. We discover peace and harmony. We rediscover that which is authentic. We discover the capacity of Presence – a Presence we all share, everywhere, in each moment, that's able to bring us exactly what's required, whenever it's required.

The task before us is simple. We are invited to take our attention off the groceries of this world and instead choose to look into the eyes of the cashier on the other side of the gap with intent to acknowledge our shared Presence. We are invited to feel this to be true.

"Hello," we may say, from this point of view. "How are you today?"

It's this simple, this obvious, this easy.

When our encounter is complete, we may say with appreciation: "Thank you for taking care of me today."

It's this simple, this obvious, this easy.

In this moment of acknowledgement, recognition, remembrance, and most of all *appreciation*, we invite Presence to consciously look through the eyes of another directly into our eyes. When we approach everyone from this point of view, we witness them becoming present. In turn, this causes us to feel present. When we look across the gap and deliberately interact with Presence, we invite an experience that's authentic.

By setting our intent to appreciate Presence in all others, we simultaneously give ourselves an opportunity to look directly into the eyes of whatever the source of everything is for us. We afford our acknowledged source an opportunity to peer back and give us a wink. We furnish ourselves with an opportunity to remember we are all connected cells within one body, one mental matrix, feeling from within one heart, and dancing within one shared vibrational resonance.

As we practice "calling out Presence" – without explaining to anyone the nature of our intent – we witness the miracle of present moment awareness. We recognize Presence awakening through seemingly total strangers in an unlimited array of unexpected ways. In moments when we least expect it, we witness the play of Presence returning this appreciation with deliberate, tender, loving gestures.

As we allow ourselves to have more and more of these unified experiences, we know without shadow of doubt that we are never alone. We also treasure the company of all life forms as unique and precious expressions of our shared Presence.

Also, when we accept that we are all unified, and we know this from personal experience, the veil lifts and we perceive everything just as it is, unfolding on purpose. Then we have discovered our purpose for "being here now in this." This purpose is to love and appreciate what we already are – without conditions.

As our experiences of Presence within this unified field of awareness increase, we remind ourselves to hold the joy of these encounters within, containing and digesting them, rather than attempting to explain them away to some "body." Being unified isn't something we need to explain to our source. It's an experience only we can appreciate.

CONGRATULATIONS!

THIS COMPLETES WEEK TEN AND OUR EXPERIENTIAL
JOURNEY THROUGH THE PRESENCE PROCESS

PART IV

POSSIBILITY

WHERE THERE'S A GARDENER, THERE'S A GARDEN

THE LIFE OF A GARDENER is an appropriate metaphor with which to communicate the nature of our shared Presence. When we roll up our sleeves and bury our hands in the earth with intent to participate fully in all of life's expressions, we bring present moment awareness into all our experiences.

To bring present moment awareness into our experiences is to become causal, and to become causal is to become an expression of that which is the causality of all. We are then conscious gardeners of life. This elevates us to a level of service by which, through example, we open the gates that lead into the cooling shade of present moment awareness for everyone we encounter.

The next part of the book brings to our awareness some of the possibilities inherent in choosing to be responsible with the garden of our unfolding experience. It reveals the potential fruits and flowers of our intent to bring the radiance of Presence into our experience in an intimate manner. These fruits and flowers are the possibilities we open the gates to by consciously choosing to show up in *this-here-now*.

There are undoubtedly many other intriguing places and experiences throughout the unified field, but right now we are here because this is where we are required to be. Only by being *here, now, in this* do we gain the wisdom and experiential momentum required to jettison us beyond the limitations of our present human experience. We don't evolve through denial and distraction, and neither do we evolve by wishing to be somewhere else. We evolve through responsibly facing and embracing the circumstances and opportunities before us in *this-here-now*.

The Presence Process began by inviting us to take a consciously connected breath, then another, and then another, until our journey of awakening into present moment awareness is fully activated. It extended this simple invitation because it's only by nurturing the life we are experiencing right here and now that the ladder into anything else is constructed.

Whether we completed this process experientially or simply absorbed the text, we set in motion an energetic intent that forever changes the course of our experience. Let us now bring greater awareness to some of the possibilities of consciously initiating this journey into present moment awareness.

FRUITS AND FLOWERS

Fruits and Flowers examine the possibilities we become open to as a consequence of embracing present moment awareness. We may already recognize some of these shifts in our life experience. As we do, let's consciously appreciate them.

WE RESPOND INSTEAD OF REACTING. This is a consequence of increasing present moment awareness. When we realize we are responsible for the quality of our experience, we are less inclined to react to our circumstances, no matter how they unfold.

On a deeper level, we know our experience is the sum of past emotions, thoughts, words, and deeds, and that reacting to anything that happens by blaming is a denial of this truth.

We also discover that, as a consequence of integrating a substantial amount of charged emotion, we are less likely to move through life "carrying a charge." We are therefore less likely to erupt emotionally and "blow our top." We are also less likely to manifest experiences that are generated by fear, anger, and grief.

Reactive behavior is unconscious behavior. The more present we become, the less we entertain this state.

WE HAVE MORE ENERGY. Before we are given an opportunity to decrease our emotional charge, we invest a large amount of energy in sedating and controlling the discomfort that emanates from our emotional body.

Also, before we realize the world functions as a mirror, serving us by reflecting what we can't perceive about our imprinted condition, we tend to use a large amount of energy dueling with reflections.

To add to this, investing in fear, anger, and grief on any level is exhausting. Holding grudges and unconsciously plotting revenge for what happened in the past is draining. Attempting to control the future so the past doesn't reoccur tires us. The moment we stop investing in reactive behavior, we experience increasing vitality.

WE OVERCOME PROCRASTINATION. In a time-based paradigm, we have many plans about what we intend to accomplish "when the time is right." However, the time is never right when we spend it reflecting on the past or pondering the future.

As we accumulate present moment awareness, we discover *the right time is right now.*

Without giving into thought, we become occupied with activity of the present instead of reminiscing about the past or daydreaming about the future. Consequently, we accomplish tasks we had planned and planned and planned, but had never been present enough to initiate.

WE COMPLETE TASKS EFFICIENTLY, EFFORTLESSLY, AND FEEL AS THOUGH WE HAVE MORE TIME IN WHICH TO ACCOMPLISH THEM. Before we discover how to integrate our unconscious mental activity, it plagues us twenty-four hours a day. As a result, when we are at work, though we may assume our full attention is on the task at hand, it seldom is. Much of our attention is involved in the unconscious conflicts that are taking place within us.

Once we integrate this, our ability to focus on our current activity increases. The consequence is that tasks that used to be challenging and draining become effortless and are completed in a much shorter period of time. We have a sense of having more time, and simultaneously a sense that everything we are attending to is happening faster.

Also, because we have less unconscious activity to distract us from current activities, we discover we enjoy and feel energized by tasks that previously drained us. Increasing present moment awareness transforms the mundane chores we once resisted into meaningful and joyful activity.

WE NO LONGER HURRY. One of the consequences of accumulating present moment awareness is a realization that, in the unfolding adventure of life, there's a time and place for everything. We realize that it's pointless to try to force into motion that which doesn't move or to attempt to stop that which is inclined to motion. We no longer push the river. We do our best to complete tasks, but when we don't finish, we are at peace with this.

We do our best, but we don't hurry madly. We realize that *to hurry is to unconsciously manifest the experience of lateness.*

As we start tapping into Presence, we realize there's no end to what life is, and therefore no point in hurrying to finish it. We trade destination-consciousness for journey-consciousness.

Not hurrying through life has the automatic consequence of improving the quality of our attention, and this inevitably increases the quantity and quality of our accomplishments.

WORKING CONDITIONS BECOME MORE ENJOYABLE. Before we entered The Presence Process, the idea of leaving our place of work and finding another job was something that occurred to many of us quite often. A consequence of "living in time" is that we seldom enjoy our means of earning an income or our place of work.

However, as we complete this process, we discover that our place of work is becoming more enjoyable. Our work becomes more interesting and effortless, we find our colleagues more enjoyable to be around, and the idea of leaving in search of greener pastures dissipates.

We realize that we are where we are required to be, and will be there until we come to a point of completion in this particular environment. We know that if and when we leave, the doors of change will open effortlessly and automatically. We realize that being in this particular space, at this particular moment of our life experience, is part of the fulfillment of our life's purpose. It is our *being here while here* that's all-important.

We enjoy our working environment more, not because *it* has changed, but because, by integrating our emotional charge, we change our experience of our environment.

WE ARE LESS RESISTANT TO THE UNPREDICTABLE CURRENTS OF LIFE. This is a natural occurrence of our "knowing" that everything in life has a time and place. Accumulating present moment awareness enables us to realize that everything that occurred in the past, especially the challenging experiences, is raw material for emotional development and the evolution of our humanity.

We realize that happiness is a transient state and therefore comes and goes. During happy moments, we enjoy ourselves, though we recognize that such times aren't necessarily geared toward emotional growth but are more like rest periods in our emotional evolution.

This is why we choose authentic joy. Authentic joy isn't an emotional state, but a state of being in which we accept all of life's offerings as *required*, especially challenging moments. Authentic joy knows that as happiness is a time for laughter, rest, and play, moments of seeming unhappiness are times for growth, introspection, and gaining strength for our journey.

In this light, what we think of as happiness and unhappiness blur into one. We are joyful in both states because we accept both as essential ingredients for achieving an integrated life experience. Embracing both brings our experience into wholeness, and this is how we tap into holiness.

Consequently, we are less resistant to life's unpredictable currents. We discover how to surrender and "go with the flow." We allow life to carry us in its ever-changing arms, knowing that no matter how it may appear in any given moment, our experience is unfolding for our highest and most noble intent.

WE EXPERIENCE SPONTANEOUS CREATIVITY. What we honor as our source isn't "a healer." What source creates can't be broken because it's manifested perfectly, and that which is manifested perfectly by definition can't experience imperfection.

However, what our imprinted self manufactures out of what has been manifested becomes imperfect because of our imprinted interpretations. Our imprinted interpretations of "what is" are delusions because they are based on an unintegrated past instead of on what's happening right now. This is why we buy into the idea that we have to heal ourselves. Once we realize that all that's required is for our experience to be integrated, and we commence this task, there's no need for the idea that we have to heal ourselves. Then our energy enters authenticity.

Healing isn't an authentic use of energy. Healing is transitional, a temporary realignment. When we consistently remain identified with the healing phase of our experience, we are like a dog chasing its tail (without having as much fun). Our shared source isn't a healer – it's a creator.

The moment we accomplish the task of integrating our experience, we enter wholeness – holiness. Subsequently, our experience aligns with the will of our shared source. The consequence is that we are creatively inspired. To be source-like, to be causal, is to be creative. To be continually concerned with the idea of healing is to limit ourselves to being a broken human "doing" instead of evolving into a creative human being.

When we choose healing as a profession, we are in danger of unconsciously choosing to remain broken as a way of living in this world.

WE FEEL MORE COMFORTABLE AROUND OUR IMMEDIATE FAMILY. Until we integrate our charged emotion, our immediate family is the clearest mirror of the inner work that awaits us. Until we realize how this mirroring works, and until we consciously choose to look into these reflections as a means of integrating our experience, it's often challenging to be in the company of our immediate family. This is because they constantly reflect aspects of ourselves we haven't yet integrated. This translates into them seemingly annoying us by "pushing our buttons."

However, the moment we attend to our integrative work, our family is no longer required to reflect our unintegrated emotional charge. Instead, we experience signs of progress through a sense of increased comfort and joy from their Presence. We feel peaceful around them. Consciously attending to our emotional integration enables us to feel at home around our family.

CIRCUMSTANCES AND PEOPLE THAT ONCE ANNOYED US NO LONGER TAKE UP OUR ATTENTION. When we consciously choose to respond to the reflection in the mirror instead of reacting to it, things that annoy and irritate us about the world appear to miraculously disappear. In actuality, they don't disappear. When we observe carefully, we realize they are still here, unchanged. It's we who have changed our inner condition and, as a consequence, our emotional relationship with our experiences.

The Presence Process stops us cleaning the mirror in an attempt to integrate our reflected blemishes.

OUR INTIMATE RELATIONSHIPS IMPROVE. Just like our family, intimate companions are mirrors. Before we consciously attend to emotional integration, we are unconsciously attracted to others because they reflect our unintegrated issues. Initially, this reflection pleases us because we feel we now have "a chance to be happy."

The idea that *this person will make us happy* is an unconscious realization of the fact that *when we integrate the imprints this particular person reflects, the quality of our experience improves.*

Unconsciously, we seek to integrate childhood imprints that originated with mom and dad. Consciously, we believe "we are in love" and have finally "found the person we are looking for." They are "the person of our dreams." Yes, they are the person we are looking for, but not because they are coming into our experience to make us happy. They are the person we are looking for because we have a sacred agreement with them to reflect exactly what requires integrating in order for us to regain present moment awareness.

When it becomes apparent that our romantic notions are just that – romantic notions, as opposed to realistic notions – we become embittered. Because we don't embrace the opportunity to work with what they reflect, the attributes that initially attracted us now annoy and irritate us. We then dress in armor and take up defensive and attacking postures. However, the moment we agree to integrate our emotional baggage, this entire scenario undergoes transformation. We discover that whatever initially attracted us is superficial, based on our sense of incompletion with our parents.

Once we achieve emotional integration within ourselves, our partner becomes transformed. Remarkably, we discover someone we appear to be meeting for the first time! We perceive them for what they are instead of for what of our past they reflected.

This change in our experience may unfold in one of two directions. Either our love blossoms into authentic intimacy, or we come to terms with the insight that we aren't meant to be intimate with each other at all. Either way, our relationship improves and becomes closer because it enters authenticity.

WE STOP INTERFERING IN OTHER PEOPLE'S LIVES. When we embrace the fact that our experience is flowing exactly as required – and that when it feels uncomfortable, it's because of our unintegrated emotional charge – we are unlikely to give other people unwarranted advice. We realize that, like us, they are doing the best with what they know and understand. They too awaken to their inherent responsibility when ready, and not a moment before.

To interfere in someone else's experience by giving them unsolicited guidance on how they are to move through their experience is to unconsciously act on the belief that their appearance, behavior, and unfolding circumstances may impact us negatively. Otherwise, why do we bother? To interfere is to "enter fear."

To interfere in anyone's experience is to blatantly deny we are all responsible for the quality of our experience. Embracing present moment awareness enables us to perceive that everyone is where they are on their path partly because of their unintegrated emotional charge, and so are we.

For this reason, we need have no fear that another's behavior will have any authentic impact on the quality of our experience. When they do appear to impact the quality of our experience, it's because they are reflecting our unintegrated charge.

We already know by now that we can't come to any authentic integration by including "the messenger" in our drama. We only achieve integration by listening to, watching, and gaining insight from the reflection they cast. Thus, as we accumulate present moment awareness, we awaken to the importance of not interfering. When we integrate our fear, we cease to enter fear because of others.

OUR SLEEP IS MORE RESTFUL. Until we consciously integrate our emotional charge, we attempt to accomplish this unconsciously. This has two consequences. Firstly, throughout the day, our conscious awareness resorts to as many sedation and control tactics as necessary to avoid dealing with "our stuff." Secondly, at night, when our conscious awareness dissolves into sleep and our unconscious awareness gains the upper hand, it begins doing its best to sort through and integrate our experiences. This unconscious activity requires energy, and hence it robs us of restful sleep.

The moment we consciously take responsibility for the quality of our waking experience, we discover our sleep pattern goes through a transitional period. Initially we may sleep more. Then we may not be able to sleep as well as we used to. Finally, our sleep pattern settles down and we enjoy a more restful sleep. We are more inclined to recall dreams that are relevant to our waking experience. This overall adjustment to our sleep pattern occurs because we are now attending to our inner work while awake instead of attending to it unconsciously during our rest.

NAGGING SYMPTOMS WE MAY HAVE EXPERIENCED FOR YEARS ARE INTEGRATED. This is a natural consequence of integrating our emotional charge. Often we embark on an experience like The Presence Process because of the impact of traumatic symptoms on our experience. However, when we have major symptomatic trauma, we predictably also have many minor symptomatic conditions that we live with and accept as part of our human experience. It's wonderful to witness how these little nagging symptoms become integrated.

LONGTIME HABITS CEASE. Lifelong habits like biting our nails or scratching and picking at our body stop. They may stop so suddenly that it may be weeks before we realize they've gone.

These types of habits, such as nervous twitches, are caused by anxiety, and anxiety is a desire to exit the present. Examine the word "anxiety," then the phrase "any exit." Notice the identical letter content. The moment we become comfortable in the present, and thus in our physical body, these nagging behaviors become integrated.

WE LOSE WEIGHT WITHOUT DIETING. Being overweight is an indication we are carrying an excess emotional charge. Dieting without resolving the underlying emotional charge is like placing band-aids on a shark bite.

We may find many ways to temporarily smother our awareness of our internal condition by forcibly sedating and controlling the outer manifestations of our inner discomfort, but until we integrate the cause of our condition, we are seldom able to eat in peace. Sooner or later we drop our guard, whereupon the weight we forcibly adjusted through dieting returns.

As we integrate our emotional charge, our weight automatically adjusts. Being overweight is an effect, not a cause. Within each big person is a big emotional charge begging for integration.

WE ENJOY BEING AROUND CHILDREN. This is a natural consequence of resolving childhood imprinting. There's a saying, "It's never too late for a joyous childhood."

The child within us retreats into a death-like state because the insecure adult we become smothers it. When we integrate the insecurities of adulthood, our child self comes out to play.

Often the adults around us can't join us in this impulse to play because they are too busy pretending to be grown up. Consequently, we naturally gravitate toward children, and they naturally enjoy our company too.

We are all children of Presence.

WE LAUGH MORE AND ARE MORE PLAYFUL. Again, it's never too late for a joyful childhood! In the present, we come to realize that an adult is a human concoction, whereas a child is a manifestation of Presence. Adults are often so serious and too busy to play. Because our adult behavior generally smothers Presence, we then feel as if we have to run the entire world ourselves, and we know what an important and exhausting job that is!

On the other hand, children are light and full of laughter. In the present, we discover there are no adults in this world. There are children who are alive, present, and playful – and children who are dead serious and working hard to keep up adult pretences.

Once we let go of past grievances and future fears, what is there to be so serious about? We are alive, and in life anything is possible. It's a misconception that vibrationally aware beings are serious, pious, and in deep contemplation of the heaviness of religious matters.

The more awake we become, the more we laugh. When we discover how to laugh at ourselves and our seemingly endless dramas, we have access to endless laughter. Whether we have the insight and courage to admit it to ourselves or not, we forget that, in the end, laughter is the medicine we are after. Hearty innocent laughter dissolves all sense of separation. Laugher is a vibrational orgasm.

OUR DIET GRAVITATES EFFORTLESSLY TOWARD EATING HEALTHILY. This is a natural consequence of being *present* in a physical body. When we "live in time," we eat but don't feel the effect of the food because we never spend long enough *present* in our body to consciously digest this aspect of the experience.

As we accumulate present moment awareness, especially on a physical level, we become increasingly aware of what different food types feel like within our body. Foods that don't sit well with us become less appealing. Foods that are alive and vital become attractive. We don't have to force this transformation through rule-based diets; we simply activate present moment awareness.

The way we eat is an effect. Often we eat as a means to sedate and control our emotional charge. We use food to stuff down a surfacing emotional charge and as a distraction from uncomfortable circumstances. Once we integrate our emotional charge, eating as a form of self-medication ceases. Then we eat not to experience false pleasure and empty satisfaction, but for the purpose of nutrition, health, and wellbeing.

Some assume that eating driven by nutritional concerns instead of for pleasure leads to a boring diet. On the contrary, foods that are alive and nutritional taste and look better. They also feel better within the physical body, as well as giving rise to clearer mental states and calmer emotional expression.

WE TAKE ACTIVE INTEREST IN OUR HEALTH. Only when we become present in our physical body do we feel the boomerang effect of its ongoing condition on our mental and emotional wellbeing.

Until we become present within it, the physical body is largely an unconscious manifestation of our unintegrated emotional states. The moment we become present within it, we are able to wield it as a causal instrument. When we activate physical Presence, it dawns on us just how privileged we are to have a body, which is a remarkable organic mechanism with more functions than can be counted. However, the body's primary function is to serve as a point of focus for the grounding of our full awareness in our present experience. Without it we can't be fully present in *this-here-now*.

It's challenging to be present in an uncomfortable body. Learning to nurture our physical wellbeing is an intimate part of accepting responsibility for the quality of our experience. Without a body, we can't dance. Without dancing, we aren't alive. Without a body, we can't be present in *this-here-now*.

Our body is our temple, for within it is the altar on which we lay our prayers of gratitude to the source of all. As we accumulate present moment awareness, we gently, lovingly, and responsibly tend to this unique expression of our shared Presence.

PEOPLE ARE ATTRACTED TO US AND ENJOY OUR COMPANY. This is because we are more authentic. Whether we realize it or not, we are all seeking authenticity. It's our nature to do so.

Whenever many people are attracted to one particular individual, we think it's because of their appearance, behavior, or life situation. However, it's seldom because of these external attributes. Rather, it's because of their unique expression of Presence. The suppressed awareness of Presence within us seeks expression and is attracted to anyone who expresses their Presence. Like attracts like.

Presence, even when it's suppressed, is attracted to Presence. Therefore, the more present we are, the more attractive we appear to others. We appear to have what they seek, even though they don't consciously realize they are seeking it. We often hear people describe this experience of magnetism in terms of someone being "larger than life." They may also state that a person has "such great presence."

WE ENJOY SOLITUDE. When to be present is challenging, we use the company of others to distract ourselves. The moment we take charge of integrating our imprinting, we become less likely to seek out the company of others for the purpose of self-distraction. We start enjoying the peace and quiet of our own company. We trade in loneliness for aloneness. To enjoy solitude is an indication we are maturing emotionally.

WE SENSE EVENTS BEFORE THEY OCCUR. This happens because Presence functions from beyond what we think of as "time." Intimately connected with the flow of life, it knows everything that has ever happened and everything that's about to unfold. By listening to our insight, it appears as though we can perceive what's going to happen in the future. In actuality, we are perceiving *the consequences of what's happening right now.*

Everything that's happening right now has consequences. We can't appreciate this when "living in time," but the more present we become, the more we intuitively tune into consequences. To us, it feels as though we know about events before they happen. In one respect, this is true. However, a consequence is something that has already happened, even when it isn't yet manifest within our field of present moment awareness.

Each moment of causality necessitates an effect. When we live in the causal point of life, which is the present moment, the inevitable effects – even though they aren't yet physically, mentally, and emotionally manifest – are already apparent to us. This is because a cause and its effect aren't two separate occurrences, but rather happen simultaneously. In "time," they appear to happen with delay. This is the trick of time. Everything is happening simultaneously in the sense that cause and effect are one. The mental body can't comprehend this simultaneity because it's to be felt, not understood.

WE EXPERIENCE SYNCHRONICITY IN THE EVENTS OF LIFE. Synchronicity is another experience that occurs when we perceive the energetic connection between causality and effect. *Déjà vu* is also a consequence of present moment awareness. *Déjà vu* occurs when our awareness touches on the effect before it becomes conscious of the causal point. When we become conscious of the causal point, we feel as though what's happening in this moment happened already. Again, this is a consequence of entering the awareness of simultaneity.

WE EXPERIENCE GREATER ABUNDANCE. Money is an outer reflection of an inner energetic flow. When our emotional body experiences severe blockages, this manifests outwardly as a lack of money. However, it's incorrect to assume that as we become increasingly present through emotional integration, we will suddenly accumulate large sums of money. The accumulation of large sums of money is born of fear, especially when this wealth is accumulated through blood, sweat, tears, and the control and manipulation of others and the external world.

As we enter present moment awareness, money becomes like bread: we manifest exactly what's required to sustain us in any given moment. We have enough for *this* moment. We don't hoard it, but instead allow it to flow freely – though responsibly – *through* us. When out of fear of hunger we buy enough bread to last years, it becomes moldy and useless before we have eaten our way through even a few loaves. Money in the present is a flow of energy that arrives in our experience in the quantity we require, when we require it – indeed, often only moments before we require it.

When we are present, we have no fear concerning the flow of money because we know how we respond to our experience is the cause of its flow. The more present we are, the less likely we are to cause ourselves discomfort, and the less likely we are to manifest lack. In each moment, we manifest enough; and because we live in the moment, we have enough. And if we feel we don't, we realize this experience too is required. We know that it's only *by realizing we have enough right now* that we have enough in all future "nows."

Financial abundance in the present doesn't mean having a lot. It means having exactly what we require, when we require it. We can think of this as living in tune with the economy of source. The economy of source doesn't require large vaults built out of fear to store immense wealth just in case tomorrow brings something unexpected. The economy of source is founded on faith, and faith is having confidence in our ability to be responsible for the quality of our experience.

There's no greater waste of energy than *to accumulate for the sake of accumulation.* To be rich for the sake of being rich is an illness born of fear and a behavior devoid of faith.

WE FEEL LESS INCLINED TO PLAN THE FUTURE. When we take care of what's happening right now, which is the only moment we can authentically attend to, our future present moments are taken care of.

Planning is a bit like floating down a river while trying to decide what course the river ought to take to reach the ocean. Such behavior is born of arrogance and delusion. There's only one course the river of life takes, and this is the will of our shared Presence.

Of course, the idea of not planning and of there being such a thing as Presence's will is threatening to the mental body. The mental body desperately believes in free will. However, the mental body believes free will is "being able to do exactly what I want, whenever I want." The mental body believes free will is the capacity to function separately from the whole. This is as deluded as thinking one may determine the course of a river by floating down it. In the human body, when a cell behaves this way, we call it cancer. When a human behaves this way, we call it "ambition" or "capitalism."

Once we set off on our journey into present moment awareness, we realize how entrained we have been by our childhood experience. We realize that while "living in time," what we think of as free will is really an unconscious reaction to life that was energetically implanted in us through imprinting. We perceive that even our mannerisms are photocopies. How can we call our life experience *free* when we have become duplicates of our parents, who are themselves duplicates of their parents?

There is only one in all creation that's free: the source of our collective expression. We connect with this collective source through Presence and present moment awareness. Connection to source isn't determined by how we move about in the outer world, but by how we enter the sanctuary of the heart within ourselves. The more we go within and align ourselves with Presence, the freer we feel.

Free will is only a valid concept in the present. There's no free will in a time-based paradigm because time-based activity is an emotional photocopy of what has gone before. There's no free will in reactive behavior. Only by aligning ourselves with what our collective source is do we restore freedom. Freedom is responsibility. When we surrender to the present, we free ourselves from "living in time." When we choose to be responsible for the quality of our experience, as our collective source is, we are free to respond to whatever is happening in any given moment.

In such a state of being, what requirement is there to plan ahead? Planning means we believe there's a possibility a wrench may be thrown into the spinning wheel of our unfolding intent. When we know we are responsible for the quality of our experience, who is there to ambush us?

WE SPRING-CLEAN OUR HOUSE AND LET GO OF "STUFF" WE HAVE HOARDED FOR YEARS. Just like excess body weight, a propensity to hoard and clutter our life with excess stuff is an effect of unintegrated emotional issues. It's a desire to hold onto the past and barricade ourselves off from the future. Once we integrate our imprinted emotional charge, we recognize accumulated stuff for what it is: clutter. Giving it away unconditionally is liberating. It causes a lightness of being.

Often thin people with strong emotional imprinting carry their excess weight in the amount of stuff that clutters their life experience.

WE MANIFEST LESS DRAMA. What is drama but an unconscious cry for attention? The moment we discover how to become our own parents – and thus to guide, teach, nurture, and integrate our own experience – is the moment we are ready to let go of a tendency toward drama. It's also the moment we naturally part company with those who wave their drama as a flag of accomplishment. The moment we relinquish our desire for drama is the moment we awaken our thirst for *dharma*. Behaving reactively prevents us from doing anything "on purpose."

CERTAIN PEOPLE MOVE OUT OF OUR SPHERE OF ACTIVITY. Not everyone seeks to integrate their past. Not everyone seeks to embrace present moment awareness. Not everyone seeks to live consciously. Those who wish to hold onto what happened yesterday and to make fearful preparations for the terribleness to come tomorrow don't enjoy the company of those who choose to awaken from such dramatic illusions.

People who choose to sleep on in a time-based fearfulness do so because they still require rest. For this reason, they gradually move out of our sphere of activity when we choose present moment awareness. This is more comfortable for them because, when they stay within the radiance of our increasing Presence, we become clear mirrors of their suppressed emotional issues.

Present moment awareness doesn't entertain blame or regret. It doesn't use life's seemingly unfair wounds as topics of conversation. Therefore, those who aren't ready to overcome their victim or victor mentality get blown like dust from the Presence of anyone who is accelerating into an awareness of personal responsibility.

OUR OUTLOOK IS NATURALLY OPTIMISTIC. And why not? When we are responsible for the quality of our experience, why not enjoy each moment? When we realize that all unexpected and challenging experiences are placed on our pathway for our highest good, we remain optimistic even in the most challenging circumstances. It's easy to be optimistic when life is easy, but it takes present moment awareness to be optimistic no matter what.

However, present moment awareness doesn't embrace a forced positive attitude. A forced positive attitude is a form of denial. When we are present in our life experience, an optimistic approach to life isn't annoying and contrived. Rather, it's spontaneous and infectious.

Negativity is a form of drama. Negativity is a state of denial. Negativity is reaction.

WE BECOME INTERESTED IN OUR VIBRATIONAL WELLBEING. Through increased present moment awareness, we experience an aspect of our being that remains unchanged no matter what. Our immortality therefore dawns on us as an authentic "knowing." We remember something that never changes. We gain increasing awareness of that which always is.

Naturally, we seek to develop a relationship with this aspect of our being because, as we accumulate present moment awareness, it becomes clearer that our shared Presence is the source of all authenticity. Hence we become inclined toward practices that stimulate awareness of our vibrational identity. Our source ceases to be a personality, limited by our religious imprinting. Our source becomes a faceless, timeless Presence, which is simultaneously *nothingness* and *the harbor of all life*. It's natural for us to become curious about this. However, unlike time-based ventures into the vibrational paradigm, our way of approaching that which is our source in the present is fueled by authenticity. *We trade in trying to understand it for a direct experience of it.*

WE CEASE SEEKING DISTRACTION. Whenever we unconsciously nurse charged emotion, we do so by finding endless ways to distract ourselves from it. Whether it's loud music, food, sport, the company of others, or work, we are constantly seeking to be busy and on the move. Our inability to be still is evidence we are seeking to cover something up.

When we keep ourselves busy, it's because we are unable to *be* – just to *be* – and thus unable to enjoy the treasure of our own beautiful being. By decreasing our charged emotion, we diminish our franticness. We naturally come to rest. When we live in a time-based consciousness, *the hardest thing to do is nothing when there is nothing to do!*

WE ARE MORE GENTLE AND COMPASSIONATE TOWARD OURSELVES.

When we don't receive unconditional love as children, we assume it's because we aren't deserving of it. This leads to unconscious self-punishment and self-belittlement.

Further, when our parents demonstrate marital and behavioral problems, as their children, we often assume it's because of our Presence. As children, we blame ourselves for everything that goes wrong. This is because we know in our heart that we are responsible for the quality of our experience.

However, in our innocence, we assume we are also responsible for the quality of our parents' and siblings' experiences. This mistaken assumption leads to a life of trying too hard, making unnecessary sacrifices, and of becoming "the helper." Becoming "the helper" is something that occurs to children of parents who experience addictions and acute afflictions.

In this world, it's normal to grow up not knowing how to nurture ourselves, and even to believe that to nurture ourselves is a sign of weakness and selfishness. This attitude changes as we move through The Presence Process. We realize that we are to nurture ourselves because unconditional love isn't something we "get," but something we are to give to ourselves – and only then are we able to give it to others in an authentic manner.

Thus we become more gentle and compassionate toward ourselves. We realize that whatever we have sought from others is what we are to first learn to give ourselves unconditionally, and only then do we develop the capacity to give it unconditionally to everyone who enters our experience. When we unconditionally give ourselves gentleness and compassion, the world mirrors this, so that our experience is of a gentle and compassionate world.

WE EXPERIENCE LESS ANXIETY. The word "anxiety" contains the two words that make up the phrase "any exit." Anxiety is a state in which we seek to escape an awareness of the present in favor of the illusion of elsewhere.

One of the attributes of The Presence Process is that it teaches us the emotional integration procedure. Mastering this tool enables us to integrate any experience, no matter how challenging. When, through consistent application of this tool, we realize we can integrate any experience, our level of anxiety decreases because the uncertainties of life no longer hold fear for us. We know we can process any event and grow from challenges by gaining insight and wisdom from them. Our uncertainty then turns into acceptance, and finally into an embracing of the whole of our life experience.

Where is the anxiety in a life we lovingly embrace?

WE ARE MORE COMPASSIONATE AND HAVE MORE PATIENCE WITH OTHERS. We become more compassionate and patient with others because we know we are in the same boat. Life isn't easy, especially when we don't know the mechanics behind the manifestation of our unfolding experience. The Presence Process empowers us by revealing these mechanics. It shows us how we are impacted by childhood imprinting, and how we are then faced with a choice to integrate this – to unlearn those behaviors that don't serve us and replace them with behaviors that do.

It's arrogant to be judgmental of another's experience when this predicament is true of all our paths. All of us are shaped by imprinting and do the best with what we are given, whether or not it appears this way on the surface. Everyone's life is a manifestation of how they aspire to unconditional love. The Presence Process assists us in developing more compassion and patience for what others are faced with by revealing the truth of this predicament in our own experience.

OUR LIFE BECOMES A JOURNEY AND NOT AN INTENDED DESTINATION.
As long as we are "living in time," our desire to *finish* whatever we are
doing is unconsciously motivated by seeking approval, acknowledgement, and unconditional love. We unconsciously believe that through
accomplishments and the tasks we complete, we will finally receive
the unconditional love we seek. Of course, this is misguided. Once we
realize nothing we do can assist us to *be,* and that nothing we do "gets"
the unconditional love we seek, we relax and reassess the situation.

While "living in time," our focus is on the beginning and end of
things, and on everything as a means to an end. However, as we enter
present moment awareness, we realize nothing begins and ends – it all
continues forever. Also, it becomes clearer that nothing ever stops,
but rather changes into something else. Present moment awareness
empowers us to tune into the eternal essence of *beingness* that exists
beyond anything we ever do.

Consequently, we slow down and stop to smell the roses. There's
no rush because, in actuality, we are going nowhere *(now here).* We
trade quantity for quality. We enjoy the moment and take our attention off outcomes.

The journey is a causal place to be, whereas the destination is an
effect we don't have to concern ourselves with because it's automatic.
Accumulating present moment awareness is an ongoing journey. Because
our source is infinite, so is the journey into source-realization. What's
the hurry? Enjoy the day, take a deep breath, smile, and be at peace.

WE EXPERIENCE SPONTANEOUS GRATITUDE. Gratitude is a good
barometer of how present we are. The more we enter present moment
awareness, the more grateful we feel for everything. Life oozes with
abundance even when we only have a cent. It flows with joy even
when circumstances appear not to be going our way. It radiates health
even when we have aches and pains.

Such gratitude is challenging to describe to anyone who hasn't yet
experienced it. This is gratitude that isn't based on comparison. This
is gratitude that requires no reason, justification, or explanation. The

gratitude we feel as we enter present moment awareness isn't only for the stuff of life, or for appearances and circumstances, but for everything life is and the endless honor of being part of it.

As we embrace present moment awareness, we perceive what flows beneath the changing surface of the world. Consequently, we feel the invisible force of what source is, embracing, holding, and moving us mysteriously yet deliberately toward a destiny. In this light, we are grateful for all our past experiences whether they were harsh or glamorous. We are also grateful for all experiences to come because we know that whatever flows toward us does so on a river of grace.

Our gratitude often feels as if it's pouring out of the pores of our skin and saturating our entire experience. Gratitude of this nature can't be forced. It isn't something we demand or go out and get. It occurs spontaneously *because* we have chosen authenticity. It causes us to gasp in awe at life because we are in it – because we *are* it.

WHAT WE REQUIRE COMES TO US INSTEAD OF OUR SEEKING IT OUT. Before we entered The Presence Process, we most likely behaved as do all who "live in time." When we wanted something, we went out and got it. We sweat blood and tears to make it happen.

Challenging work is warranted as long as it's joyful work. However, once we activate present moment awareness, we discover that this sort of behavior starts diminishing. We become more like The Medicine Buddha, who sits still, eyes closed, palms open upward. Whatever The Medicine Buddha requires effortlessly appears in those beautiful palms.

We all have the same capacity. This capacity increases as we gain present moment awareness. We discover that when we unconditionally focus on something with accompanying felt-perception, if it's required, it effortlessly appears. We become magnets for what we require. We notice that the more effortlessly we place our unconditional felt-attention on what we require, the more effortlessly it manifests. This is because Presence is also in everything and everyone. It's the director behind all of life's movements.

When we choose the "blood, sweat, and tears" path, which is paved with fear, doubt, and lack of faith in the connectedness of life, Presence allows us to function this way until it exhausts us. This is because Presence adheres to non-interference. But when we release control and allow Presence to bring what we require through faith and trust, then so *be* it. This is one of the teachings of the Presence of The Medicine Buddha. The Medicine Buddha frequency is within us all, waiting to be activated through present moment awareness.

WE FEEL A DEEPER SENSE OF CONNECTION WITH NATURE. Life on this planet, whether manifest as a bird, tree, or cloud, contains present moment awareness. It contains the same present moment awareness we activate through The Presence Process. This is because there's only one Presence and it resides within all. Everything is its manifestation and expression. The more we tune into it, the more this relationship is reflected in our world experience. We then naturally resonate with all life forms.

As we enter present moment awareness, we experience moments when it appears as if birds and butterflies are intimately aware of us. This is because *they are*. It's when we "live in time" that we mistakenly believe nature is unconscious and oblivious. Nature only appears oblivious when we are. Each plant we pass and each breeze that ruffles our hair is aware of our Presence.

Initially, this is challenging to accept and even harder to comprehend because, as a result of ancient imprinting, we assume nature is ignorant and unaware. If something can't talk, we assume it's inferior. If something can't walk, we behave as if it's dead. For the most part we behave as though nature is inanimate, and we assume birds sing simply to make a noise. But nature is alive, infinitely intelligent, and aware. Just like other humans, nature reflects us. The more present we become, the more connected with nature we feel.

Only a person who isn't present harms nature. Only a person "living in time" kills for sport. In "time," our heart center is closed and we can't feel the impact of our activity on the life forms around us.

The more present moment awareness we accumulate, the more conscious we become of the effect we are having on our natural surroundings and of how intimately we are connected to them. By accumulating present moment awareness, we walk gently through this world. Consequently, the natural world walks gently alongside us. We are unified within it.

WE BECOME PART OF THE NATURAL CYCLES. The more present we become, the more aware we are of the energetic cycles that roll through the unified field. In fact, it's accurate to state that the entire unified field is an energetic cycle.

When we "live in time," we perform rituals and ceremonies because it's full moon, winter solstice, or summer solstice. However, as we enter present moment awareness, we operate differently. We no longer feel we have to attend to these ceremonies, yet we discover we still acknowledge nature's cycles. For example, we may decide on the spur of the moment to have a nighttime picnic. As we lay our picnic blanket beneath the stars, we look up and notice the full moon rising. Or we may decide in the moment to spring clean our house, and when we have completed the task, someone informs us a planet has gone retrograde and this is supposedly a good time to "clean out the clutter."

These synchronistic incidents occur because when we anchor ourselves in the present, we acknowledge the natural cycles within our unified field without having to make a show of it. Because these cycles become part of our normal experience, we don't need to do anything special, extra, or out of the ordinary. We acknowledge them as a normal part of our experience because we are present in the moment they unfold. We feel them and respond accordingly. We *become* the cycles and no longer function as separate entities that require the performing of activities to acknowledge them. We become them and therefore no longer need to "observe" them.

WE PERCEIVE THE WINDOW DRESSING OF THE WORLD. One of the many consequences of The Presence Process is that it suffocates pretentiousness. We therefore don't need to wear special clothes to realize how special we are. We don't need to wave a banner to let people know we are here. We don't need to give ourselves Native American names so we feel the currents of our indigenous self flowing through our day-to-day life. We don't need to put a sign on the door declaring ourselves "open for business."

Once we enter present moment awareness, we aren't even required to advertise our craft. We strive to *be* it, and Presence brings to us those who require our service. We let people around us know what we are doing *by being it,* as opposed to talking about it. This approach applies not only to the metaphysical professions, but to everything. Again, this is the teaching of The Medicine Buddha.

We also discover we don't need to seek out those whose services we require because they appear within our experience in the moment we are ready to interact with them.

Many of us are living like this already. We don't advertise because we know Presence is omnipresent. We don't attempt to profit from others by selling ourselves. We don't attempt to cleverly manipulate others into making use of our services. We don't seek out clients, then string them along so as to keep their business as long as possible. We perfect our art and let Presence bring to us those who require our attention. This is the economy of source.

WE NO LONGER SEEK THE EXTRAORDINARY. When we are strangers to the present, we seek out the extraordinary. We do so because we can't appreciate the inherent magnificence and beauty of the present we already occupy. This is one of the reasons we resort to special clothing, Native American names, superficial working titles, and other forms of inauthenticity.

However, as we accumulate present moment awareness, we perceive how silly we are when we behave this way and enjoy a good laugh at our pretentious behavior. This laughter returns us to authentic behavior. It's hearty laughter at ourselves that frees us from this self-important nonsense.

As we enter present moment awareness, we naturally discontinue searching for the extraordinary. When we are present within each ordinary moment of our experience – whether we are showering, eating, washing the dishes, or chatting with our neighbor – our entire life is extraordinary. We discover that it isn't seeking out the extraordinary that makes for an extraordinary life, but that it's in our capacity to take each seemingly ordinary moment and embrace the extraordinary energy of Presence flowing through it.

We relax and enjoy each moment as it is, for it's extraordinary just the way our collective source orchestrates it.

OUR CAPACITY FOR TRUSTING OUR INSIGHT BLOSSOMS. This is the final step we take to free ourselves from thinking, planning, and attempting to control the world. Our attempts to control the world are attempts to control our collective source. Source plays along and lets us entertain all manner of drama, but in the end, we accomplish nothing.

To relieve ourselves of this pointless plight requires us to reconnect with our capacity for insight, because insight is the voice of source. Insight is silent and still. It doesn't shout above the arrogant voice of the controlling mental body. It speaks clearly, and when we discover how to listen to it, it tells us everything we need to know. Because this voice comes from beyond time, it knows everything that has ever happened and everything about to happen.

When we listen to and trust our insight, we no longer need to plan our day. We walk into it and pay attention to each moment as it unfolds. Each moment reveals how to respond to the next. We no longer require shopping lists, but instead walk through the shop with our shopping cart and remain receptive to insight. When we allow it, insight replaces our alarm clock and even the watch on our wrist. It also talks through anyone and anything. It may cause a window to blow shut to tell us a storm is coming, or a neighbor's dog to bark to awaken us from an afternoon nap. It may even talk through our superior at work, or just as easily through a song on the radio. However, we have to train ourselves to listen – not just to hear with physical ears, but to listen and receive with our heart.

The challenge is that insight doesn't necessarily make sense because it speaks from beyond the position we are in on our current timeline. But when we obey, we realize it has our most noble interest at heart. It alerts us to impending accidents and natural disasters just as readily as it informs us we left a tap running or are low on milk.

Trusting our insight is the greatest of accomplishments because to accomplish this is to open a line directly from source's mouth into our inner ear. Then we require no intermediaries – no priests, fortunetellers, or even weather forecasters. We mainline source. Then, where is fear? Where is anxiety? These disperse and we walk directly and intimately into the vision source has for us. We live in awe at the miracle called life.

Learning to live *is* learning to listen. Listening is receiving. When we are able to listen, we realize we always receive all we require.

WE FEEL BLESSED WITH PURPOSE. By going through The Presence Process, we realize there's nothing we may do that can make us either more or less than what we already are. As "beings," we are already perfect and unchangeable. Maybe our experience is out of balance, but we now know how to integrate this.

That we are perfect as we already are is the realization we are encouraged to reach out and grasp. We recognize that our authentic purpose isn't a job we are supposed to be doing. Rather, it is to be here, now, in this, where we are currently placed. Through the vehicle of The Presence Process, we are invited to consider that there is no greater purpose than to show up and be available and useful through being fully present and paying attention. By accomplishing this, we become source's eyes, ears, hands, and feet. We walk, talk, live, and love for source. Our Presence *is* source's Presence.

When we allow this to be so, we live life deliberately, and everything we do is on purpose. We just are. We have no agenda, plan, or interpretation. We drop all conditions. Life becomes a "need to know" experience in which we trust that we know what we are required to know in the moment we need to know it. Such is our relationship with source.

We take nothing, interfere with nothing, interrupt nothing, and control nothing. Our life experience and its contents become a box of tools used to stimulate our individual and shared evolution. We live to love, and love to live.

WE MAKE AN AUTHENTIC CONTRIBUTION TO THIS WORLD. As we enter present moment awareness, it becomes obvious that the highest frequency of activity is *to serve* – to serve the whole by taking care of the part within our experience. As we accumulate present moment awareness, this enthusiasm to serve erupts from within; and when we follow its beckoning, it leads into a joyous and deeply satisfying experience.

There is no more blessed place to stand than in the center of a life experience dedicated to unconditional service. This is the source of the eternal fountain of unconditional love. This is the top of the highest mountain we can climb. To have an opportunity to wear the wings of joyful service is the greatest gift we bring to our heart.

The footprints of loving service emerge from and lead into the center of source's heart. First we serve ourselves by restoring present moment awareness. Then we serve our family by seeing them as perfect, whole, required to be just as they are, and a blessing to our every step. Then we serve our community by walking wide awake through it without judgment and concern. Then we serve our city by holding a vision of liberation for all from the fog of time. Then we serve our planet by standing at the center of our experience and allowing source to be as present as possible within each breath.

Then, as authentically as we are able to, we look out across the unified field and smile at the stars, moon, and sun. For the greatest service of all we may render on earth is to stand awake and state in silent certainty:

I am here, now, in this, awake and alive. I am a human being, and yet so much more. I am vibration fully present and conscious within matter. Through our shared Presence, I look upon you with love, and therefore with recognition. I am here to remember you as me, and me as you. Let us awaken together from the spell of time and sing the song called Life Eternal, now and forever.

RADIATING PRESENT MOMENT AWARENESS RESPONSIBLY

As we reawaken,
Let us gently leave the bed,
Quietly tiptoe out of the darkened room
And into the morning light.
Let us play here.
Let us not shake others in their beds.
They are sleeping because they require rest.
When they reawaken and hear us playing,
They shall come and join us.

The Presence Process invites us to rise up from our dreamtime and walk through our experience of this world as examples of authentic responsibility. It teaches us we are to step into the experience of present moment awareness for ourselves. We can't do it for another, and no other may do it for us.

In order for our journey to be authentic, the steps taken toward liberation from a time-based awareness and into present moment awareness are taken for and by ourselves. Once we pick up the pace, our devotion to this quest radiates this awareness into each cell of each life form blessed by our Presence. It's at this point in our journey that we consciously embrace the task of radiating present moment awareness responsibly.

To wake others up just because we perceive them to be asleep is foolishness. It's arrogance, interference, and ignorance. Sleep isn't a mistake, but has purpose. A seed sleeps until it sprouts. It sprouts not only because it's ready for life, but because all life forms around it are also ready to support its awakening. To force a seed to sprout is to perceive it in separation and consequently disregard the intimate participation of all parts of the unified field in the miracle of its awakening.

To discuss the task of radiating present moment awareness responsibly, I'm going to step back from describing our collective journey into present moment awareness and once again re-enter my individual experience. Sharing my experience of awakening into the resonance of non-interference is the best way to pass this instruction on. This instruction is vital, for the more present we become, the more responsible we are required to be. Such knowledge calls forth integrity. Without integrity, we cause harm.

Our increasing level of present moment awareness enables us to clearly perceive the plight of others as they sleepwalk their way through this world. If you have awoken a sleepwalker, you know what state of disorientation they experience. The best course of action to take when we encounter sleepwalkers is to avoid fully awakening them, and instead gently guide them to the safety of their bed, where they may rest in comfort and awaken naturally. To shake them awake is a dangerous mistake. I had to discover this lesson the hard way. I share this insight with you now so your experience may be gentler and infused with more responsibility than mine initially was.

As already explained in the introduction to this book, The Presence Process was uncovered through my intent that such a procedure should exist, and I discovered it by walking into and through it myself. I didn't intend this to be about "enlightenment." I still don't. In fact, I suspect I'm the only one in my world who is currently unenlightened. This is possibly because I don't believe in such a mentally driven, destination-oriented concept.

I have a strong feeling that once I fully integrate my imprinting and re-enter the eternal present, everyone will already be there waiting patiently for me. The banner they wave will say, "What took you so long?" It's at this point of my journey that I anticipate dropping to my knees and laughing hysterically at my folly. This particular bout of laughter is the medicine I am after. However, because I love the concept of service (serve us), I have intended that my entry into ever-lasting present moment awareness should dawn on me gradually and methodically so I might clearly map the terrain. I have chosen this approach so my footprints might serve as an example for others who are interested in such a journey. This is my small contribution to the *dharma* of humanity. I know there's a paradox interwoven here, but this is what my life reveals itself as: a paradox immune to the comprehension of the mental body, but clearly apparent to the intent of the heart.

When I initially began to walk into my experience of gathering present moment awareness, I did so unconsciously, as a desperate means to "heal myself." I began this journey by entering the world of healing, not because I initially sought to become a healer, but because I was in pain. But as I became exposed to the different modalities of the healing arts, I also simultaneously found myself carried away by the possibility of being able to affect not only my condition, but also the condition of others.

There is enormous nutrition for self-importance in approaching healing as "a profession." It sneaks up on us without any warning. It happened to me, and I have witnessed many fall prey to this malady.

Before I restored any semblance of harmony to my own experience, I was already attempting to heal the whole world. I thought of myself as "a healer," though I camouflaged my inflated self-importance by humbly admitting to being "a self-healer." Secretly, I cherished the idea of wielding some invisible, mystical, and magical capacity that would bring comfort to the suffering, rest to the weary, and hope to the desperate. This attitude is perhaps an expected side effect of religious imprinting.

Drunk from the notion of saving my world from its desperate plight, I soon forgot about my task of healing my own suffering, becoming practically power-hungry in search of perfecting my capacity to heal the ailments I saw reflected everywhere in the world. Of course, my reflections in the world played along, so that the more I wanted to heal the world, the more unbalanced the world appeared.

Eventually, this pathway of self-importance, which appeared to be "paved with good intent," led to a dead end. After ambitiously opening my own healing practice, I soon became increasingly troubled, while the people I attempted to "heal" remained as stuck as I was. My experience of affliction then began to overwhelm me, threatening to drown me. Consequently, I ran as fast as I was able from anyone who appeared to need my help. I was unable to bear hearing another complaint, moan, or groan because it was becoming painfully obvious I didn't have the capacity to do anything authentic about it.

For about two years, I suffered from deep physical distraction, mental confusion, and emotional turmoil. I felt shipwrecked of all vibrational awareness and stranded on an island of disappointment. This condition became so acute that I became fearful of losing my bodily and mental faculties. I had long since lost touch with my heart. I had long since betrayed my integrity. I was bewildered and unable to comprehend how the pathway of good intent I had embarked on had led me into such desperate circumstances.

It was only when I reached the point of absolute hopelessness that I was able to hear and listen to the wise words of another: "When are you going to take your advice? When are you going to do for yourself what you are attempting to do for others? When are you going to heal your own experience?"

This moment of realization, and my willingness to end my foolish and arrogant rampage to heal the world, was the moment I began climbing out of the pit of "the wounded healer." I looked into the mirror and saw clearly how my life hung by a thread, and that one more moment's arrogance might manifest an experience of severing this thread. I realized I was unable to heal anyone else, and I had to admit that none in my world needed a healing of their experience more than I did.

As always, the world played the role of my trusted and obedient mirror. As long as I convinced myself it needed *my* help, it reflected this deluded condition. It beckoned for my assistance from every direction. It overwhelmed me with its pitiful cries. There was no end to its misery. But the moment I realized it was I who required assistance, and shelved my arrogance and pride long enough to ask for guidance, authentic assistance came forward in all shapes and forms to lift me from my pit of self-importance. Only then did my world bring forward wise teachers who began revealing how I was to nurture, guide, heal, and instruct myself. As each of these teachers imparted their lesson, they also departed as quickly as they appeared, so as not to allow me to become reliant on them. They revealed the task, but left me alone to carry it out. There was no carrying. There was no interference. They lovingly placed their lesson before me, then quietly stepped away so any choice made was mine alone. They approached without pity or sympathy and departed without concern. They offered authentic self-empowerment and asked for nothing in return.

This became the foundation of my approach to and construction of The Presence Process. From the moment I began making myself available to facilitate this journey, I declared myself to be no more than a willing student of present moment awareness. I am no teacher. I am a willing but mediocre student – I know this now. It's our shared Presence that's responsible for any achievement that now graces my experience.

I have done my best to keep the door of my heart and mental body open so others may continue to be my teachers. In essence, everyone who came to be personally facilitated through this process was my teacher. Each of these individuals came and placed their teaching at my feet. Through their commitment to activate their experience of present moment awareness, they solidified the integrity of this process. On the surface, it appears I was facilitating them and constructing this process, but this wasn't the case. I was willing to discover how to efficiently activate present moment awareness through establishing an authentic relationship with our shared Presence. They arrived, sent by the Presence, to show me the way.

In this light, each individual who entered this process by allowing me to sit and act as a facilitator enabled the writing of this book. They remain the authentic heroes of this endeavor. This book is a gift placed in your hands through each of them. I don't for a moment assume that I healed them of anything. At all times, I have done my best to keep it clear in my heart that I was integrating my own experience and learning as much as I could about present moment awareness by watching and listening to anyone who arrived to show me how to further improve this process. In this respect, life is my teacher, and I its student.

Today, as I have already stated within this text, I no longer even use the word "heal." I prefer the word "integrate." I could never, under any circumstance, be comfortable being called "a healer." However, if a label is to be placed on my activity, I admit to being fond of the term "integrationist."

The process we call The Presence Process unfolded from watching how others charted their course into present moment awareness and from mapping my footprints through the lessons these individuals placed before me. The process came from asking big questions, then patiently allowing the answers to manifest as integrated physical, mental, and emotional experiences. Everything about The Presence Process is gathered from authentic present moment experience – and also from experiences of utter distraction. However, the foundation is firmly built on one word: experience. This is why this process impacts everyone who enters it.

In my heart, I know all who consciously choose to read this book and complete this process, taking a leap of faith into their emotional abyss, activate the experience of "raising themselves from the dead." Conscious integration of our imprinted emotional charge is the pathway walked by the bravest of the brave. The Presence Process is indeed an act of faith created by an act of faith, and all who enter it in the light of such faith are rewarded by receiving exactly what's required.

It's essential to remember that The Presence Process as an experiential journey may not be appropriate for everyone. Please don't make the error of ever thinking this way. *Because* they are ready, those who are ready for the process require no persuasion or convincing. Those who aren't ready naturally show their lack of interest or resistance.

This isn't an experience others are to be sold on just because it works for us. This is a journey to be entered experientially only by those who are ready for authenticity. Some of us may receive exactly what we require simply by reading it. Besides, no matter which level of entry we choose, we all plant seeds in the garden of present moment awareness – and each and every seed is acceptable, welcome, and celebrated. We may only plant one single tiny seed, but it may turn out to be the seed of a mustard tree or a baobab.

Remember that by completing this journey – by reading our way through and participating experientially in the process – we transform our entire perceptual matrix, and hence our experience of the world. Our world changes when we change our experience of it. As our experience unfolds from this point, realize that The Presence Process has profound consequences that have to be experienced to be comprehended.

Through our ongoing experience, we radiate present moment awareness into the experience of everyone we encounter. This consequence continues and grows for the rest of our life on this planet – and beyond. Through our shared Presence, we are able to share the bounty of what we have given to ourselves through this experience with all we encounter in our world. Some eat of what we have planted and grown with gratitude, while others ask how they too may plant their garden of present moment awareness. Knowing the difference between the two groups prevents us from making the mistake of interfering.

I haven't gone into any case studies in this text. However, as I bring closure to this part of our journey together, there is one encounter I'd like to share. By looking deeply into it, we are able to recognize the possibilities inherent in activating present moment awareness. When the penny drops, we are in awe at what we really are – and at what is possible when we "do unto ourselves unconditionally as we would have others do."

THE STORY OF CLIVE AND NADINE

One day a man called Clive phoned and asked me whether I facilitate children. He said he had a twelve-year-old daughter called Nadine who had recently been confined to a psychiatric institution. She had been diagnosed as having a bipolar mental disorder and was being administered Lithium.

Clive related that he was recently divorced, and his daughter had consequently been living with his ex-wife. Apparently, after their divorce proceedings, Nadine, unbeknown to him, had taken to strange and unpredictable behavior. This behavior included violent outbursts and apparent acts of mental derangement. It escalated so rapidly that his wife agreed, through the guidance of a psychiatrist, to have Nadine medicated and institutionalized.

Clive told me angrily that when he heard about this, he immediately rushed to the institution and removed his daughter, despite the protest of the staff. Now, he explained, he had a severely drugged and unpredictable twelve-year-old in his house and wanted to know whether I would facilitate her. My reply took him off guard: "No. But if *you* are willing to come and experience this work, she will be able to integrate her condition."

I briefly explained to him that when we have children, unless we resolve our own childhood imprinting, it's automatically passed onto them. I told him that until children are able to integrate what we imprint upon them, they cannot have their own authentic experience. I told him that all troubled children are reflections of troubled parents.

I then asked him what his ex-wife's response was to their daughter's condition. He said she was obviously concerned, but satisfied that the psychiatric institution would "deal with it" – even if it meant Nadine lived an institutional life laced with Lithium. She couldn't cope with Nadine at home, and she didn't intend to. He said that although *she* was apparently unable and unwilling to take on Nadine, he had to because he couldn't cope with the idea of his daughter remaining in this predicament another moment. He said he felt traumatized by witnessing her condition.

I told him that from our brief conversation, because of his deep concern for his daughter, and because *he* had approached me with this predicament, it was evident his daughter's situation was to a larger extent a reflection of his unintegrated childhood issues. I explained that this was why he was "the deeply concerned one." I said: "There is nothing wrong with your daughter, Clive. She is reflecting your unintegrated childhood imprinting. When you integrate your suppressed emotional charge, she will simultaneously regain wellbeing."

Understandably, he was startled. He said he hadn't heard of such an approach. I then asked him what happened to him when *he* was a twelve-year-old. There was a silence on the phone. Then his voice came back weakly: "My father left us. How did you know something happened when I was twelve?" I briefly explained the seven-year cycle. I then asked whether he recognized that his past circumstances were repeating right now, like clockwork, in his daughter's life experience. Could he see that his recent leaving of his daughter because of the divorce was a repeating pattern that was playing out within her experience? He replied that until this moment, he was unaware his daughter's condition had any connection with his troubled youth.

To this day, I don't think Clive really digested what I said about "emotional imprinting" or the nature of the seven-year cycle until he completed the process himself. I believe he initially agreed to my approach of first integrating his experience rather than me facilitating his daughter because he was desperate and because, like him, I strongly disapproved of Nadine's medicated predicament. It was also profoundly insightful for him to make the connection between his daughter's current predicament and his own unintegrated emotional condition.

Clive agreed to enter The Presence Process immediately. He also agreed to calculate how to gradually wean Nadine off her Lithium in such a way that she would be off the medication in the time it took him to complete his journey through the process. Bear in mind that the version of the process Clive experienced through personal facilitation isn't what we go through in the book. In addition to the process as presented within this book, personal facilitation involved one three-hour facilitated breathing session per week, accompanied by sessions of personal mirroring by myself, together with three three-hour water sessions in very warm water. None of this is to be attempted alone.

I won't tell you that what Clive went through with Nadine over the course of this ten-week period was easy, but it was an authentic experience for both of them. Because of his commitment to completing the personally facilitated version of The Presence Process (a service I no longer offer), the intimacy of a father and daughter relationship was resuscitated, and joyfulness gradually seeped back into their home.

For the first three weeks, Clive continued to attend to the process fueled primarily by faith and the desperation of a concerned father. I personally had no doubt about the inevitable consequence of his quest because I have witnessed over and over the integrative capacity of The Presence Process. He appeared to have no alternative but to persist, and I'm sure that for the first few weeks, he clung to my absolute certainty about the possibility of accomplishing integration.

As Clive touched on and integrated the traumas within his own emotional body, miraculous shifts manifested. He had arrived home from work to discover sudden, inexplicable changes in Nadine's behavior. He had arrived at his session with me shaking his head in disbelief. "She isn't shouting at me anymore" became "she sat in the kitchen and spoke to me last night," which became "she started doing the dishes with me last night without my even asking her to," which then became "she put her arms around me in the car today and told me she loved me."

As Clive's ten weeks concluded, Nadine was back in school, completely off her medication, doing whatever teenage girls do. His ex-wife was startled, especially when Clive dropped Nadine off to spend some time with her. Nadine's approach to her schoolwork was also transformed to such an extent that her teacher phoned Clive with glowing reports.

As Clive left after completing his final session with me, he asked, "Why does the world not know about this work?" Of course, I smiled, because I know there's a time and place for everything. He said he wanted to write a book about what had happened. I knew this was his way of saying how grateful he was for the fruits and flowers of present moment awareness. I sincerely hope he one day writes Nadine's story for the Clives and Nadines of this world. If not, his voice is heard through the sharing of this case study.

Clive and Nadine's story is just one of many. I have chosen to share their story with you because I intend you to know in your heart that The Presence Process isn't about us going around healing this world or anyone in it. It's about us having the guts to integrate our own experience of it. This process isn't to be used for interference. We aren't to suggest to someone that they do The Presence Process so they will become the type of person we think they ought to be. Remember that the road paved with good intent often leads into hellish outcomes, especially when our unconscious intent is to change others so they fit neatly into our picture of life. When we don't like what we perceive about others, we are to change our perception by integrating the relevant emotional charge within us, not by tinkering with the outer circumstances we observe. The Presence Process is intended as a journey we take for and into ourselves, by ourselves. But as we perceive through Clive and Nadine's story, the miracle of it is that when we unconditionally activate present moment awareness, all benefit.

Authentically activated present moment awareness radiates like the scent of ripe peaches.

THE ORGANIC UNFOLDING OF PRESENT MOMENT AWARENESS

It was only after I overcame my misplaced desire to "heal the world" that I started my journey toward authentic wholeness. I began by looking at myself and working with the obvious imprints that were causing discomfort in my immediate experience. Then I looked to my family, as if into a mirror, and used this reflection to perceive more of what I required to integrate.

Our immediate family members are the clearest and most honest reflections of our unintegrated imprinting. Anything and everything that appears "wrong" with our immediate family members, to the point that it emotionally upsets us, is *our issue*. This is challenging medicine to swallow, but there is no exception to this rule. Our family mirrors us – this is what makes them our family. When we make the mistake of attempting to clean the mirror to cope with unpleasant reflections, we add to the debris of unhappy families. But when we embrace our immediate family as those who love us enough to play the role of honest reflection, we accomplish miracles.

Once upon a time I ran from my family. I chose any company but theirs. Today, because of the blessings and insights inherent within present moment awareness, I look at my immediate family and perceive them as they are: perfect. Everything I sought to change about them in the past is now everything I miss about them when they aren't physically present in my experience. Today I am blessed with a joyful family, not because I changed any of them, but because I adjusted my experience of them through what they reflected. They are created perfect. It was my perception of them that was clouded. They aren't their imprinting, but are unique expressions of our shared Presence.

Once we attain an awareness of peace within our family, we then radiate present moment awareness into our community, then into our city, our country, and finally over our continent and across our planet. I embrace this intent as my ongoing journey.

This book isn't written to change my planet and the people I share it with, for we are already created perfect. We aren't our imprinting, and therefore not the appearance, behavior, or circumstance projected by it. However, I send this book out as an invitation to anyone who is currently having an experience that's uncomfortably charged. This book will assist anyone to change the quality of their experience by instructing them how to take responsibility for their emotionally charged predicament.

To date, I haven't been able to change anyone. I thank source for making it so, for I don't seek to interfere with the expressions of our shared Presence within this beautiful creation. I now know that when something is amiss within my experience, it's because I perceive it amiss.

How do I know when I'm present and when I'm not? When I look into my experience of the world and perceive circumstances from the past that I think should have been different, and when I start making plans to change the way circumstances are unfolding right now, I know I'm living in a distracted place called "time." Time is a place where nothing is ever right – now. But when I observe my world and perceive its beauty, its perfect imperfection, its fullness of life – and when, for no reason at all, I feel gratitude for being in it, for each moment and particle of it – I know I am right here, right now.

It has taken me a long "time" to embrace "the everything" life is. I am now deeply in love with it all, for it's all an expression of what source is to me. There isn't one freckle on the face of life I seek to change. Of course, I still have my buttons pushed; but this is only because I still have imprinting to integrate. In sickness and health, in riches and poverty, in youth and old age, in sleepiness and in waking, I love and cherish each moment.

Life *is* my source, and present moment awareness the altar upon which I lay my prayers of gratitude. Now, I want for nothing. Now, there is nothing I do not want. Now, I have what I require and require what I have. How can it be any other way? If it is, it's because I have departed the moment. In my heart, I now feel the warmth and bubbling smile of our endless and eternally shared Presence. As long as this journey continues, I gladly take the ride.

I know there are doors opened through the activation of present moment awareness that go beyond the capacity of what may be written in this book. These are states of beingness communicated only through our personal experience of present moment awareness. This is the abyss I continually fling myself into as recklessly as I know how. These are the adventures I invite you to navigate into. These are the big questions I encourage you to ask.

Contrary to what the time-based world may claim, we aren't meant to bring peace to this planet. Such a notion is delusional and a distraction. This planet is neutral. As such, it's the perfect "setup" for anyone who is ready to evolve through the rite of personal responsibility. We are here because we are "set up to be." We are here because we are invited "to be" despite the distraction of endless doing. This Earth school is a grand hall of mirrors. Notice that *Earth* and *heart* are the same word with the letters rearranged.

We are here, now, in this, to discover that we may realize peace here, now, and in this, only when we authentically offer an awareness of this vibration to our own heart. When we offer an awareness of what peace is to ourselves, the mirror this world is laughs at the play of it all. Then an awareness of the peace that's already given, and that always will be, cascades in from every direction.

PART V

CONTINUANCE

THROUGHOUT THE PRESENCE PROCESS, we have planted more seeds than it's possible to count. This journey represents the springtime of our reawakening into present moment awareness. By completing this process, we ensure the garden of our unfolding experience becomes full and bountiful – so much so that we are able to invite others in to share our cool shade and enjoy the beauty and bounty of our fruits and flowers. We live continually within the resonance of great possibility, and others feel this. This is, of course, as long as we consciously take care of the seeds we have planted.

As we reach completion of this text, know that "completion" according to The Presence Process doesn't mean "finishing." Completion of this particular journey means we have entered a state of awareness in which we are ready and willing to accept full responsibility for the quality – the causal felt-aspect – of our experience. It means we have elevated ourselves into living at the causality of our awareness. Living consciously within the causality of our awareness is akin to continually sowing seeds in fertile ground. It's a state of continued ripening.

In addition to entering causal consciousness, completion according to The Presence Process also means we are now saturated with the awareness of personal responsibility. Therefore, as the seeds we plant with consciously felt experience, thoughts, words, and deeds break through the soil and come to light, we are willing and eager to water and take care of them. We are intent on living each moment of life consciously because we know there's no other way to be.

We endeavor to embrace each moment of our experience in a manner that waters and nurtures our present moment awareness. We now know how to accomplish this: by choosing response over reaction, and thereby being a vehicle and not a victim or victor. This final moment of The Presence Process briefly examines our road ahead. It offers us some valuable insight into the resonance of living as "a cause" and the responsibility of embracing such a profound intention. It also gifts us with a tool for consciously approaching vibrational awareness.

FREEDOM IS RESPONSIBILITY

You have now successfully completed your journey through The Presence Process, and there are only a few more insights to be shared before we close this book. Before you go any further, acknowledge yourself for reaching completion of this beautiful and profound journey. Only you know what you went through, so only your appreciation of your experience is valid. Know that whatever experience you had, and will continue to have as a consequence, is valid. It's your treasure from which to mine ongoing insight.

Completion of an experience like this, whether we read The Presence Process or entered experientially into it, is no small accomplishment. You accomplished something authentic. You activated authentic movement in the quality of your experience. You may have gone through personal hell to get to this point, so it's meaningful to stop, gently connect your breathing for a moment, smile inwardly, and enjoy this moment. You have done well. You have blessed yourself, your life experience, and all those with whom you now come in contact. Well done!

Fortunately, this isn't the end of anything. This moment marks a continuation point of a profound journey into an ongoing experience of present moment awareness.

Essentially, what we have accomplished by completing The Presence Process is turning the ship of our life experience around and pointing it in a direction that at last serves us. We are now heading out of, instead of further into, the time-based mentality. We are ripe to reap the fruits and flowers of this journey forever because it's a journey that inevitably delivers our awareness into eternity. Our experience of the world will no longer be what it was. We are now gently reawakening from a long unconscious dream by consciously grasping the gifts of an authentically lived life experience.

This is where living as a responsible human being becomes important.

Just because we are now moving in the right direction doesn't mean we take our hands off the steering wheel. Even though living responsibly empowers our experience to flow seemingly more effortlessly, our capacity for awareness of responsibility isn't equipped with an automatic pilot button. There's nothing unconscious about responsibility. On the contrary, now more than ever, we are required to embrace a hands-on approach to steering the quality of our experience. From this point onward, it's beneficial to keep in mind the following analogy:

A pilot flying a plane seldom stays on course. They are continually correcting their course because the plane, buffeted by the winds of atmospheric turbulence, is constantly being pushed off the intended flight path. Consequently, the pilot is constantly adjusting the course of the plane to compensate. Consistent compensation is required to ensure the flight path leads to the intended destination.

Remember that, by completing this book, we have initiated authentic movement within many aspects of our experience. We are now like a train that was once stationary, but that is now moving along the rails at higher and higher speed. When we now choose not to take responsibility for the quality of each moment, we inevitably crash. When we suddenly stop the locomotive of our intent to remain present and intensify our relationship with present moment aware-ness, we feel the heavy weight of the carriages representing the dif-ferent aspects of our experience piling onto and derailing us from our conscious journey into authenticity. This isn't meant to appear threatening. This is the predicament now unfolding, since with increased awareness comes increased responsibility.

Crashing is the consequence of allowing ourselves to become unconscious again. Crashing is allowing ourselves to return to a deathly dance with imaginary reflections of an unresolved past. Crash-ing is allowing ourselves to continue to unconsciously project fear, anger, and grief onto the neutral screen of the world. Crashing is allowing ourselves to become physically distracted, mentally confused, and emotionally unbalanced. Crashing is choosing to become irre-sponsible about the consequence of the as-yet unintegrated charges within our emotional body.

When we now choose to crash by not being responsible for main-taining and increasing present moment awareness, this time we can-not plead ignorance about the mechanics of our experience. This time, when we become unconscious, we make a conscious choice to become so. Crashing isn't necessary. However, we may still manifest the expe-rience every now and then just to remind ourselves that being respon-sible is preferable.

It's our responsibility to remain steadfast in our intent and to make required adjustments when we lose focus – in other words, to respond. We will inevitably have experiences in which our awareness appears to plummet, causing us to become confused and to seemingly unravel the fabric of our intent. Why? Because the atmospheric tur-bulence of life, and our experience of the energetic cycles of the phys-ical, mental, and emotional unified field, constantly bump us off course. We therefore remember how to respond. While we are alive in this world, we are required to respond consciously to our experience.

Our intent is our flight path. When we feel ourselves being tossed into unconsciousness by "time," how then do we consciously respond? How do we compensate and make the required adjustments?

We stop whatever we are doing and connect our breathing until present moment awareness is restored. It's this simple. It's this obvious.

Consciously connecting our breathing restores present moment awareness and reminds us of our intent when the turbulence of our experience causes confusion. Consciously connecting our breathing rescues us from the wreckage of any crash we may manifest. By committing to make our 15 minutes breathing practice as much a part of our daily routine as brushing our teeth, we insure ourselves against Presence-decay. Our breathing *routine* is our responsibility because it ensures we have consciously established a *route in*to ourselves, which is where all navigational adjustments are made. Our breathing routine is our safety belt in times of excessive turbulence, our jaws of life in times of calamity, and our compass through all confusion.

We are and always will be the center of our experience. Our experience is only happening *because* we are in it. Therefore, it's our responsibility to constantly recommit to being as present as possible. It's our responsibility to keep the awareness of what peace is alive within ourselves by consciously *choosing to feel peaceful for a few moments each day.* It's our responsibility to unconditionally give ourselves what we seek to receive. It's our responsibility to be open to receiving unconditionally what we enjoy giving. It's our responsibility, through whatever practice we most respond to, to consistently steer the ship of our experience gratefully into the heart of our authentic vibrational self. It's our responsibility to remember our innocence and to nurture our spontaneous joy, playfulness, and creativity. It's our responsibility to give ourselves unconditional love. It's our responsibility to remember to stop every now and then to appreciate the eternal precious experience called "the present," which we are given so we may take another consciously connected breath. It's our responsibility to live as if fully alive.

When we review The Presence Process, starting from the beginning of the book, we will be astounded at how many perceptual tools we are given throughout the text to supplement our journey. We are now well equipped to consciously navigate this awesome journey called life. By rereading this book whenever it feels appropriate, we also discover we have a greater comprehension of the insights it contains. This in itself is a barometer of how much and how swiftly our awareness has grown. It will surely inspire us to continue consciously reawakening into the unlimited and breathtaking potential of a conscious relationship with our shared Presence.

After a period of integration, we may, like many others, choose to repeat this experience or reread this text to access deeper insight. This process may be repeated as often as we feel necessary. It always meets us where we are and leads us into greater depths of present moment awareness. Our experience of it is always valid.

ROSES HAVE THORNS

One of the insights laid before us through The Presence Process is that life is like a rose, and roses have thorns. Our collective source created roses to be the symbol and scent of love and loving. Our source also deliberately adorned these beautiful flowers with sharp thorns. This divine arrangement reminds us about balance, stimulates integration, and reawakens us to gentleness and respect.

We have all felt discomfort. We have already each experienced so much physical, mental, and emotional discomfort in this one life experience that our tendency is to consciously and unconsciously seek a state in which we are eternally joyful. Such a state of beingness is possible here, but it doesn't come from choosing a path that has "a destination" or a path in which we practice exclusivity. Because our source is infinite, the journey into source-realization is an eternal one. Because source created everything, then *everything* is to be embraced when we are integrating what source is.

The way to achieve authentic joy while in this world isn't through pushing certain experiences away from us, while pulling others toward us. Joy isn't about reaching a point of endless happiness. This isn't what life is about at all. Any preoccupation with intending to feel good all the time, to have our circumstance easy all the time, and to achieve complete and instant integration in every aspect of our experience is delusional. Life is both sides and ongoing. Life is always and all ways.

A path into an authentically joyful experience is only possible when we embrace each experience life offers as required. Yes, this is challenging. Joy stems from embracing the beauty, the fragrance, *and* the thorns of life. This may not make complete sense right now because we may still be attempting to flee one state of being in favor of another. However, it will make sense in due course as we learn how to feel our way through it all. By continuing to practice what we have realized through The Presence Process, without focusing on an endpoint to our journey, we inevitably enter a joyful frequency. Joy is the inevitable consequence of all that The Presence Process initiates. Within the frequency of patience, all planted seeds sprout, and all blossoms bear fruit.

It's important, especially when the going gets tough, to remind ourselves that everything in this life is an expression of our collective source, no matter how we may interpret it in any given moment.

To unconditionally embrace, instead of to resist, is the key to experiencing integration.

We cannot enter a full awareness of our inherent holiness – our wholeness – by excluding any expression we perceive on the physical, mental, emotional, or vibrational face of source. This is what growing up and becoming fully human invites.

There's a way to know whether we are in tune with the present or not. We are able to go up without assuming that going down means "the end," and we are able to go down without assuming we will never go up again. Up and down, down and up – it's one and the same joyride through the experience of life. When we are attached to neither the up nor the down, then we are seeing with source's eyes. Then the endless joyride becomes truly joyous.

The only place we will ever find to be home while we are in this experience is in the endless present moment in which we already reside. Our home is our eternal present moment awareness. Aspiring to be at home within ourselves – to be fully present while in this world – is a quest. By seeking no other place of refuge, we are seldom disappointed. Present moment awareness isn't a destination but an infinite journey. We therefore cultivate infinite patience and compassion within ourselves, for ourselves. We endeavor to unconditionally give ourselves exactly what we require for this journey.

The more aware we become, the clearer it is that just because roses have thorns doesn't mean we are meant to bleed, although at times we may. The thorns are here to remind us to move about in this world with present moment awareness, to not be in a hurry, and to be as gentle with ourselves as is the texture of a rose petal. In this way, we perceive how the thorns of life adorn our pathway to facilitate us into greater awareness.

There is another lesson inherent in this royal flower. Just because a rose has thorns doesn't mean it requires fixing. The thorns communicate that beauty in this creation is to be handled with love, care, attention, and the respect inherent in present moment awareness. The Presence Process is an ongoing invitation to each of us to hold ourselves in this way, and to be living examples that this is possible for everyone.

THE CAPACITY OF PRESENCE

Let us remember what a blessing we are to everyone who enters our experience when we consciously choose present moment awareness.

We don't need to know the impact our present moment awareness has on others for it to leave its mark. Present moment awareness radiates automatically and effortlessly. It moves silently beneath the surface of things, bringing the light of remembrance into the darkness of forgetfulness. Even just a moment of conscious present moment awareness is enough to touch another's life in such a way as to confirm the blessing of life itself.

Consciously wielded present moment awareness plants seeds of compassion that melt heartache and hardship in everyone we meet. As we move through our experience of the world in this manner, harmony is restored in our wake because present moment awareness radiates directly from our source. It knows no order of difficulty and moves beyond the confines of conditions and limitations. It brings about what's required.

Present moment awareness sends out the promise of joy. It rekindles the memory within others of the eternal within themselves, an expression that's more authentic than anything the world offers. Awakening others to what we all share, our present moment awareness invites them to experience being unified. When we consciously choose to be present with others, they are set on a path that enables them to remember what's authentic. Consequently, they remember their source. Remembering our source brings reawakened awareness into our experience of everything.

To restore harmony to the quality of our experience, we don't require any special qualifications. We aren't required to study any course or practice any intricate modality in order to bring an awareness of what peace is to all we meet. Neither do we need to enroll in any special course in order to unleash the full potential of unconditional love. We don't have to state one single word in order to reveal what's valid. To become examples of vibrational awareness, we don't need to wear a particular color of clothes, eat special foods, or adopt a magical posture. We don't require any rituals or chants to unleash the capacity of our source.

We aren't required to *do* anything in order to *be* present. All that's required is that we choose to be present.

Our heartfelt present moment awareness carries with it the full power, glory, and indescribable potential of the unified field. Present moment awareness integrates all barriers created by fear, anger, and grief. It integrates wounds inflicted through unconscious behavior arising out of our unintegrated emotional charge. It instantly dissolves misunderstanding. Our calming present moment awareness is the balm that soothes all experience infected by the perceptual virus of "time." Present moment awareness forgives anyone of anything, and everyone of everything. It gives comfort to the lonely and rest to the weary. It is home for the lost.

Our choice to show up and be present in our experience empowers others to show up and be present in theirs. In turn, they are able to share their present moment awareness with others. Present moment awareness therefore ignites a chain reaction that grows infinitely brighter. Present moment awareness is an eternal flame of awareness that, once shared, radiates infinitely. There is nothing in creation that can extinguish it when we consciously choose to reawaken and share it.

Given unconditionally, present moment awareness allows our collective source to be present physically, mentally, and emotionally in our experience of this world. It enables unconditional love to be expressed despite all conditions. By sharing our present moment awareness, we *know* our collective source is love. Then, and only then, are we being responsible for the gift called "life."

A PARTING GIFT

CONSCIOUSLY APPROACHING VIBRATIONAL AWARENESS

When we are complete with our experiential journey through The Presence Process, we may ask: "What now?"

In answer to this question, allow me to share a daily practice I call "consciously approaching vibrational awareness." To discover the consequences of applying this practice, it's recommended we commence each day with the practice. It's a simple, practical means of aligning ourselves with the causal point of all life: the vibrational current flowing through ourselves and all manifestations we call "creation."

The vibrational tool offered here isn't religious or spiritual. Rather, it's a perceptual approach that honors the manner in which our human experience flows outwardly from its unified source. Through its daily application, we train our capacities to follow the natural flow of our awareness back into our source.

Engaging in this practice daily is a means of remaining causal in all our inner and outer activities. When consistently applied, the consequences of wielding this perceptual tool are self-evident, experienced as noticeable perceptual shifts in our daily experience.

PART I:

1 Sit comfortably, cross-legged or on a chair, with your back straight but relaxed. Make sure you aren't cold.

2 Keep your eyes closed for the entire practice.

3   Connect your breathing for 15 minutes. (As per The Presence Process, this means breathing in and out without any long gap or pause between breaths.)

4   Breathe intensely enough to clearly hear your own breathing.

5   Preferably breathe in and out through your nose only. But if your nose is blocked, breathe in and out only through your mouth.

6   In sync with the connected breathing, mentally repeat the expression: "I am here now in this." I (during the in-breath) am (during the out-breath) here (during the in–breath) now (during the out-breath) in (during the in-breath) this (during the out-breath).

PART II:

1   After about 15 minutes, inhale as deeply as possible through your mouth, filling your lungs to capacity, then hold this breath to the count of 20 (or less if this is too much).

2   Release your breath through your mouth.

3   Repeat this intake, holding and counting to 20, followed by an out-breath, three times.

PART III:

1   Now take your attention off your breathing and allow it to rest at the point your awareness resides when you are

"present with eyes closed." This inner point, slightly above and between the physical eyes, is the eye center.

2   While at rest within the eye center, mentally repeat "I am here now in this" for about 5 to 10 minutes.

3   When you become aware that your attention has wandered away from the words you are repeating into other unconsciously generated thoughts, gently bring your attention back and continue the deliberate repetition.

4   Become aware of the two distinct places awareness is able to reside during this practice: present in deliberate repetition at the eye center, and wandering unconsciously away from the eye-center into the dream state called "thinking" (about past and future).

5   Don't be concerned about this unconscious wandering. Simply observe it. Be with it unconditionally.

PART IV:

1   Cease all mental repetition.

2   Using felt-perception, become aware of all sensations that arise in and around your body. No matter how it's perceived, this felt-experience is an encounter with the vibrational field.

3   Sit with this felt-experience of the vibrational field for a few moments.

PART V:

1   Cease conscious feeling of the overall vibrational field and focus only on *listening*.

2   First listen for a few moments to whatever sounds are heard within the world. Listen to these sounds without condition. Listen to them as if audibly "receiving them" – as if you are now a receiver of these audio vibrations. Allow yourself to perceive all these outer sounds, no matter what they are, as being emitted by the one unified causal point of all that is. As if all these accumulated outer sounds make up "God talking."

3   Gently withdraw your awareness from these outer sounds and allow it to once again rest at the point of inner Presence, the eye-center. This time, while residing at the eye-center, listen for sounds that come from *within*. Whatever is heard is valid. If nothing is heard, listen to this nothingness.

4   While listening to these sounds, or the nothingness, make sure your attention remains at the eye-center.

5   When you become aware that your attention has wandered away from listening at the eye-center, into following unconsciously generated thoughts or external sounds, gently bring it back and continue listening.

6   Become aware of the two distinct places attention is able to reside during this practice: present in deliberate listening at the eye-center, and wandering unconsciously away from the eye-center in the dream state called "thinking" (about past and future).

7   Don't be concerned about this unconscious wandering, but simply observe it. Be with it unconditionally.

8   Listen inwardly for about 5 minutes, longer if you feel moved to.

9   This state of "listening," of "being a receiver," is vibrational contemplation. *Listening* is how the heart initially feels the resonance of the vibrational.

Once we are listening to any inner sound, or to the nothingness, we are at *the doorway of our inner portal into vibrational awareness.* Whatever occurs beyond this point is ours to contain.

The efficiency of this practice isn't in *what we hear inwardly,* but in our capacity to remain in a state of listening. This state of listening – of consciously being a receiver – empowers us to become open to receive all we require for our daily encounters directly from our unified source. As our capacity to listen evolves, so also does our capacity to receive.

This vibrational practice isn't about perfection, but about full participation in our human experience from "a causal point of you." Don't *try*. Relax into it and enjoy the inevitable consequences. Effortlessness comes from effortlessness. May this practice eternally bless you and all you love with all you require.

Our Service Territory Expands

Since introducing Eckhart Tolle to the world with *The Power of Now* in 1997 (followed by *Stillness Speaks, A New Earth,* and *Milton's Secret*), NAMASTE PUBLISHING has been committed to bringing forward only the most evolutionary and transformational publications that acknowledge and encourage us to awaken to who we truly are: spiritual beings of inestimable value and creative power.

In our commitment to expand our service purpose—indeed, to redefine it—we have created a unique website that provides a global spiritual gathering place to support and nurture individual and collective evolution in consciousness. You will have access to our publications in a variety of formats: traditional books, eBooks, audiobooks, CDs, and DVDs. Increasingly, our publications are available for instant download.

We invite you to get to know our authors by going to their individual pages on the website. We also invite you to read our blogs: The Compassionate Eye, Consciousness Rising, Conscious Parenting, and Health. Enjoy the wisdom of Bizah, a lovable student of Zen, presented in daily and weekly entries.

We are each in our different ways both teachers and students. For this reason, the Namaste spiritual community provides an opportunity to meet other members of the community, share your insights, update your "spiritual status," and contribute to our online spiritual dictionary.

We also invite you to sign up for our free ezine *Namaste Insights*, which is packed with cutting edge articles on spirituality, many of them written by leading spiritual teachers. The ezine is only available electronically and is not produced on a set schedule.

What better way to experience the reality and benefits of our oneness than by gathering in spiritual community? Tap into the power of collective consciousness and help us bring about a more loving world.

We request the honor of your presence at
www.namastepublishing.com